F. P Badham

The Formation of the Gospels

F. P Badham
The Formation of the Gospels
ISBN/EAN: 9783743395367
Manufactured in Europe, USA, Canada, Australia, Japa
Cover: Foto ©Lupo / pixelio.de

Manufactured and distributed by brebook publishing software (www.brebook.com)

F. P Badham

The Formation of the Gospels

THE FORMATION
OF
HE GOSPELS.

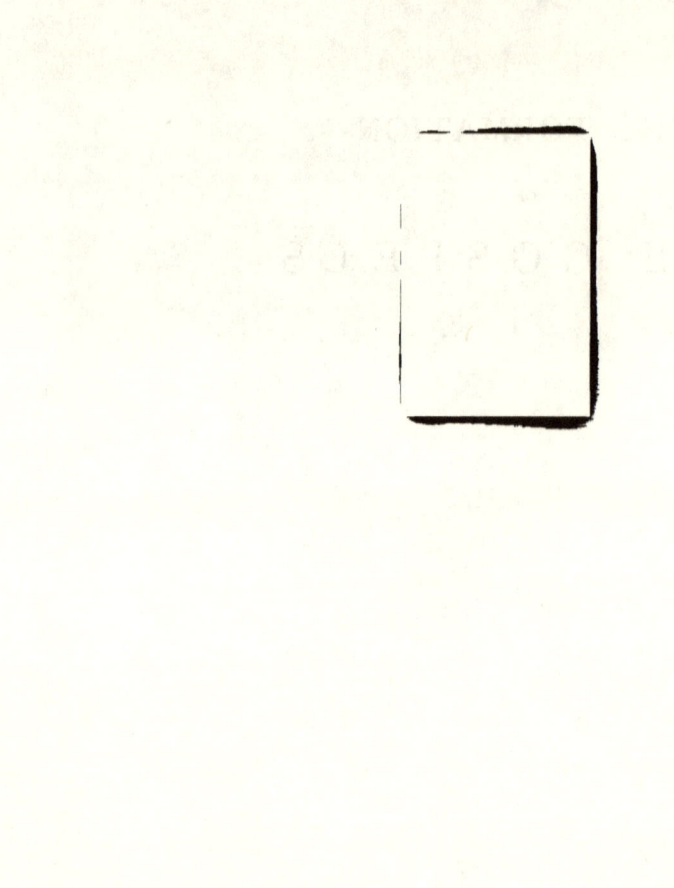

THE FORMATION

OF

THE GOSPELS

BY

F. P. BADHAM, M.A.
EXETER COLLEGE, OXFORD

SECOND EDITION, REVISED AND ENLARGED

LONDON
KEGAN PAUL, TRENCH, TRÜBNER, & CO. L^{TD}
PATERNOSTER HOUSE, CHARING CROSS ROAD
1892

The rights of translation and of reproduction are reserved.

PREFACE.

THE ensuing attempt to solve the synoptic problem is based primarily on the doublets and inconsistencies from which none of the synoptic gospels is free, and on the differences of order by which all three are distinguished.

No pretence is made to completeness of treatment. A construction-theory is sketched, which must stand or fall by the test, "Will it work?" The locks to be opened are too many and complicated for any but the right key to fit.

To enable this test to be applied easily—for however complex and artificial the theory may appear at commencement, in conclusion it is extremely simple—I have appended the text (A.V.) of the synoptic gospels, with certain distinction of type.

It will be seen that to a certain extent, the results are new—they are certainly arrived at by a new process—to a certain extent, old. The dual base of the triple tradition has already been recognised in the theory of an "Ur-Matthæus," an "Ur-Markus;" but another principle of cleavage is here substituted for one which incessantly invokes the redactor, frequently offends by revealing " Ur-Matthæus" in S. Mark, and " Ur-Markus" in S. Matthew, and finally leaves us in possession of an " Ur-Matthæus" and " Ur-Markus" very much more closely related than the relationship of S. Matthew to S. Peter at all requires. So again as to the great journey pericope of S. Luke; certain of its peculiarities have already been recognised, but not the laws which they illustrate here.

The principles of analysis adopted are few and definite. In one or two cases only is room left for any arbitrariness in applying them. The analysis proceeds by clear fixed rule.

ARGUMENT.

CHAP.		PAGE
I.	That patristic evidence is not incompatible with the following theses	1
II.	That there is a complete gospel (Petrine, it will appear presently), peculiar to S. Matthew and S. Luke; and that the remainder of the synoptic record, the so-called "triple tradition," at its base in S. Matthew and S. Mark, is dual	10
III.	What growth of our canonical gospels the acceptance of these theses involves	10
IV.	That a primary case, firstly, for bisecting S. Matthew and S. Luke, and secondly, for bisecting S. Mark and the remainder of S. Matthew, is presented by certain doublets	11
V.	That the case for bisecting S. Matthew and S. Luke is strengthened by certain incongruities in both; and that the sections of S. Matthew and S. Luke, involved by these doublets and incongruities, are solidly distinguished, "Petrine" from non-Petrine, by the fact that the former are altogether absent from S. Mark .	24
VI.	That these "Petrine" sections form a complete gospel in themselves, and are alien to the remainder of S. Luke	25
VII.	That they are foreign in S. Matthew	27
VIII.	That they are bound together and distinguished from others by certain peculiarities of arrangement . .	28
IX.	That they are further bound together and distinguished from others by their absolute independence . .	30
X.	That there is evidence, from certain phenomena in Tatian's Diatessaron, that they once had a separate life of their own	32

CONTENTS.

CHAP.		PAGE
XI.	That they are bound together, distinguished from others, and connected with Luke i. 5–ii. by certain phenomena in the Acts of the Apostles	43
XII.	Also in the Epistle to the Hebrews	53
XIII.	That internal and external evidence connects these sections with S. Peter	58
XIV.	And with them Mark xvi. 9–20	62
XV.	That the primary case for bisecting S. Mark and the non-Petrine part of S. Matthew, A B, is strengthened by certain incongruities in both	64
XVI.	That the solidarity of A and of B, the groups in which the sections involved by these doublets and incongruities are arranged, is shown by certain differences of order in S. Mark and A B	68
XVII.	That this bisection of S. Mark and A B restores old connections, and interrupts none of any importance	74
XVIII.	That the solidarity and individuality of A and of B is shown by certain peculiarities of style and tendency	76
XIX.	That the text of A and B has been abbreviated in S. Mark, not expanded in A B; that the differences with which it appears are mainly such as to prove the priority of A B; consequently, that certain obstacles to bisection, peculiar to S. Mark, are due to the redactor	81
XX.	That the traces of redaction in A B are slight; that Matt. i., ii. is not an accretion, but an integral part of A	85
XXI.	Date and order of the documents proposed	94
XXII.	That the existence of the documents proposed is evidenced by certain phenomena in the "Gospel according to S. John"	97
XXIII.	Also in the "Gospel according to the Hebrews"	103
XXIV.	Illustration of the construction-theory proposed from the records of the Resurrection	107

THE GOSPELS WITHIN THE GOSPELS 125

THE FORMATION OF THE GOSPELS.

I.

By far the earliest information bearing on the Synoptic problem is that given by Papias. As to the exact date of Papias there is some uncertainty, but at any rate it was not such, in the opinion of Eusebius, as to render acquaintance with apostles an absolute impossibility. Here is the information:—

"Mark, having become the interpreter of Peter, whatever things he remembered he wrote accurately, but not in the order in which Christ spoke or did them. For he was neither a hearer nor a follower of the Lord's, but afterwards, as I have said (*v. r.* "as it is said") of Peter's, who used to frame his teaching to meet the immediate wants of his hearers, and not as though he were attempting to make a connected narrative of the divine words (*v. r.* "Logia"). So Mark committed no error in thus writing down some things (ἔνια)[1] as he remembered them to have been spoken; for he took special heed to omit none of the things that he had heard, and to state nothing falsely."

---

[1] The imputation of disorder which has just been cast on S. Mark's work in general is scarcely qualified by "ἔνια"; for in the most disorderly gospel possible, the Baptism, the call of disciples, the Passion, would fall of themselves into their proper place. The causes of disorder adduced would not affect S. Mark's work in a few particulars merely. Or it may be that in the use of "ἔνια" John the Elder is viewing the *whole* Christian record, to which S. Mark had only contributed a share.

Matthew composed the Logia in the Hebrew (*i.e.* Aramaic) dialect, and every one interpreted them as he was able."—EUSEBIUS, *H. E.*, iii. 39.

This information Papias gives on the authority of "John the Elder,"[1] who evidently belonged to an earlier generation.

Putting aside all external considerations, the following appears a natural inference from John the Elder's statement. At the close of the first century, or beginning of the second, there existed, firstly, several gospels akin in matter and form, divergent in text, discrepant in particulars, and a gospel in Aramaic, more or less resembling them; secondly, an independent gospel, distinguished from the gospels abovementioned by quite different arrangement. John the Elder's hearers asked him to explain these phenomena, and this first of harmonists complied with their request, telling them that the substantially-akin, textually-divergent gospels were irresponsible and somewhat licentious translations of the Gospel in Aramaic,[2] and that the peculiarly arranged gospel was the work of an apostle's secretary, who depended entirely on the order of the apostle's discourses.

John the Elder's explanation may not have been altogether correct, but we are left facing the phenomena on which he comments. Let us now endeavour to find such documents as his comments require.

---

[1] The phrase with which Papias introduces the information about S. Mark, "John the Elder said," presumably governs the information about S. Matthew too. The two statements resemble one another, and seem to go together.

[2] John the Elder says that S. Peter's interpreter "wrote accurately," "committed no error," "took special heed not to omit or to add." But the interpreters of S. Matthew's Logia "interpreted as they best could." Their procedure is contrasted with S. Mark's.

THE FORMATION OF THE GOSPELS.

There is no very valid ground for denying John the Elder's reference to our canonical S. Matthew. The expression "Logia"—sometimes translated "sayings"—does not at all exclude the idea of an historical narrative. This is shown by its usage in the New Testament, and by Papias himself. And though critics are now generally agreed that our canonical S. Matthew, as a whole, is no translation from an Aramaic original, yet this objection cannot be far pressed, for in very early times we find an Aramaic gospel current under S. Matthew's name, "The Gospel according to the Hebrews," and an impression widely prevalent that this was the original of our canonical S. Matthew. That this impression was erroneous, the fragments extant of "The Gospel according to the Hebrews" are held to prove. But their kinship to our canonical S. Matthew is often very curious. Even a scholar like Jerome, after careful study of both documents, assented to the prevalent notion of their relationship. And it does not appear that John the Elder's position was such as to guarantee him against error.[1]

Proof, indeed, is wanting that "The Gospel according to the Hebrews" existed in John the Elder's days, but there is a presumption that it did: for in the third quarter of the second century we find it treasured in

---

[1] The balance of evidence is decidedly against the sometimes attempted identification of John the Elder with John the Apostle. For Papias speaks of "what *was said* by Peter, or Andrew, or Philip, or Thomas, or James, or *John*, or Matthew, and what Aristion and John the Elder *say*," and we have Eusebius on our side in drawing the natural inference that two Johns are referred to. Nor is it likely that Papias would have placed an apostle behind any Aristion.

Dionysius of Alexandria informs us that there were two tombs at Ephesus inscribed "John." And in the Apostolic Constitutions (vii. 46) John the Apostle makes mention of "John, ordained Bishop of Ephesus by me John."

Malabar, and quoted as authoritative by Hegesippus in Rome. Earlier in the century it is similarly quoted (so at least most critics are of opinion) by the author of the seven Ignatian Epistles. There are reasons for inferring that it was employed by Papias.[1] And certain expressions of Epiphanius are usually taken as implying its acceptance by Cerinthus, John the Elder's contemporary.

When, in addition to all this, we find from internal evidence—as we shall presently—that neither our canonical S. Matthew, or the other synoptic gospels contain any "sayings" other than integral parts of the narrative, and recognise the fact that no traces of an Aramaic original can be discerned in the variation between the narratives in gospel and gospel,[2] the chances that John the Elder had in view "The Gospel according to the Hebrews" when he spoke of Aramaic Logia appear overwhelming.

Let us assume, then, that John the Elder refers to our canonical S. Matthew and to "The Gospel according to the Hebrews." But he refers to the former only as one of a class. Where are the other members of the class, the Greek gospels, substantially like, textually differing from our canonical S. Matthew?

---

[1] Eusebius, after enumerating the sources from which Papias drew, concludes by telling us that "he recounts a history . . . which the Gospel according to the Hebrews also contains."—*H. E.*, iii. 39.

[2] The one or two variations between gospel and gospel, which might possibly have arisen from independent translation—Matt. ix. 16 (Mark ii. 21); xii. 29, *cf.* Luke v. 36; xi. 21, 22—will be taken as independent reports of words originally uttered in Aramaic. Such variations only occur in Christ's speeches.

There are of course certain variations in the narrative too, but they are counterbalanced by ten times as many coincidences, and moreover, are found in all portions of the narrative alike—in the "dual traditions" (the sections common to S. Matthew and S. Mark, S. Mark and S. Luke, S. Luke and S. Matthew), as well as in the "triple tradition."

THE FORMATION OF THE GOSPELS.

Whether indeed they really stood in any closer relationship than our canonical S. Matthew to "The Gospel according to the Hebrews" is more than doubtful. For in Jerome's days, and long before, a proper translation of "The Gospel according to the Hebrews" was a desideratum. And John the Elder's error in the case of our canonical S. Matthew leaves us sceptical as to the value of his opinion in the other cases. But where are the documents that can have done duty as "translations"—documents whose curious relationship to one another, and to our canonical S. Matthew, John the Elder can have thought he could plausibly explain by referring it and them to the same Aramaic original? Such documents are to hand—our second canonical gospel, and the correspondent sections of the third. This identification will relieve us from the necessity of desiderating documents which have perished, leaving no other vestige, and from the awkwardness, otherwise resultant, of having to admit that John the Elder says nothing about the "triple tradition," the most interesting and important point in the synoptic problem.

Let us now see whether or not the first of John the Elder's statements prevents our including the second canonical gospel in his category of "translations."

The more we scrutinise the second canonical gospel, the less it answers to the document which John the Elder's first statement requires. It is no hastily constructed document. On the contrary, its construction evinces considerable art and care. Nor does it contain likely subject-matter for an apostle's occasional discourses. Doctrine and parable we should expect, not minute incident, artistic touches, and scenic effect.

Nor does the origin of the first document described by John the Elder lead us to expect a gospel virtually coincident in scope with his second document, which originated so differently. But above all, it is John the Elder's comment on the DISORDER of this first document that precludes our identifying it with the canonical S. Mark; for the latter is by all appearance the most orderly gospel we possess. Definite notes of time, "on that day," "immediately after," abound. How are we to reconcile this with the fact that John the Elder's S. Mark "stated nothing falsely," "committed no error," "wrote accurately"?

The natural inference from John the Elder's statement is that it is from the standpoint of his second document that he impugns the chronology of his first. But the chronology of our canonical S. Mark is virtually identical with that of our canonical S. Matthew. And such differences as there are, are demonstrably deep and structural.

Let us see if there is any other standpoint from which John the Elder can have launched his "disorder." Certainly not in our third canonical gospel, for, with one insignificant exception [1] (the reason for which will appear presently), every one of the sections common to the second canonical gospel, and the third, reappears in the latter in exactly the same position. Certainly not in the fourth gospel, for, with regard to the Johannine chronology, our canonical S. Matthew, S. Mark, S. Luke sin equally.

It remains, then, that John the Elder's second document is to be sought elsewhere than in our canonical S. Mark. Where? Here again guidance is afforded

[1] In Luke viii. the visit of Christ's mother and brethren is placed *after* the parable of the sower instead of *before*, as in Mark iii., iv.

by an apparent omission of John the Elder's—his mysterious omission to refer to S. Luke. For the distance from which he evidently looks back to the composition of the Matthæan documents is greater than allows us to assume his absolute ignorance of our third canonical gospel. It is likely that John the Elder's statements about gospel-formation are in some measure complete. It is unlikely that his first document has been allowed to perish entirely. And so it follows that this first document must include the portions of the canonical gospels which his second does not—roughly, the matter peculiar to S. Luke.

Let us now consider how far this estimate of John the Elder's statements is corroborated by the attitude of Papias.

Critics are generally of opinion that before the death of Papias our Synoptic gospels were current in their present canonical form. But if our estimate of John the Elder's statement is correct, Papias would not look at them in quite the same way as his contemporaries. With what he believed to be the Aramaic original of the triple tradition in his hands, and with the remainder of the Synoptic gospels in a separate form, he had two standards to judge by. Certain portions of our Synoptic gospels would appear less valuable to him than others.

Papias tells us that whenever he met any one who had seen an apostle, he made a point of inquiring what the apostle had said, " And I have not scrupled to add (to my " Exposition of the Scriptures of the Lord ") what I have learned. For I did not think what came to me in the books of so much value as what I could gain from the yet living voice." Papias can scarcely mean to say that he preferred what he was told S. Matthew and S. Peter had said to what he knew S. Matthew and S. Peter's secretary had written. But it is obvious that "the books" to which he refers are books which his contemporaries held in high esteem. They can scarcely be the works of heretics, as Dr. Westcott suggests, for Papias would scarcely apologise for subordinating such books as these to genuine apostolic reminiscences.

One of the fragments extant of the "Exposition of the Scriptures of the Lord" illustrates this conception of Papias's attitude. He avers that "Judas walked about this world, a sad example of impiety," despite the fact that in Matt. xxvii. the traitor's suicide follows as an immediate consequence of Christ's condemnation.

Here, then, in the statements of John the Elder and Papias, we have evidence of the existence of two other gospels besides the canonical. Let us see how far the attitude of other second century fathers is consistent with this conclusion.

Examples have already been given of the wide acceptation of "The Gospel according to the Hebrews." Evangelical matter contained elsewhere than in our canonical gospels is cited as authoritative in 1 Clement, and the Epistle of Barnabas, and by Justin, and "Ignatius." Writers of the second century, whose exclusive use of our canonical gospels is beyond question, are rather difficult to find. The conservative view, with its clear-cut lines, leaves the lofty position of these uncanonical gospels unaccounted for, and also, we may add, their strange consanguinity with the canonical. The relationship seems other than that of child and parent.

THE FORMATION OF THE GOSPELS.

It is not till the second half of the second century that we first find distinct proof of our canonical gospels occupying a unique position, and even then their position is not very assured. The fact that they were widely superseded by Tatian's Harmony evidences certain weakness in their prescriptive rights. And the so-called "interpolations" found especially in Tatian's text, in the old Latin and old Syriac versions, and the Codex Bezæ, reveals greater plasticity than one would expect in documents generally regarded as quite unique of their kind, and each derived from one standard apostolic autograph.[1]

All attempts to explain away the force of the facts above noted create a portentous gap. In Luke i. 1 we hear of "many" gospels—containing, as we may infer from the very slight additions which the fathers are able to make to the sacred narrative, much the same matter as those we possess. Finally, we find the three in exclusive possession of the field. A transition style is needed to link the two periods together.

Reasons are suggested in the ensuing pages for supposing that the three are composite—a development of the "many;" that there were Tatians before Tatian; and that the "interpolations" in Tatian's text, the old Latin, old Syriac, and Codex Bezæ are chips and shavings, indicative of seams and jointing.[2]

---

[1] Tertullian makes mention of the autographs of Epistles. Peter of Alexandria makes mention of the great standard copy of the Fourth Gospel at Ephesus. But we never hear of autographs of the Synoptic gospels, though there was often every reason for appeal to them, *e.g.*, by Irenæus, against Marcion and the Ebionites, whom he accused of mutilating and corrupting the sacred text.

[2] The ordinary view accounts for many of these various readings by supposing that one gospel has been interpolated from another. This does not adequately account for a certain regularity which is observable. There is never any attempt to foist any of the peculiar matter of the third canonical gospel into the second.

Before closing this brief survey of the external evidence against the conservative view of the origin of the Synoptic gospels, it is perhaps worth while calling attention to a passage in the apocryphal "Acts of Barnabas." Here TWO reputed Matthæan documents are mentioned—a "Book of Words" and a "Book of Works."[1] These Acts are assigned by Lipsius to the fourth century, but the passage in point is sufficiently curious to suggest the likelihood of derivation from some earlier authority.

II.

My theses are these:—

1. That our canonical S. Mark cannot in whole or part be identified with the document described by John the Elder, but that there is a document, peculiar to S. Matthew and S. Luke, and alien to the remainder of both, which answers to John the Elder's description.

2. That the lowest stratum of the triple tradition is generally to be found in our first canonical gospel, occasionally in our second, and that this lowest stratum consists of *twin* gospels.

III.

The working out of these theses involves the following construction-theory:—

1. Previous to the destruction of Jerusalem S. Matthew's disciples possessed two gospels (denoted in the ensuing pages by the symbols A and B), the former written before, and the latter (a sort of supplement) after, the flight to Pella. A and B were speedily combined.

[1] Βίβλος τῆς φωνῆς τοῦ θεοῦ, καὶ θαυμάτων καὶ διδαγμάτων σύγγραμμα.

2. Somewhat later a Pauline Christian with A and B, and A B in his hands, but with little original knowledge, produces an improved harmony, our second canonical gospel; his aim being, as one gathers from his omissions, to supersede A B, but not A and B.

3. S. Mark in Rome (*circ.* A.D. 72), knowing nothing of the fore-mentioned documents, writes down what he remembers of the "Preaching of S. Peter."

4. S. Luke combines the "Preaching" and our second canonical gospel, occasionally showing his acquaintance with the other documents above-mentioned.

5. Certain sections of the "Preaching" interpolated into A B, complete our first canonical gospel.

IV.

I subjoin tables of the doublets in S. Matthew, S. Mark, and S. Luke. It is not necessary to identify all the incidents and sayings which are here contrasted. History repeats itself, and our Lord may have reiterated His maxims frequently. But it is unlikely that the earliest evangelists, with a plethora of material, would reproduce such reiteration in writing. In the case of didactic incidents, they would naturally record one of a kind. At the risk of overshadowing those doublets which are really impressive, I have endeavoured to make the list complete, both in order to avoid the appearance of suppressing instances which were inconvenient, and also because even the least impressive tend to remove a preliminary objection to any cleavage whatever of our canonical gospels, by diminishing the number of lacunæ resultant. It will be part of our object to show that certain fragments of the canonical gospels form gospels complete of themselves.

DOUBLETS IN PREACHING OF PETER.

1. This is Elijah, which is to come. xi. 14.

2. The sign of Jonah. xii. 41.

3. Deputation from John. Parable of the children playing at weddings and funerals. John came neither eating nor drinking, and they say, He hath a devil. The Son of man came eating and drinking, and they say, Behold a friend of publicans and sinners. xi. 2-19.

4. More tolerable for Sodom. xi. 24.

5. Trees known by their fruit. xii. 33-35.

6. Unfruitful trees shall be hewn down and burnt. iii. 17.

7. Some of them shall ye scourge in your synagogues, and persecute from city to city. xxiii. 34.

8. Whosoever shall speak a word against the Son of man, it shall be forgiven him. But whosoever shall speak a word against the Holy Spirit, it shall not be forgiven. xii. 32.

9. Every idle word that men shall speak, they shall give account thereof in the day of Judgment. xii. 36.

10. Ye shall not see Me henceforth, till ye shall say, Blessed is He that cometh. xxiii. 39.

11. Whosoever humbleth himself shall be exalted. xxiii. 12.

12. Greatest be your servant. xxiii. 11.

13. Your Father knoweth ye have need of things. vi. 32.

14. What ye hear in the ear, proclaim upon the housetops. x. 27. (Cf. "What ye have spoken in the ear in the inner chambers shall be proclaimed upon the housetops." Luke xii. 3.)[1]

15. All things ye would that men should do unto you, do unto them : for this is the law and the prophets. vii. 12.

16. I thank Thee, O Father, Lord of heaven and earth, that Thou hast revealed these things unto babes. No one knoweth the Son save the Father. And He said to the disciples, Blessed are your eyes, for ye see. xi. 25 ; xiii. 16 ; cf. Luke x. 19-24 : "Behold, I have given you authority over all the power of the enemy."

---

[1] It is evidently because the Petrine interpolator recognises this doublet that the text of the Preaching in Matt. x. 27 is paraphrased. The priority of the text preserved in Luke xii. 3, and the genuineness of the doublet, are shown by the fact that in Luke xii. 3 the saying

S. MATTHEW—I.

AB.

Elijah is come already. Then understood they that He spake of John. xvii. 12, 13.

The sign of Jonah. xvi. 4.

{ John's disciples say, We fast, and thy disciples fast not. Sons of the bride-chamber. Why eateth your master with publicans and sinners? ix. 10-15.

John came in the way of righteousness, and ye believed him not. xxi. 32.

More tolerable for Sodom. x. 15.

Trees known by their fruit. vii. 16, 17, 18, 20.

Unfruitful trees hewn down and burnt. vii. 19.

In their synagogues they will scourge you. . . . But when they persecute you in this city, flee into the next. x. 17, 23.

Every blasphemy shall be forgiven: but the blasphemy against the Spirit shall not be forgiven. xii. 31.

Whosoever shall say to his brother, Raca, shall be in danger of the judgment. v. 22.

Ye shall not have gone through all the cities of Israel, till the Son of man be come. x. 23.

Whosoever shall humble himself, the same is greatest. xviii. 4.

Greatest be your servant. xx. 26, 27.

Your Father knoweth what things ye have need of. vi. 8.

Enter into thy inner chamber and pray; and thy Father, which seeth in secret, shall recompense thee (openly). vi. 6.

Thy neighbour as thyself. On these two commandments hangeth the whole law and the prophets. xxii. 39, 40.

Peter said, Thou art the Son of God. And Jesus answered, Blessed art thou; for flesh and blood hath not revealed it unto thee, but My Father which is in heaven; and against my Church the gates of hell shall not prevail. xxvi. 16, 17, 18.

---

appears in exactly the same connection as in Matt. vi. 6, *à propos* of Pharisaic hypocrisy.

Another example of paraphrase on the part of the Petrine interpolator, dictated by similar considerations, is supplied in Matt. xvi. 27 (cf. Mark viii. 38).

17. Give not that which is holy unto the dogs. Ask and it shall be given you: for every one that asketh receiveth. If ye, being evil, give good gifts unto your children, how much more shall your Father in heaven give good things to them that ask Him. vii. 6-11.

18. If they say, Behold, He is in the wilderness; go not forth: Behold, He is in the inner chambers; believe it not. Be ye ready: for in an hour that ye think not the Son of man cometh. xxiv. 26, 44.

DOUBLETS IN

A.

1. Two blind men healed. Dumb devil cast out. Pharisees say by Beelzebub. ix. 27-34.

2. Went about all the cities, teaching in their synagogues, and preaching the gospel of the kingdom, and healing all manner of disease and all manner of sickness. But when He saw the multitudes, He was moved with compassion for them. And He called unto Him His twelve disciples. ix. 35-x. 1.[1]

3. They will deliver you up to councils. And brother shall deliver up brother to death. And ye shall be hated of all men for My name's sake. x. 17-22.

4. He that endureth to the end shall be saved. Ye shall not have gone through all the cities of Israel, until the Son of man be come. x. 22, 23.

5. When they persecute you in this city, flee into the next. x. 23.

6. Whosoever shall give unto one of these little ones a cup of cold water. x. 42.

7. Taking up the cross. x. 38.

8. He that findeth his life shall lose it. x. 39.

9. If thy hand or foot offend thee, cut it off. If thine eye offend, pluck it out. xviii. 8, 9.

10. Whoso putteth away his wife. xix. 9.

11. Ostentation of the Pharisees. xxiii. 5, 6.

12. Swearing by heaven, God's throne. xxiii. 16-22.

13. This is My beloved Son. iii. 17.

14. His disciples follow. viii. 23. Cf. Mark i. 36.

---

[1] "And He went up into the mountain." This is needed to make the parallel complete. That something has slipped out of the text in ix. 35-x. 1 is evident from xi. 1, "He departed THENCE." Some

And she cried, and He answered her not a word. But she came and worshipped Him, saying, Lord, help me. And he said, It is not meet to take the children's bread, and cast it to the dogs. But she said, Yea, Lord. Then Jesus answered, Be it as thou wilt. And her daughter was healed. xv. 21-28.

If any man shall say, Lo, here is the Christ, or, Here; believe it not. Watch, for ye know not on what day your Lord cometh. xxiv. 23, 42.

S MATTHEW—II.

B.

Blind and dumb devil cast out. Pharisees say by Beelzebub. xii. 22-24.

Went about in all Galilee, teaching in their synagogues, and preaching the gospel of the kingdom, and healing all manner of disease and all manner of sickness. And seeing the multitudes, He went up into the mountain. And His disciples came unto Him. iv. 23-v. 1.

> They shall deliver you up to tribulation. Ye shall be hated of all nations for My name's sake. Ye shall be delivered up of kin. xxiv. 9, 10.
>
> He that endureth to the end shall be saved. And this gospel shall be preached in the whole world, unto all the nations, and then shall the end come. xxiv. 13, 14.
>
> When ye see the abomination in the holy place, flee to the mountains. xxiv. 15, 16.
>
> When gave we thee drink? Inasmuch as ye did it unto the least of these My brethren. xxv. 37, 40.

> Taking up the cross. xvi. 24.
> Whosoever would save his life shall lose it. xvi. 25.

> If thine eye offend thee, pluck it out. If thine hand offend, cut it off. v. 29, 30.
> Whoso putteth away his wife. v. 31.
> Ostentation. vi. 2, 5.
> Swearing by heaven. v. 33-37.

This is My beloved Son. xvii. 5.
His disciples came unto Him. v. 1.

---

locality must have been mentioned previously. That this locality was "the mountain" we shall ultimately be able to deduce from Mark iii. 13.

15. Withdrew into the parts of Tyre and Sidon. xv. 21.
16. The sign of Jonah. xvi. 1-4.
17. Mercy, not sacrifice. ix. 13.
18. Four thousand fed. Fragments collected. Embarkation for the west side of the lake. xv. 32-39.
19. Power to bind and loose given to the Twelve. xviii. 18.
20. Love thy neighbour as thyself—to the lawyer. xxii. 39.
21. Paralytic healed. ix. 1-8.
22. Christ's power over the sea—storm stilled. viii. 23-27.
23. Christ's teaching about children—a child in the midst. xviii. 1-4.
24. Tribute. xxii. 15-22.
25. Every plant which My Father planted not shall be rooted up. xv. 13.
26. To him that hath shall be given. xiii. 12.
27. Faith to remove mountains. xxi. 21.
28. Contention who should be greatest. xviii. 1-4.
29. Ceremonious purifications. The outside of the platter. xxiii. 24-26.
30. Announcement of the Passion in Galilee. xvii. 22, 23.
31. Announcement of the Passion on the way to Jerusalem. xx. 17-19.
32. Hosanna—from the multitude. xxi. 9.
33. False Christs, false prophets. xxiv. 23-25.
34. Nation against nation and kingdom against kingdom. xxiv. 7, 8.
35. On this generation. xxiii. 36.
36. Supper in the upper chamber. xxvi. 17-29.
37. Christ's exclamation on arrest: "Are ye come out as against a robber? But all this is come to pass that the scriptures might be fulfilled." xxvi. 55, 56.
38. Mockery by the high priest's servants. xxvi. 67, 68.
39. Night trial before the Sanhedrin. xxvi. 57-68.

40. Wine (*v.r.* vinegar) and gall. xxvii. 34.
41. There was a great earthquake. And the watchers did quake, and became as dead men. xxviii. 2, 4.

42. Go into Galilee; there ye shall see Him. xxviii. 7.

Came into the parts of Cæsarea Philippi. xvi. 13.
Sign of Jonah. xii. 38-40.
Mercy, not sacrifice. xii. 7.
Five thousand. Fragments. Embarkation. xiv. 13-22.

Power to bind and loose given to S. Peter. xvi. 17.
Thy neighbour as thyself—to the ruler. xix. 19.
Paralytic. viii. 6.
Storm stilled. xiv. 32.
Blessing children. xix. 13-15.

Temple-rate. xvii. 24-27.
The tares. xiii. 24-30.

To him that hath shall be given. xxv. 29.
Faith to remove mountains. xvii. 20.
Contention. xx. 20-28.
Purifications. Not that which entereth into the mouth defileth. xv. 10, 11, 15-20.
Announcement to Peter. xvi. 21.
Announcement after the Transfiguration. xvii. 9.

Hosanna—from the children. xxi. 15.
False Christs, false prophets. xxiv. 5, 11.
Wars and rumours of wars. xxiv. 26.

This generation shall not pass. xxiv. 34.
Supper in the house of Simon. xxvi. 6-13.
Thinkest thou that I cannot beseech my Father? How then should the scriptures be fulfilled, that thus it must be? xxvi. 52-54.
Mockery by Roman soldiers. xxvii. 27-31.
Morning trial before the Sanhedrin. xxvii. 1. Cf. Luke xxii. 66-71.
Vinegar. xxvii. 48.
The earth did quake. Now the centurion, and they that were with him, watching Jesus, when they saw the earthquake, feared exceedingly. xxvii. 51, 54.
Go into Galilee; there ye shall see Me. xxviii. 10.

DOUBLETS IN A.

1. The voice of one crying. i. 3.
2. Teaching from a boat (πλοῖον). iv. 1.
3. They besought that they might touch the border of His garment. vi. 56.
4. He suffered not the devils to speak, because they knew Him. i. 34.
5. And He called unto Him the Twelve, to send them forth. And He gave them authority over the unclean spirits. And they gather themselves again unto Jesus. vi. 7.
6. And His friends went out to lay hold on Him. iii. 21.
7. The report of Him went into all the region of Galilee round about. And they came to Him from every quarter. i. 28, 45.

8. The commission of investigation. Pharisees from Jerusalem. vii. 1. Cf. Matt. xv. 1.
9. And many other things they have received, washings of cups and pots. And He said to them, Full well do ye reject the commandment of God, that ye may keep your tradition, and many such like things ye do. vii. 4, 9, 13.
10. After the feeding of the four thousand,—Why reason ye because ye have no bread? Do ye not yet understand? Have ye your heart hardened? viii. 17.[1]
11. After the manifestation of Christ's power over the sea. The amazement of the disciples. iv. 41.
12. If any man would be first, he shall be last of all, and minister of all. ix. 35.

13. And they sought how they might destroy Him: for they feared Him, for all the multitude was astonished at His teaching. xi. 18.

---

[1] The priority of Mark viii. 17 to Matt. xiv. 33 is shown by the fact that the latter makes S. Peter's confession almost valueless.

[2] I omit those doublets which are also contained in S. Matthew,— Nos. 2, 3, 14, 15, 18, 22, 23, 28, 31, 32, 34, 35, 37, 38, 39, 40. These quoted are to be considered in connection with the parallel passages in S. Matthew, for their presence in the second gospel is not more significant than their absence in the first. Let the consequences be tried of completing Matt. xii. 15, 16 out of Mark iii. 7–19! So with nearly all

S. MARK.[2]

B.

> Behold, I send My messenger. i. 2.
> Teaching from a boat (πλοιάριον). iii. 9.
> As many as had plagues pressed upon Him, that they might touch Him. iii. 10.
> And the unclean spirits cried, Thou art the Son of God. And He charged them that they should not make Him known. iii. 12.
> And He appointed Twelve, that He might send them forth to preach, and to have authority to cast out devils (*v. r.*, and to heal diseases). iii. 14, 15.
> And there come His mother and His brethren. iii. 31.
> And a multitude from Galilee followed, hearing what great things He did; and from Judæa and Jerusalem and Idumæa. iii. 7, 8. Cf. Matt. iv. 24.
> Pharisees from Jerusalem. iii. 22.

Ye leave the commandment of God, and hold fast the tradition of men (*v. r.*, "washings of cups and pots, and many such like things ye do"). vii. 8.

After the five thousand,—They understood not concerning the loaves; but their heart was hardened. vi. 52.

The amazement of the disciples. vi. 51.

Whosoever would become great among you, shall be your minister: and whosoever would be first among you, shall be servant of all. x. 42, 43.

And they sought to lay hold on Him; and they feared the multitude. xii. 12.

---

the passages in the second gospel—its picturesque details aside—which are absent in the first. Mark xi. 25 is absent after Matt. xxi. 22, because of Matt. vi. 14, 15; Mark x. 15 after Matt. xix. 14, because of Matt. xviii. 3; Mark iv. 21-24 after Matt. xiii. 23, because of Matt. v. 13, vii. 2, x. 26. A is sacrificed in S. Matthew and B in S. Mark, or *vice versa*. Sometimes, as in the last-mentioned instance, the sacrifice in S. Matthew is to the Preaching.

14. And it was the third hour, and they crucified Him. xv. 25. Cf. xvi. 4 (k.)

15. He bought a linen cloth. xv. 46.

DOUBLETS IN

Preaching of Peter.

1. There is nothing covered up, that shall not be revealed; and hid, that shall not be known. xii. 2.

2. No man, when he hath lighted a lamp, putteth it in a cellar, neither under the bushel, but on the stand, that they which enter in may see the light. xi. 33.

3. Unto every one that hath shall be given; but from him that hath not, even that which he hath shall be taken away from him. xix. 26.

4. Healing on the Sabbath, cleansing leprosy, raising the dead, forgiving sins. xiii. 10-17; xiv. 1-6; xvii. 12-19; vii. 11-17, 48.

5. Mission of the seventy—no purse—no wallet—in that same house remain—even the dust we do wipe off. x. 1-12.

6. Call of Zacchæus, the publican. He is gone to lodge with a sinner. I am come to seek and save the lost. xix. 1-10.

7. Circuit of Galilee. viii. 1.

8. The scribes and Pharisees began to press upon Him vehemently, and to provoke Him to speak of many things; laying wait for Him, to catch something out of His mouth. xi. 53, 54.

9. Taking up the cross. xiv. 25.

10. He that denieth Me in the presence of men shall be denied in the presence of the angels. xii. 9.

11. Whosoever shall seek to gain his life shall lose it. xvii. 33.

12. Must suffer many things and be rejected. xvii. 25.

13. Contention who should be greatest. xxii. 24.

14. What shall I do to inherit eternal life? asks the lawyer. x. 25.

[1] 15. Blessed is the womb that bare Thee. Blessed rather are they that hear the word of God, and keep it. xi. 28.

[1] 16. And the Pharisees, lovers of money, scoffed. And He said,

---

[1] It is to be noted that "Blessed is the womb" occurs in exactly the same connection, viz., in connection with the charge of possession by Beelzebub, and the demand for a sign, as "Thy mother and brethren stand without," in S. Matthew. Cf. Mark iii. And just as the inquiry

And they crucify Him. And from the sixth hour there was darkness. xv. 24, 33. Cf. Matt. xxvii. 45.

They bought spices. xvi. 1.

S. LUKE.

S. MARK.

{ Nothing is hid, that shall not be made manifest; nor secret, that shall not be made known. viii. 17.
No man, when he hath lighted a lamp, covereth it with a vessel, or putteth it under a bed; but putteth it on a stand, that they which enter in may see the light. viii. 16.
Whosoever hath, to him shall be given; and whosoever hath not, from him shall be taken away even that which he thinketh he hath. viii. 18.

Healing on the Sabbath, cleansing leprosy, raising the dead, forgiving sins. iv. 31–37; vi. 1–11; v. 12–16; viii. 40–56.

Mission of the Twelve—nor money nor wallet—there abide—shake off the dust. ix. 1–6.

Call of Levi, the publican. Ye eat and drink with sinners. I am not come to call the righteous, but sinners. v. 27–32.

Circuit. iv. 15, 44.

The principal men sought to destroy Him, and they watched Him, and sent forth spies that they might take hold of His speech. xix. 47; xx. 20.

Taking up the cross. ix. 23.

Whosoever shall be ashamed of Me, of him shall the Son of man be ashamed, when He cometh in the glory of the Father and the holy angels. ix. 26.

Whosoever would save his life shall lose it. ix. 24.

Must suffer many things and be rejected ix. 22.

Contention who should be greatest. ix. 46.

What shall I do to inherit eternal life? asks the ruler. xviii. 18.

Thy mother and brethren stand without. My mother and brethren are those which hear the word of God and do it. viii. 21.

And a certain ruler said, All these (commandments) have I ob-

---

of the rich young ruler appears in S. Matthew and S. Mark in close proximity to the divorce decision, so in S. Luke does "The Pharisees, lovers of money, scoffed."

Ye are they that justify yourselves in the sight of men, but God knoweth your hearts: There was a certain rich man, clothed in purple, &c.

17. They shall not leave in thee one stone upon another. xix. 44.

18. They shall say, Lo, there! lo, here! go not after them. xvii. 23.

19. There shall be signs in sun and moon and stars; and upon the earth distress of nations, in perplexity for the roaring of the sea and the billows. xxi. 25.[1]

20. When they bring you before the authorities, be not anxious how or what ye shall answer, or what ye shall say: for the Holy Spirit shall teach you in that hour what ye ought to say. xii. 11, 12.

21. Then shall they say to the mountains, Fall on us; and to the hills, Cover us. xxiii. 30.

22. In that day, he on the housetop, and his goods in the house, let him not go down to take them away: and let him that is in the field, likewise return not back. xvii. 31.

23. The days shall come when they shall say, Blessed are the barren, and the wombs that never bare, and the breasts that never gave suck. xxiii. 29.

24. Woe to the Pharisees. xi. 37-52.

25. And He received a cup, and when He had given thanks. xxii. 17.

---

[1] The phenomena mentioned in Luke xxi. 11 are practically the same as those mentioned in verse 25—comets and eclipses, tremors of the earth, and tidal waves.

served from my youth. Jesus said, How hardly shall they that have riches enter into the kingdom. xviii. 18-30.

There shall not be left here one stone upon another. xxi. 6.
Many shall come, saying, I am he; and, The time is at hand: go not after them. xxi. 8.
There shall be earthquakes, famines, and pestilences: there shall be terrors and great signs from heaven (*v.r.* "and tempest"). xxi. 11.
Settle it therefore in your hearts, not to meditate beforehand, how to answer: for I will give you a mouth and wisdom. xxi. 14, 15.

Then let them in Judæa flee to the mountains. xxi. 21.

Let them that are in the midst of her, depart out; and let not them that are in the country, enter therein. xxi. 21.

Woe unto them that are with child, and to them that give suck in those days. xxi. 23.

Woe to the Pharisees. xx. 45-47.
And He took the cup in like manner after supper. xxii. 20.

V.

Consideration of the second and third tables of doublets may be postponed for the present. Our business is with the first and fourth—with the sections anticipatively classified as Petrine. The doublets above instanced are not all very decisive, but cumulatively they have a certain force. And it cannot be objected that they are selected arbitrarily, for in both cases *the sections labelled Petrine are distinguished* en bloc *from the opposite sections by their entire absence from the Gospel according to S. Mark.* I am not referring merely to the texts above cited, but to the paragraphs they involve.

The evidence of the doublets may be supplemented by certain inconsistencies, or at least textual incongruities, especially in S. Luke. Thus:—

The substitution of the Petrine equivalents for the accounts given in S. Mark of Peter's call, the reception at Nazareth, and the trial before Caiaphas, produce the result that in Luke iv. 38 Peter's call is preceded by a reference to Peter's discipleship; in iv. 31, 32, 36, 37, a description of Christ's first visit to Capernaum, and the amazement of the inhabitants, follows a reference (v. 23) to many mighty works done there already; and in xxii. 71, the members of the Sanhedrin ask, "What FURTHER need have we of witness?" when no witness at all has been recorded. So too the omission of the journey "beyond Jordan" (Mark x. 1) leaves inexplicable Christ's presence at Jericho (Luke xviii. xix.), Jericho not lying on the road from Galilee to Jerusalem.

Again, in Luke ix. 51, Christ has "steadfastly set His

THE FORMATION OF THE GOSPELS. 25

face to go to Jerusalem," and it is expressly stated that " the days were come that He should be received up." But between this start and the arrival in Jerusalem (xix. 29-40) so large an amount of matter is interposed as to destroy the whole balance of the gospel.

Pursuing the lines just suggested, and then to the sections thus demarcated, adding others in which similar peculiarities of style and diction are observable,[1] one arrives at the result indicated by red-letter in the gospels appended to this volume.

VI.

It will be perceived that the main-stock of the "Preaching," according to this scheme, lies between Luke ix. and xix. Let us examine this great section. Have we here a real account of Christ's last journey to Jerusalem ? or the main-stock of a record, covering the whole period of our Lord's life ? The references to locality point to the latter conclusion. Thus :—

In ix. 52 Christ is already in Samaria. His face is "*steadfastly set*" towards Jerusalem. In x. 13-15 He is addressing Chorazin, Bethsaida, and Capernaum. In x. 25-37 the answer to the lawyer, apart from the position the lawyer occupies in the triple tradition, suggests by the scenery employed—the road from

[1] The unity of the remainder of the third canonical gospel after the parts common to the second have been subtracted (for this is what the above method will be found to amount to), is shown by numerous peculiarities of style and diction. Among the words and expressions peculiar to the "Preaching" may be noticed—ἐπαιτεῖν, ἐπανέρχεσθαι, βαλάντιον, σαροῦν, υἱοὶ τοῦ αἰῶνος τούτου, ἐκμυκτηρίζειν, χρεωφειλέτης, διαγογγύζειν, συκοφαντεῖν, τὰ πρὸς εἰρήνην, πρεσβεία, κόπρια, σκάπτειν, ἀμφιεννύναι.

Jerusalem to Jericho—that He is present in Jerusalem. In x. 38 He is in the village of Martha and Mary. In xi. 53 He is thronged by scribes and Pharisees; and the preceding denunciation of the Pharisees, quite apart from the position it holds in the triple tradition, must surely have been uttered in Jerusalem: "Ye who build the tombs of the prophets," "Zachariah, whom ye slew," would have sounded inappropriate elsewhere. In xii. 1, the "many thousands pressing" on Christ carry the scene back to Galilee. But the eschatological parables in vers. 35–48—the bridegroom's servants waiting, the thief breaking through, the steward making ready—suggest the very last days of the ministry, and consequently Jerusalem. In xiii. 1–9 the reference to the tower of Siloam is to a structure close at hand; "*present some at that season* who told Him of the Galilæans whose blood Pilate had mingled with their sacrifices," suggests attendance at a feast; and the fig-tree to which the vinedresser has come seeking fruit three seasons, and which he will leave for another year, suggests that Christ is present in Jerusalem, not for the first time, or the last. In xiii. 22 Christ is "journeying through cities and villages to Jerusalem;" and in xiii. 31 He is in Herod's dominions—"Get thee hence: Herod would kill thee;" but in the next verse He is lamenting over Jerusalem. In xiv. 25 He is again journeying—"great multitudes accompanied Him." But the paradoxical metaphor in xvi. 9, "eternal tabernacles," suggests in sight the perishable booths of reed, erected in Jerusalem during a celebration of the greatest of Jewish feasts. In xvii. 11 Christ is "on the way to Jerusalem, passing through the midst of Samaria and

Galilee."[1] The imagery in xviii. 9-14—the Pharisee praying—suggests proximity to the Temple; but Christ is far away from it in xviii. 31—"Behold, we go up to Jerusalem."

VII.

The Matthæan sections which we have distinguished as Petrine are never of the warp and woof of S. Matthew. Sometimes they interrupt the narrative, and always they can be removed without leaving any wound. Moreover, *they all occur in S. Luke in a different context*, so that we are obliged to make our choice; and as the Preaching occurs in S. Luke in far larger blocks, it is obviously S. Luke's contexts that ought to be preferred.

Comparison with the passages in S. Mark parallel to those in S. Matthew, where the following Petrine sections are inlaid, Matt. iii. 7-10; xii. 27, 28, 30; xiii. 16, 17; xxiv. 26-28; xxvi. 52-54, shows how lightly these sections occupy their present position. The narrative runs as smoothly or smoother without them.

In Matt. v. 25, 26 the "adversary" is our enemy unforgiven; but in Luke xii. 57-59 the "adversary" is Christ Himself, with whom Israel would do wisely in making peace.

The discursus concerning anxiety (Matt. vi. 21-34) seems out of place in a legislative section; and the inculcation of persistency in prayer (vii. 7-11) harks back to a subject which has been treated already (vi. 5-13).

The relationship of Matt. viii. 5-13 to Luke vii. 2-10

[1] Tatian's text appears to have added, "It was the time of the Passover" (*vide* "Harmoniæ Tatiani," Ciasca, p. 53). This can scarcely be considered an interpolation from John v. 1, as Ciasca suggests, for John v. 1 has been employed by Tatian already (*vide* "Harmoniæ," p. 39).

is at present inexplicable, but the removal of vers. 7–10 from the former passage leaves us with two narratives of the same event which are perfectly independent.[1]

The answers to worldly disciples (Matt. viii. 19–22) interrupt the embarkation; and the request, "Let me go and bury my father," sounds unsuitable at such a moment.

The deputation from John (Matt. xi. 2–30) follows strangely after the inauguration of a circuit.[2]

In Matt. xii. 32–37 there is some bathos in the terrible denunciation of a particular type of blasphemy being immediately followed by the general reference to " idle words."

The "blessedness" of the disciples (Matt. xiii. 16, 17) seems cramped by the context. Contrast Luke x. 23, 24.

The lament over Jerusalem (Matt. xxiii. 37–39) distinguishes itself by the use of "Ἱερουσαλήμ." Elsewhere in S. Matthew one always finds the form "Ἱεροσόλυμα."

The eschatological fragment (xxiv. 37–51) comes not inappropriately, but it only replaces, as will appear presently, a shorter passage of like import—Mark xiii. 33–37.

VIII.

A very marked trait of the sections we have labelled Petrine is their peculiar arrangement. The arrangement is generally subjective, not chronological.

---

[1] In Matt. viii. the centurion comes himself. In Luke vii. he does not presume to come, but sends a deputation.
[2] The reason, however, why this contest should have been chosen is not far to seek. Verse 5 pre-supposes cures of leprosy, deafness, paralysis, blindness, and a raising of the dead.

In Luke xiv. the word "supper" is the keynote. Christ is invited to a supper. Then follows His advice as to the behaviour of His followers when they are invited, and when they issue invitations themselves. Then follows the parable of the last great supper to which all the world is invited.

In Luke xv. "love for the lost" is the link connecting the hundredth sheep, the tenth piece of silver, the prodigal son.

In Luke xvi. the word "riches" is the keynote. The steward acquires riches for his old age, rulers scoff who are righteous and rich, and Lazarus lies at the gate of Dives.

In Luke vii. the meal in the house of Simon the Pharisee, and the unction by a sinner, follow the deputation from John, because of the sentence at the termination of the latter, "Behold a gluttonous man, a friend of sinners."

In Luke xii. 1–12 we find three perfectly distinct ideas—hypocrisy, persecution, and sin against the Spirit, connected by links which dissolve entirely on close scrutiny. In the former case, the link being "revelation of secrets," of Pharisaic untruth, private piety, or the gospel; in the latter, the mere word "blasphemy."

In Luke xvi. 16, 17, "The law was UNTIL John," and "not a tittle of the law shall fall," are linked together on account of their very inconsistency.

Examples of similar connection might be multiplied. Surely here we have just such links as one might expect an evangelist to forge who had heard an apostle reporting speeches of Christ, but was himself unaware of their historical occasion.

The fact, already mentioned, that the Petrine arrangement is different in S. Matthew and S. Luke, proves that in one direction or the other that arrangement was not regarded as authoritative.

IX.

The most distinctive trait of the Petrine sections is their independence. In the red sections at the close of this volume, not a single example will be found of textual relationship to the uncoloured, as to events. The speeches of Christ occasionally approximate (cf. Matt. vii. 24–27, xxiii., xxv. 24–30; Luke vi. 47–49, xi. 37–52, xix. 21–27), but this approximation is not closer perhaps than one might expect in two independent faithful reports.[1] It must be remembered, too, that some twelve years elapsed before the Apostles separated, and during this time they must have frequently repeated the most characteristic of Christ's speeches in one another's hearing. As to speeches, there was a prototype to conform to; as to events, of course none.

In the lists of doublets, a good many examples have already been given of such parallelism as obviously can only be accounted for by assuming the concurrence in our canonical gospels of two quite distinct streams of tradition—the most striking, perhaps, being afforded in the eschatological prophecies, scattered in the one case, focussed in the other; formally independent, substantially coincident. Collating one gospel with

[1] If closer, of course there remains the alternative of a mixed text to fall back on. But the verbal divergence in these cases is much greater in the Greek. It seems safer to allow the predominant colouring to govern.

another, placing all the Petrine sections on this side and all the non-Petrine sections on that, this parallelism can be made almost complete.

There is the sermon on the mount, and the sermon on the plain; the parable of the talents, and the parable of the pounds; the parable of the virgins, and the parable of the bridegroom's attendants; the lawyer of Mark xxii., Mark x., and the lawyer of Luke x.; the murmuring at Nazareth, Matt. xiii., Mark vi., and the riot at Nazareth, Luke iv.; the call of Peter in Matt. iv., Mark i., and the call in Luke v.; the unwashed hands of the disciples, Matt. xv., Mark vii., and Christ's own hands unwashed, Luke xi.; the mockery by Pilate's soldiers, and the mockery by Herod's; the unction at Bethany, and the unction by a sinner; the request of James and John for the highest seats, Matt. xx., Mark x., and the contention who should be greatest, Luke xxii.,—in both cases Christ's cup, and thrones of judgment being promised to the Twelve, Matt. xix. 28, Luke xxii. 30. In Matt. xxiv., "Iniquity shall abound, love wax cold," and in Luke xviii., "Shall the Son of man find faith on the earth." In Matt. xxvi., "Put up thy sword," and in Luke xxii., "Suffer thus far." In Matt. xxv., to the sheep on the right hand, "Come, inherit the kingdom prepared for you: for I was hungry and ye gave me meat;" in Luke xii., "Fear not, little flock: it is your Father's good pleasure to give you the kingdom. Sell that ye have, and give alms." In Matt. xxi., Mark xi., "If ye have faith and doubt not, ye shall not only do what is done to the fig tree, ye shall say unto this mountain, Be thou taken up and cast into the sea. And when ye stand praying, forgive;" in Luke xvii., "If thy brother sin, forgive him. If ye had faith ye would say unto this sycamine tree, Be thou rooted up and planted in the sea."[1]

X.

Some thirty years before the close of the second century, a harmony of our canonical gospels was composed by Tatian. The object of the following chapter is to show that besides our canonical gospels, Tatian possessed the sections herebefore classified as Petrine, in a separate form—in fact, that his work was not, as it is generally styled, a "Diatessaron," but rather, as Tatian himself styled it (according to Victor of Capua), a "Diapente," a harmony of *five*.

The Diatessaron has not come down to us intact, and we are compelled to collect its contents in more than one direction. We have—

1. A commentary on the Diatessaron (containing numerous extracts) by the great Edessan teacher, Ephraem. This commentary, only extant in an Armenian version, has been translated into Latin by Moesinger ("Evangelii Concordantis Expositio, Venetiis," 1876).

2. An Arabic version of an orthodox recension of the Diatessaron. This has been translated into Latin by Ciasca ("Tatiani Evangeliorum Harmoniæ, Romæ," 1888).

3. Quotations from the Diatessaron in the "Acts of Addai," "Teaching of the Apostles," "Acts of Barsamya," "De fato" of Bardesanes, and other

---

[1] Notice, too, that the import of the parable which follows the command to forgive frequently in Matt. xviii. is the same as in Luke xvii.—the unmerciful servant, the servant not thankworthy—What a fraction of our debt and duty to God we can ever pay!

Edessan documents (Ante-Nicene Library, vols. xx., xxii.);[1] also, according to Zahn, in the Homilies of the Persian sage, Aphraates.

Let us deal first with Moesinger's work.

It is not, perhaps, of very great significance that Tatian identifies the lawyer of Luke x. with the lawyer of Matt. xxii., Mark xii. (p. 195); the discourse concerning ablutions at the Pharisee's dinner-table with the Corban discourse (p. 138); the riot at Nazareth, Luke iv., with the murmuring recorded in Matt. xiii., Mark vi. (pp. 128–131)—for it may be urged, by way of extenuation, that in these three cases S. Luke had already made his choice. But it is of the greatest significance that Tatian sometimes gets behind S. Luke and identifies things which are there explicitly distinguished, making it clear that in his opinion S. Luke had not carried far enough the identification of the second canonical gospel and the Preaching. Thus he identifies " Blessed is the womb that bare Thee " with " Thy mother and brethren stand without " (p. 122; contrast Luke viii., xi.); identifies the rich

[1] We have an express statement in these documents themselves that the Diatessaron was adopted in public service at Edessa (Ante-Nicene Library, vol. xx., second part, p. 25), and their gospel references are sufficiently allied to the fragments of the Diatessaron in Ephraem's Commentary to prove that this statement is no interpolation. For example, in the "Acts of Thaddæus" it is said that "Christ appeared first to *His mother* and other women, and to Peter *and John* first of the disciples, and afterwards to the eleven" (Acta Apostolorum Apocrypha, ed. Lipsius, pars prior, p. 277)—this remarkable idea of an appearance to the Blessed Virgin (adopted, it may be noticed, by S. Ambrose and other Western writers) arising from the fact that Tatian had identified the Mary of John xx. with the Virgin, instead of the Magdalene (Moesinger, pp. 29, 54, 269, 270). That John was in the company of Peter when Christ appeared to the latter, the biographer of Thaddæus may have inferred for himself, but it is just worth noticing that in Ephraem's Commentary, John xxi. 19*b*–22 is cited immediately after " Touch me not," and before " He breathed on them " (Moesinger, p. 271).

C

young ruler with one of those Pharisees whose love of money and legal righteousness provoked the parable of Dives and Lazarus (pp. 168–174; contrast Luke xvi., xviii.); identifies the denunciation of ceremonialism at the Pharisee's dinner-table with the great final denunciation of Pharisaism (p. 211; contrast Luke xi., xx.).

Equally significant is the frequency with which Tatian transposes. Whether this arises from S. Luke's having attempted to amend the Petrine order, and Tatian's harking back to the original document, or from an attempted amendment on the part of Tatian, we need not now stop to inquire. *Primâ facie*, it is likelier that the earlier evangelist was the more audacious. But it is sufficient that in Tatian's work certain sections of S. Matthew and S. Luke are treated exceptionally. Among these transpositions may be noted:—The Servants waiting the Bridegroom's return (p. 219);[1] "Who hateth not father and mother" (p. 118); The unjust judge (p. 190); The Pharisee and publican (p. 181); Martha and Mary (p. 98); "The Galileans who perished" (pp. 165, 166); "The angels of these little ones," Matt. xviii. 10 (p. 105). Nor can any of these transpositions except possibly the first be accounted for by the exigencies of harmony, seeing that the passages alluded to only occur in the sacred narrative once.

Of course, it follows from what has been just said that Tatian generally ignores the *setting* of the Petrine sections in S. Matthew and S. Luke. To take the most striking instance, one searches his harmony in

---

[1] Tatian evidently connects this parable with that of the Ten Virgins.

vain for the great journey pericope. The verse by which this pericope is governed (Luke ix. 51) is, as will be found presently, transposed; and between Luke ix. and xix. several journeys to and from Jerusalem are allowed to intrude. In fine, Tatian extends Luke ix.–xix. over the whole period of the ministry.

But if it is Tatian's task to break up and transpose, it is also sometimes his task to reunite. He uniformly complements the Petrine sections in one gospel out of the Petrine sections in the other, *e.g.*, in Matt. vii. 6–12, out of Luke xi. 5–13 (p. 73); in Luke x. 21, 22 out of Matt. xi. 25–30 (p. 117). And he disregards the foreign matter which divides Luke vii. 50 from Luke x.

And now to turn from Moesinger's work to Ciasca's.

Ciasca's text fully confirms all the peculiarities above noted in Moesinger's commentary, and enables us to lengthen the list considerably:—

The call of S. Peter recorded in Luke v. is identified with that recorded in Matt. iv., Mark i. (p. 9).

The utterances recorded in Luke xvii. 1–10, "If thy brother sin, forgive him," "If ye had faith as a grain of mustard-seed, ye would say to this sycamine, Be planted in the sea," are identified with those which in S. Matthew and S. Mark follow the fig-tree blasted (p. 58).

The eschatological discourse recorded in Luke xvii. is identified with that recorded in Luke xxi. (pp. 73–75).

The utterance recorded in Luke xii. 11, 12, "Be not anxious what ye shall answer," is identified with that recorded in Luke xxi. (p. 73).

The utterance recorded in Luke xii. 54–56 "When ye

see a cloud rising in the west," is identified as answer to the demand for a sign in Luke xi. 16 (pp. 25, 26).

To the instances of transposition may be added, The rich fool (p. 50); "Go tell that fox" (p. 43); "Wilt thou that we call fire from heaven" (p. 68); "Easier for heaven and earth to pass" (p. 25); "Are there few saved?" (p. 54); "The Pharisees pressed on Him vehemently," Luke xi. 53-xii. 3 (p. 72); "Father, forgive them" (p. 92).[1]

To what has been said regarding the general breaking up of the great journey section, it may be added that Tatian makes the "scribes and Pharisees" of Luke xi. 53, Jerusalemites; and to Jerusalemites addresses the parable of the barren fig-tree (pp. 72, 165, 166).

And a new point may be noticed—Petrine matter is *repeated*. "And the multitudes, knowing the place, came to Him, and He welcomed them, and them that had need of healing, He healed," this verse is quoted in its canonical context (Luke ix. 11), and then again after the parable of Pharisee and Publican (pp. 33, 57).[2] Tatian, it seems, found it in the latter position in the Preaching, but owing to its very different allocation by S. Luke, he fancied it had been omitted altogether. Another example of such repetition, "If the mighty works had been done in Sodom that have been done in thee, it would be an inhabited place to this day," this verse is quoted in its canonical context

---

[1] "Father forgive" is found in a similar position in the Apostolical constitutions (Ante-Nicene Library, vol. xvii. p. 134).

[2] It is interesting to notice that on this second occasion, where Tatian's text is, *ex hypothesi*, based on the Preaching directly, a clause of Luke ix. 11 is omitted, which, by criteria suggested presently, is shown to be an addition of S. Luke's own—"taught them things concerning the kingdom of God."

against Capernaum (Matt. xi. 23*b*, 24), and then again (not indeed in Ciasca, but in Moesinger, p. 230), after some address to *Jerusalem*.[1] As it stood in the Preaching, its application must have been ambiguous.

To enable a just estimate of the significance of the facts above-noted, it is necessary to complete the investigation, and examine Tatian's method of procedure with regard to other portions of the sacred history— the triple tradition and S. John. Here it will be quickly perceived that his method is quite different. He never identifies events repeated in the same gospel —is unallured by the most tempting opportunities. Even when it is in different gospels that the same event recurs, he is reluctant. Thus he distinguishes the deaf-dumb-blind cures of Matt. ix., xii.; Mark vii., viii.; Luke xi. He distinguishes the call of Matthew (Matt. ix.), the call of James, the son of Alphæus (Mark ii.),[2] and the call of Levi (Luke v.), (Ciasca, pp. 11, 12). His transpositions, though sometimes surprising—for he differs from most modern harmonists, in declining to recognise the chronology of the fourth gospel as paramount—are due (with two exceptions) to some exigency of harmony, as, for example, when he postpones the visit of Nicodemus to the end of the ministry, this arising from his preference for the position which the cleansing of the Temple, and the challenge " By what authority " occupy in the triple tradition. The two exceptions alluded to are these: he places the conversation with the

---

[1] No accidental slip of Ephraem's. In the Apostolical Constitutions, ii. 60, Resch discovers evidence of a declaration by Christ that Sodom should be justified before Jerusalem. Resch does so without noticing the corroborative testimony of Ephraem.

[2] Tatian, like D, read "James" in Mark ii. (*cf.* Moesinger, p. 58). In Ciasca's text, "James" is corrected to "Levi."

woman of Samaria *after* the cure of the nobleman's son, the leper in proximity; and he places the widow's mite *before* the great disputations in the Temple. Here, indeed, the disturbance of the canonical arrangement appears somewhat wanton.[1] It may be noticed, however, that the leper and the mite are only attached in their canonical context lightly. The leper indeed suits its context very ill.[2] But allowing the utmost significance to these exceptions, it still remains that Tatian does not transpose non-Petrine matter to anything like the same extent as Petrine. Tatian's method of procedure then may be summed up as follows: 1. He takes the triple tradition as a basis. 2. He adapts the fourth gospel to the triple tradition with the least necessary violence. 3. He fits the Preaching into this framework with all manner of licence—in other words, singles out certain sections of S. Matthew and S. Luke, and treats them in a way for which justification must be sought outside the limits of our canonical gospels.

But this theory of a fifth gospel, the Preaching, in Tatian's hands involves certain ulterior consequences.

1. If Tatian possessed the Preaching, it must have been known to earlier authorities—certainly to Justin (Tatian's master), and to Clement of Rome.

---

[1] In the former case *contact with the unclean* is the thought running in his mind. Unwashen hands! Conversing with a Samaritan! Not repelling a Canaanite! Giving speech to a Gentile! Touching a leper! In the latter case the thought is *the worthlessness of Pharisaic piety.* A Pharisee praying! A Pharisee giving alms!

[2] Tatian might argue, "He could no more enter into a city," but here is Christ entering Capernaum! "Tell no man," but does not this accord better with Christ's attitude at a later period, that pointed to in Mark vii. 36, 37? "He withdrew into the deserts, and multitudes came to him from every quarter"—how well this will preface the congregation of the four thousand!

2. If Tatian possessed the Preaching, he would not merely act as he has been shown to, he would also make some additions to the canonical text (for a comparison of the Petrine sections in the first gospel and the third, makes it evident that some few fragments of the Preaching have been lost [1]), additions similar in character to those Petrine verses which are peculiar to the first gospel.[2]

Both consequences can be faced. Agrapha are found, as already mentioned, in 1 Clement and Justin, some of them very significant. In the former, for example, "It were good for that man if he had not been born, rather than that he should cause one of my elect to stumble"—not a loose quotation of Matt. xviii. 6; Mark ix. 42, "Whoso causeth one of my little ones to stumble, it were better that a mill-stone were hanged about his neck," for Clement cites this immediately afterwards. Rather, it is a parallel.[3] It is significant, too, that so many of Justin's evangelical references should be to matter contained only in the

---

[1] If the number of Petrine verses peculiar to the first gospel be taken as a criterion, the number of verses missing will be about forty.

[2] S. Luke omits Matt. xi. 14 as superfluous (cf. Luke i. 17); omits Matt. xi. 23b, 24, as a redundancy; omits Matt. vi. 34; vii. 6; xii. 36, 37, as "hard sayings." Illustrative of this last motive, one may notice his omission of two sections of the second gospel—"If hand or foot offend," and the reluctant miracle in Syro-Phoenicia. Why he should omit the call to the heavy-laden is not easy to see. Possibly this was a post addition, absent in S. Luke's copy. But it is doubtful whether it belongs to the Preaching at all. It joins on almost equally well with the precedent section as with the subsequent; in the former case the connection would be between the formal Sabbath rest and the true rest found in Christ, between Christ's light burden and the burdens of the lawyers "grievous to be borne"; in the latter case, it would be as follows: "All power is mine. I call whom I will. Come unto me ye weary, and I will give you all your desire."

[3] In Luke xvii. 2 this Petrine text is superseded by Mark ix. 42. But it has not disappeared without leaving traces. We have the order of the clauses inverted, and a v.r., "εἰ μὴ ἐγεννήθη."

Gospel of S. Paul's disciple, bearing in mind Justin's strange attitude towards S. Paul, whose name he never mentions, whose epistles he never refers to. With greater force this argument applies to the Clementines. An author, hostile to S. Paul, habitually filling S. Peter's speeches with matter peculiar to S. Luke! In Ciasca's text extra-canonical readings occur very seldom, but this proves little, for a comparison of Ciasca's text with that preserved in Ephraem's Commentary makes it evident that in the former an orthodox censor has been at work, adding, altering, and excising.[1] It is therefore in Ephraem and the other Edessan writers before-mentioned, and in Aphraates that we must look for any additions to the canonical text that Tatian may have made. These sources sometimes furnish us with "agrapha" which are also found in the earlier authorities. Extra-canonical quotations and references common to writers, who, *ex hypothesi*, must have possessed the Preaching, and to writers who can only have had access to the Diatessaron! Here, for example :—

1. "Be merciful, that ye may obtain mercy: forgive that it may be forgiven you" (ἐλεεῖτε ἵνα ἐλεηθῆτε, ἀφίετε ἵνα ἀφεθῇ ὑμῖν). These agrapha are quoted in 1 Clement in connection with Matt. vii. 1, 2; Luke vi. 36–38, and cannot be explained away by supposing that Clement is quoting loosely, for they are also quoted by Polycarp. "ἐλεεῖτε" reappears in Aphraates (ed. Bert., p. 90), "Let us be merciful as it is

---

[1] The text has been conformed to the Peshito. Tatian's omissions (*e.g.*, the genealogies—Epiphanius tells us that Tatian omitted these, and all relating to Christ's Humanity) have been supplied, and readings not found in the Peshito have been excised, *e.g.*, "Woe to us! Woe for our sins! for the desolation of Jerusalem draweth nigh." *Vide* Moesinger, p. 248; Ante-Nicene Library, vol. xx. p. 31, &c.

written, that God may be merciful to us." "ἀφίετε" is extant in Ciasca (p. 18).¹

2. "Good must needs come, but blessed is he through whom it come" (the corollary of Luke xvii. 1), is quoted in the Clementines, and by Aphraates (ed. Bert., p. 70). "What thou wouldst not have done to thyself, do not to another" (the corollary of Matt. vii. 12; Luke vi. 31), is quoted in the Clementines, and by Bardesanes (Ante-Nicene Library, vol. xxii. pt. ii. p. 90). "There shall be sorrow in heaven over the least that is lost" (the corollary of Luke xv. 7, 10), is referred to in the " Quis dives salvetur" (XLI., XLII.; cf. Apost. Const. viii. 47, canon 52), and quoted by Ephraem (Moesinger, p. 163).

3. "Your speech shall not be vain, but filled by deed," is found in the Διδαχή, and referred to as a precept of Christ's in the Acts of Addai, "Christ commanded that we practise in deed what we preach in word" (Ante-Nicene Library, vol. xx. pt. ii. p. 29).

4. "He who prays must first look well to his gift, that there is no spot to be found on it, and then he shall offer it up, lest his offering remain on earth,"² is quoted by Aphraates (ed. Bert., p. 66), and referred to in the Διδαχή, "Let no one that hath a dispute with his fellow come together with you until they be reconciled, that your sacrifice may be pure." It looks like the Petrine parallel to Matt. v. 23, 24.

5. "Take nothing from any man, and possess noth-

¹ In Resch's "Agrapha" one finds "ἀφίετε" taken as the equivalent of S. Luke's "ἀπολύετε." But Resch is evidently wrong, for the Diatessaron contains BOTH.

² These last words, "lest his offering remain on earth," show that the blemish to be avoided is lack of brotherly love. The reference is to Gen. iv. 7, LXX., "Thy offering returns to thee." The smoke of Cain's offering hung heavy.

ing on earth, for your possession is in heaven." In whole or part this is frequently quoted as a saying of Christ's by the Edessan authorities. The last clause, or something very like, is quoted as a saying of Christ's by Justin (De Resurrectione, ix.); and a probable allusion to the whole verse occurs in the Clementines (Hom. viii. 21).

6. "On the first day of the week Christ rose again, and on the first day of the week He rose upon the world, and on the first day of the week he ascended" (Ante-Nicene Library, vol. xx.; Edessan documents, p. 38; *cf.* pp. 13, 36, 40, 90).[1] This statement is exactly paralleled in the Epistle of Barnabas, "We ought to keep the first day of the week with gladness, for on the first day of the week Christ rose, and, having manifested Himself, ascended."

Our theory then of a fifth gospel, the Preaching, in Tatian's hands, involves no isolated phenomenon. The agrapha in the early authorities lead up to such a theory. Leading away from Tatian, one notices a "Gospel of Peter"[2] in use at Rhossus; and a widely diffused "Prædicatio Petri," not indeed identical with our "Preaching," but perhaps based on it.

That the Preaching ultimately disappeared is not very extraordinary. It was, *ex hypothesi*, followed by S. Luke's Gospel very quickly, and as re-arranged there was far better suited for general use. Its narrow circulation could not guarantee it against corruption. And no room for it was left when once our second

---

[1] The idea that Christ ascended on a Sunday is closely connected in the Edessan documents with the further idea that Christ remained on earth after His Resurrection FIFTY days.

[2] Serapion speaks of it as "consisting for the most part of the right word of the Saviour, but with some things super-added." Origen indirectly informs us that it contained an account of the Infancy.

canonical gospel was generally received as S. Mark's. Three evangelists were well-known by name, and three gospels were needed to correspond—three only. The Preaching would ultimately be regarded as a mutilated adulterated S. Luke.

XI.

At this point it becomes necessary to digress temporarily into a side field. The connection between the "Gospel according to S. Luke" and the "Acts of the Apostles" is so close, that no theory respecting the former can thoroughly commend itself, unless its consequences can be followed out in the latter. Besides this, there are several important sections of the gospel, notably Luke i. 5–ii., for the classification of which the gospel by itself affords inadequate indications, and it is natural to look for additional light in the sister document.

Manifestly, it is on internal evidence that the Acts question must be decided. As Renan observes, "Of Christ we possess four accounts, of the Apostles only one."

In the "Gospel according to S. Luke" we have detected three ingredients,—there is the canonical S. Mark, the "Preaching of Peter," and the work of the redactor, presumably S. Luke. The first of these three ingredients being obviously absent in the Acts (for between Acts and the canonical S. Mark not the slightest similarity exists of style and diction), the question now to be examined is this—Whether it is the author of the Preaching, or S. Luke, that we hear in the Acts, or both? for the connection between the gospel and the Acts appears too close to allow the supposition of any considerable new authority in the latter. Let us endeavour to discover S. Luke's own particular style.

S. Luke's own particular style can, *ex hypothesi*, be partially discovered by the following tests:—

1. By comparing the passages common to the second canonical gospel and the third. The new expressions and phrases in the latter will be S. Luke's own.

2. Similarly, by comparing the passages of the Preaching, common to the first canonical gospel and the third,—for though, *prima facie*, there is equal likelihood of the original Petrine text being preserved in the latter, yet when we come down to particulars, and examine each difference on its own merits, this likelihood will generally be found to disappear (cf. Luke vii. 21; Matt. xi. 3, 4).[1] And in the same direction, viz., to the freer editing on the part of S. Luke, point the verbal coincidences between the Petrine and non-Petrine portions of the third canonical gospel, and the absence of such in the first.

Also we have to compare the account of the appearance at Emmaus in Luke xxiv. with that contained in Mark xvi. 9–20: for this appendix to S. Mark will be shown in Chapter XIV. to belong to the Preaching: and that the original Petrine account has been expanded in Luke xxiv., not abbreviated in Mark xvi., appears from the dependence of Luke xxiv. 22–24 on non-Petrine sections.

3. By noting the expressions common to the sec-

---

[1] S. Luke has to justify "the blind receive their sight." Compare, too, Matt. vi. 23, "$εἰ\ οὖν\ τὸ\ φῶς\ τὸ\ ἐν\ σοὶ\ σκότος\ ἐστίν,\ τὸ\ σκότος\ πόσον$," with Luke xi. 35, "$σκόπει\ οὖν\ μὴ\ τὸ\ φῶς,\ τὸ\ ἐν\ σοί,\ σκότος\ ἐστίν.$" The original must have been "$εἰ\ οὖν\ τὸ\ φῶς,\ τὸ\ ἐν\ σοί,\ σκότος\ ἐστίν.$" S. Luke is the further away.

tions of the Preaching contained in S. Luke, and to those portions of Luke xxiv., which not being paralleled in Mark xvi. 9–20, *ex hypothesi*, represent the lost ending of the canonical S. Mark, or something equivalent.[1]

4. With the vocabulary afforded by these three tests in our hands, let us next examine the "we" sections of Acts, confining ourselves strictly to the sections in which the "we" actually occurs; for however necessary to a complete sense the contexts may appear, yet there is the antecedent possibility to be reckoned with of an earlier document to which "we" sections have been added as after-touches. That after-touches they are, supposing such earlier document to have existed, and not part and parcel of that earlier document, the critics are in a majority who admit. The author, then, of the "we" sections is in all probability either the sole author of Acts or the completer. No later hand has gone over his. Moreover, he had no collaborator, the intimate connection of the "we" sections with one another being such as to preclude any plurality of authorship. With this much premised, to proceed:—

Here in Acts xvi. 9–18 we find:—
κατακολουθεῖν, παραγγέλειν ἐξελθεῖν, πνεῦμα πυθῶνος (cf. δαιμονίου, Luke iv. 33), μένειν (= lodge), διανοίγειν. εὐαγγελίζεσθαι, συνέρχεσθαι, ἀνάγειν (= embark), αὐτῇ τῇ ὥρα, ἐγένετο δέ, παραβιάζεσθαι—in eight verses eleven expressions which the redactor of the gospel is alone in using, or for which he has shown a predilection.

Similarly in Acts xx. 5–16; xxi. 1–18:—
προέρχεσθαι (2), ἱκανός (= πολύς, 3), βαθύς, ὁμιλεῖν, ἀνάγειν (3), ἐγένετο δέ (2), ἑξῆς, πλεῖν, κατέρχεσθαι, (2), τιθέναι τὰ γόνατα (2), ἀποσπασθῆναι, ὑποστρέφειν,

[1] For special justification of this hypothesis, *vide* Chapter XXIV.

ἡσυχάζειν, συνέρχεσθαι, ἀποδέχεσθαι, παραγίνεσθαι, πείθεσθαι, κατάγειν, δὲ καί, σύν (4), ζητεῖν (followed by inf.).

Again in Acts xxvii.–xxviii. 16 :—

ἑξῆς (2), πλεῖν (3), κατέρχεσθαι, ἀποτινάσσειν, χαρίζεσθαι, ἀνάγειν (6), κατάγειν (2), πείθεσθαι, ἰσχύειν, ἅπτειν (= to kindle), ῥίπτειν, ὑπάρχειν (4), σταθείς, ἡμέρα γίνεσθαι (3), θρὶξ ἀπὸ τῆς κεφαλῆς ἀπολεῖται, ἐνώπιον, προσάγειν, προσδοκᾶν (3), βουλή, ἱκανός (= πολύς, 2), συναρπάζειν, κατέχειν, ἀποδέχεσθαι, βραχύ, διιστάναι, ἐπιγινώσκειν (2), καὶ αὐτός, τὰ περί, συνέχεσθαι (πυρετῷ), σύν (2), ζητεῖν (followed by inf.).

The full force of the foregoing list becomes evident when we contrast the relationship of these "we" sections to the Preaching. TO THE "WE" SECTIONS AND THE GREAT JOURNEY PERICOPE (Luke ix.–xix.) THERE IS LITTLE COMMON AND NOTHING PECULIAR. Nor must be forgotten the smallness of the field to which we have been confined in gleaning the vocabulary of the redactor of the gospel. The foregoing list, then, appears sufficient to establish the identity of the redactor of the gospel and the author of the "we" sections. And so we have here a fourth test for the discovery of S. Luke's own particular style, the phraseology of the "we" sections being his very own.

5. This fourth test leads to a fifth. The dedication to Theophilus (Luke i. 1–4), the strict classical form of which contrasts so strongly with the Hebraic narrative subsequent, has affinities with the "we" sections and with the sections connected.[1] But we are not limited to this indirect indication of authorship. There is the argument from remainders. Order or connected-

[1] Cf. Acts xviii. 25, 26 ; xxvi. 4, 5. Among other points of contact between the "we" sections and Luke i. 1–4 may be noticed a fondness for quadrisyllables, especially in termination.

ness ("καθεξῆς") is about the last quality to be attributed to the Preaching. Acquaintance with previous evangelistic efforts ("πολλοὶ ἐπεχείρησαν") precludes an author absolutely independent, such as the peculiarities of the Preaching have been shown to require. And the earliest tradition extant of the origin of the Preaching accords ill with the idea of "careful investigation" ("παρηκολουθηκότι ἀκρίβως").

At first sight, indeed, it occurs as an objection that the limits within which our theory requires us to confine S. Luke's activity are too narrow to justify the writer's claim in Luke i. 2 to have received the sacred tradition from men "who from the beginning were eye-witnesses and ministers of the word," but on closer scrutiny this objection disappears. S. Luke does not necessarily claim to have received the tradition from eyewitnesses himself, but only to be a member of the community to which such tradition was delivered. This is shown by his use of the first person just previously— " πεπληροφορημένων ἐν ἡμῖν "—for only in the sense of being their co-religionist could he reckon himself one of those among whom the events of Christ's life " found accomplishment."

To sum up now the general result of applying these five tests. There are certain words and phrases unmistakably S. Luke's own in the earlier part of Acts, but there are at least four times as many in the later. The second half of Acts, the history of S. Paul, is mainly original work of S. Luke's, but not altogether; and there are a few, a very few, traces of S. Luke's handiwork in the first half of Acts, the history of S. Peter.

It will now be our object to show that the remainder of Acts, after the subtraction of S. Luke's work, is a continuation of the Preaching.

1. The first half of Acts contains a quite independent account of the death of Judas,[1] and refers to and agrees with the Petrine sections of S. Luke,[2] *e.g.*, as to the trial before Herod, the persistent attempts of Pilate to release, and the superiority of Annas to Caiaphas (Acts i. 18, 19; iii. 13, 14; iv. 6, 27).[3] There is a likeness too between Cornelius, and the centurion of Luke vii.

Among the words and expressions, otherwise peculiar to the Petrine sections of S. Luke, may be noticed, ἀναδεικνύναι, ἐκτενῶς, ἀναβαίνειν εἰς ἱερόν, κρούειν θύραν, προσδοκία, ποιεῖν ἐκδίκησιν, προϋπάρχειν, ζωογονεῖν, ἴασις, αἴρειν φωνήν, ἀνασπᾶν, ἀνακαθίζειν, διισχυρίζεσθαι.

2. The Epistle to the Hebrews, as will be shown in the next chapter, is closely connected both in style and thought with the Gospel according to S. Luke and the Acts. But now that the gospel has been cut in two, it will be found that the connection with the epistle is confined to the sections classified as Petrine. Consequently there is an inference that the sections of Acts which contain affinities with the epistle are Petrine too. The earlier part of Acts contains many more affinities with the epistle than the later.

3. Except on the theory of S. Paul's return to the East after the imprisonment recorded in Acts xxviii., it follows almost inevitably that the author

---

[1] From which Matt. xxvii. 8 appears to be an interpolation. The old Latin supplies "Aceldama." Or Acts i. 19 may be borrowed from the above passage by S. Luke.

[2] And sometimes disagrees with the non-Petrine sections of S. Luke. For example, the contrast of Baptism with water and Baptism with the Spirit is put into John's mouth in Luke iii. 16; but into Christ's in Acts i. 5; xi. 16. The quotation from the Baptist's Preaching in Acts xiii. 25 does not accord with Luke iii. 16; or the reference to the entombment in ver. 29, with Luke xxiii. 50, &c.

[3] Caiaphas is the High Priest in Matt. xxvi. 3, 57; but Annas in the Preaching (Luke iii. 2; Acts iv. 6).

THE FORMATION OF THE GOSPELS. 49

of the Pastoral Epistles (not S. Paul) had certain portions of Acts in his hands, and not others. He knows of the troubles S. Paul underwent "at Antioch, Iconium, Lystra," 2 Tim. iii. 11 (the order is the same as in Acts xiii., xiv.); he knows of the tears which the Ephesian elders shed at Miletus, 2 Tim. i. 4; he knows the terms of S. Paul's valedictory address, 2 Tim. ii. 9, 19; iv. 7; he knows of the mission of Erastus to Greece, and the absence of his name in the list of S. Paul's companions from Greece, 2 Tim. iv. 20 (cf. Acts xix. 22; xx. 4); he knows that Trophimus accompanied S. Paul "as far as Asia;" but he does not know (unless indeed in 2 Tim. iv. 20, the *v. r.* "Melita" be adopted) that Trophimus further accompanied S. Paul to Jerusalem (cf. Acts xx. 4, xxi. 29); and he does not know the length of S. Paul's imprisonment at Cæsarea, 2 Tim. iv. 13, 20. In fine, the author of the Pastorals appears to be acquainted with those portions of Acts which belong to the Preaching, and unacquainted with those which are the original work of S. Luke. And this inference is strengthened by the test of language, for the language of the Pastorals is exceptionally allied to that of the Preaching (*cf.* 1 Tim. v. 18; 2 Tim. ii. 12, 26).

4. Some of the later part of Acts is sufficiently connected with the earlier to make it clear that the disappearance of S. Peter from the scene marks no MS. ending. There is a keynote struck in Acts i. 8, "Be my witnesses in Judea, and in Samaria, and unto the uttermost part of the earth," which involves a termination in Rome,[1] and as the subsequent account

---

[1] If S. Mark did not accompany Aristarchus and S. Luke to Rome, he is soon found there in their company (Col. iv. 10; Philem. 24).

of witness in Judæa and Samaria is part of the history of S. Peter (notice, too, the resemblance of Acts i. 11 to iii. 19), there is an inference that S. Peter's biographer gave some account of witness in Rome too. In the same direction point the often noted conformities of S. Peter and S. Paul. Both healing congenital lameness; both falling into trances; both in conflict with magicians; both offered worship; both bound with double chain; both supplying the gift of tongues by the imposition of hands; inaugurating their ministries by similar sermons; healing, the one by cloths from his body, the other by his shadow. For in some cases, at any rate, the Pauline parallel is couched in the language of the Preaching. All that S. Luke can have done is to have somewhat heightened the parallelism. And in one notable case, S. Paul has been robbed to pay S. Peter, in the matter of eating with the Gentiles (Acts xi. 3, 12; cf. Gal. ii.), as though the writer would show that the title "Apostle of the Uncircumcision" was not S. Paul's exclusively, that the merit of opening a door to the Gentiles and establishing a common table belonged to S. Peter as well.[1]

5. There are certain incongruities in the text of Acts which can be best explained by supposing that more than one hand has been at work, and these incongruities generally follow the lines already indicated. Agabus is introduced in xxi. 10 as though he had not been mentioned previously in xi. 28; churches of Syria and Cilicia are written to and confirmed in

[1] The Pauline parallel to Acts xi. 3, 12 may have been excised by S. Luke, as derogatory to S. Peter. But the emphasis laid in Acts xi. on S. Peter's advance appears significant, when we remember his subsequent recession.

xv. 23, 41,[1] of the foundation of which nothing appears to be known to the author of Acts ix. 30, xi. 25. Saul's companions in ix. 7 "stood speechless, hearing a voice, but beholding no man," but in xxii. 9, xxvi. 14, they "fell to the earth," "beheld the light, but heard not the voice."[2] The exordium in xiii. 1 comes strangely after xi. 19–30; xii. 25.

In this connection the various readings in Acts call for notice, *e.g.*, xv. 33, 34; xviii. 4, 5; xix. 1. How closely they are connected by phraseology with the rest of the text![3] How naturally they are accounted for, if the genesis of Acts be such as is suggested! They look like interlineations of S. Luke's own, or corrections showing through his erasure.[4]

To sum the matter up. The earlier part of Acts is by the author of the Preaching, and a not neglectable portion of the later.

Let us now examine Luke i. 5–ii. in the light of this conclusion. These two chapters will be found to contain the following words and expressions peculiar to the Preaching, διελθεῖν ἕως, ἔναντι θεοῦ, χεὶρ κυρίου, βραχιὼν κυρίου, Δαυὶδ παῖς (θεοῦ), ἐπιδεῖν, τί ὅτι, φόβος ἐπί (exc. Rev. xiii.), ἀναζητεῖν, μεγαλεῖα (θεοῦ), στεῖρα,

---
[1] The wording of this letter is evidently S. Luke's. Compare "ἐπειδὴ πολλοὶ ἐπεχείρησαν, κἀμοὶ ἔδοξεν, παρηκολουθηκότι πᾶσιν, γράψαι σοι" and "ἐπειδὴ τινες ἐτάραξαν ὑμᾶς, ἔδοξεν ἡμῖν, γενομένοις ὁμοθυμαδόν, πέμψαι." This absolute use of "ἔδοξεν" is peculiar to Luke i. 3 and Acts xv.

[2] S. Luke's hand is shown by "ἔμφοβος," "καταπίπτειν."

[3] Thus Acts xv. 34 contains three of S. Luke's characteristic expressions = ἔδοξεν (absolutely), αὐτοῦ, ἐπιμεῖναι.

[4] Thus the *v. r.* in xix. 1. "And having determined to go up to Jerusalem, he was hindered by the Spirit (and passing through the upper country, he came to Ephesus)," seems to be the Petrine equivalent to xviii. 18–28. These eleven verses are couched entirely in S. Luke's special style. Perhaps S. Luke's informants were Aquila and Priscilla. The Edessan tradition tells us that "they accompanied S. Luke to the day of his death."

THE FORMATION OF THE GOSPELS.

ποιεῖν μετά, λατρεύειν (abs., exc. Hebrews), ποιεῖν ἔλεος, καθότι, ὀδυνᾶσθαι, ἡμέρας ὁδός, σκιρτᾶν, στρατία, ἐν (= among), φάτνη, πνεῦμα ἐπέρχεται, ἀνθ' ὧν (except 2 Thess. ii. 10), τόπος ἐστί (= there is room), εὐλαβής, ὕψιστος (absolute), θρόνος Δαυίδ, ἀπογραφή, ἐπισκέπτεσθαι (of God), σιωπῶν μὴ δυνάμενος λαλῆσαι (constr. cf. Acts xiii. 11; xiv. 8), δόξα ἐν ὑψίστοις καὶ εἰρήνη. Δέσποτα—δοῦλος σοῦ, ὅρκον ὤμοσε, κατὰ τὸ ἔθος, ὑπομένειν.

And surely the following are from one hand:—

Mine eyes have seen Thy salvation,
A light for revelation to the Gentiles,
And the glory of Thy people Israel (Luke ii. 30, 32).
Salvation unto His people,
For the remission of their sins,
To shine upon them that sit in darkness (Luke i. 77, 79).

I have set Thee for a light of the Gentiles,
For salvation unto the uttermost part of the earth (Acts xiii. 47).

Open the eyes (of the Gentiles), that they may turn from darkness to light, that they may receive remission of sins—proclaim light both to the people, and to the Gentiles (Acts xxvi. 17, 18, 23).

He hath raised up a horn of salvation for us,
In the house of His servant David,
As He spake by the mouth of His holy prophets,
Which have been since the world began (Luke i. 69, 70).

Of this man's seed (David's) hath God, according to promise, brought unto Israel a Saviour (Acts xiii. 23).
God hath sworn with an oath that of the fruit of his (David's) loins, he would set one upon his throne (Acts ii. 30).
Whereof God spake by the mouth of His holy prophets,
Which have been since the world began (Acts iii. 21).

That he might remember mercy,
As He spake unto our fathers,
Towards Abraham and his seed for ever (Luke i. 54, 55).

Men of Israel, ye are sons of the covenant which God made with your fathers, saying unto Abraham, "In thy seed shall all families be blessed" (Acts iii. 25).

To remember His holy covenant.	The promise made unto the fathers, God hath fulfilled unto our children (Acts xiii. 32, 33).
The oath which He sware unto Abraham our father (Luke i. 72, 73).	The promise made of God unto our fathers (Acts xxvi. 6).

XII.

The peculiar affinities of the Epistle to the Hebrews with S. Luke's Gospel and the Acts have often been noticed. As the case now stands, these affinities are all with the "Petrine" sections.[1]

The following words and expressions are peculiar to the Epistle and the Preaching:—

ἐκλείπειν, παλαιοῦν, ἱλάσκεσθαι, τὸ ἄκρον, εὔθετος, ἀνώτερον, ἀναστάσεως τυγχάνειν, εἰς τὸ παντελές, μέτοχος, πόρρωθεν, στόμα μαχαίρας, τὸ ἀληθινόν, (ἁρπαγή, ἀποδεκατοῦν except Matt. xxiii. 23, 25). (ἐκζητεῖν, ἀποδιδόναι λόγον except 1 Pet.), χρεία ἐστίν (exc. Rev.).

[1] The only exceptions to this rule that are furnished in the gospel, "συναντᾶν," "παροικεῖν," have no significance whatever, for the presence of these words in Heb. vii. 1, 10; xi. 9 is explained by reference to the LXX. Gen. xiv. 17; 1 Chron. xvi. 19.
The exceptions furnished in Acts—in the final "we" section—"ἀσάλευτος," "βοήθεια," "ἀναδέχεσθαι" (there is "ἄστρον" too, but the presence of this word in Heb. xi. 25 is explained by reference to the LXX. Ex. xxxii. 13), are at first sight slightly disturbing; but as they are ἅπαξ λεγόμενα here and in Hebrews, and are used in different senses, there is nothing to preclude our attributing the coincidence to accident.
The following consideration reassures us—that the only alternative, the attribution of the affinities with Hebrews to S. Luke himself, is a sheer impossibility: for the words which are commonest in the gospel, words proved by the tests of Chapter XI. to be S. Luke's own, are altogether absent in the Epistle—παραχρῆμα, παραγίνεσθαι, ὑπάρχειν, καὶ ἐγένετο and ἐγένετο δέ (introductory), ἐνώπιον, ὑποστρέφειν, ἐφιστάναι, ἱκανός, πλήθειν, συνέχειν. So, too, the words commonest in the "we" sections—κατανᾶν, προσλαμβάνεσθαι, &c.

διατίθεσθαι, ὁ ἡγούμενος, ἀπαλλάσσειν, ἀνορθοῦν, ἦχος (= sound), διαβαίνειν.

ἀρχηγός, ἐσώτερος, σχεδόν, ἀναθεωρεῖν, ὕπαρξις, πατριάρχης, ἐκ ὀσφύος, μετὰ παρρησίας, μετὰ δακρύων, μετ' εἰρήνης, ἐργάζεσθαι δικαιοσύνην, ὑμνεῖν (with acc.), πειρᾶσθαι, λόγος παρακλήσεως, ἐπιστέλλειν, καταφεύγειν, ἀποδίδοσθαι, παροξυσμός, προσφέρειν προσφόραν, Αἰγύπτιος, εὐλαβεῖσθαι.

The thoughts, too, are very often similar:—

"The sign to the Ninevites," alluded to in Luke xi. 30, was the wild stranger crying, "Yet forty days and Nineveh shall be overthrown"—not the whale. So the Hebrews are told, in the fourth decade after the crucifixion, the last before the destruction of Jerusalem, that their day of grace is almost past—the forty years' provocation nearly complete; it is others who will enter Canaan.

As Christ, in the Preaching, falls "into an agony," and prays "more earnestly," His sweat becoming "as blood," so in Hebrews "He offered up prayers and supplications, with strong crying and tears, unto Him that was able to save Him from death."

As in the Preaching, so in the Hebrews, we hear of the "righteousness" of Abel and his wakeful blood; Samuel as inaugurator of prophecy; the voice, "This day have I begotten Thee;"[1] the "perfection" of Christ through suffering (*cf.* Luke xiii. 32); the necessity for final perseverance; Christ's liability to human infirmity;[2] "seasons of restitution."

[1] The *v. r.* in Luke iii. 22, "This day have I begotten Thee," belongs *ex hypothesi* to the Preaching.
[2] It is not without reason that the ox has been taken as the emblem of the third evangelist.

S. Stephen's apology (Acts vii.) is especially noteworthy in this connection, almost every reference to the O. T. being paralleled in the Epistle. Pharaoh's destruction of Hebrew children; the escape of Moses and his great renunciation; the burial of Jacob's sons; the promise to Abraham and his homelessness in Canaan; the forty years' wandering; the rest given by Joshua; the heavenly archetype of the Temple; the mediation of Angels at Sinai; that Moses was "ἀστεῖος," became "ἔντρομος" at the Bush, led Israel through the "ἐρυθρὰ θάλασσα."

Especially noteworthy is the very similar relationship of the Preaching and Hebrews to 1 Peter.[1] Among the words and expressions peculiar to 1 Peter and Hebrews may be noted—ἀντίτυπος, ἔννοια, ῥαντισμός, ἑκουσίως, ἐπισκοπεῖν, κατασκευάζειν κιβωτόν, παρεπίδημος. And διὰ βραχέων ἐπέστειλα is not unlike δι' ὀλίγων ἔγραψα. But it is rather in thought than in word that the two epistles approximate. In both we hear of Purification, Redemption, Atonement by blood, the Lamb without blemish, the pattern afforded by Christ, priesthood of Christians, their spiritual sacrifices, their homelessness on earth, their abiding heritage in heaven. The Paulinism of Hebrews has been commented on frequently, but it would be impossible to select any five chapters from S. Paul's epistles, which present as many points of contact with Hebrews as 1 Peter.

It is chiefly for the sake of Luke i. 5–ii. that we have made this digression. The affinities of Hebrews with Luke i. 5–ii. are quite as great as with the other parts of the Preaching.

[1] The connection of the Preaching with 1 Peter is pointed out in the next chapter.

The following words and expressions are peculiar to Luke i. 5–ii. and the Epistle:—

λύτρωσις, τελείωσις, τάξις (of priestly rank), ἱεράτεια, ὑπογράφεσθαι, Ἀαρών, ἰδεῖν θάνατον, τὸ ἁγιόν (exc. Matt. vii. 6), λατρεύειν (abs., exc. Acts xxvi. 7), δόγμα (= decree), εὑρίσκειν χάριν.

Luke i. 5–ii., like Hebrews, is full of priest, and Temple, and altar, and offering, and incense.

The Blessed Virgin hears, "A sword shall pierce thine heart, that thoughts of many hearts may be revealed." Similarly, in Heb. iv. 12, the word of God is compared to a sword "piercing even to the dividing asunder of soul and spirit, of both joints and marrow, and quick to discern the thoughts of the heart."

So again, when we read in Heb. xii. 22–24—"Ye are come to Mount Zion, to hosts of angels, to the church of the first-born enrolled in heaven, and to Jesus"—we are reminded of that enrolment when S. Joseph and S. Mary brought up their first-born Son to David's city, and shepherds and angels did Him homage. In both cases there seems to be an allusion to Psalm lxxxvii., describing the extension of the citizenship of Zion to the world:—

> "This one was born there,
> Yea, of Zion it shall be said, This one and that one was born there,
> The Lord shall count, when He writeth up the peoples,
> This one was born there."

The evidence then of the Acts and of the Epistle to the Hebrews goes strongly to support the connection with the Preaching of Luke i. 5–ii., separated so often from the rest of the Gospel. Luke i. 5–ii.

must be Petrine. And there is very little room left for S. Luke.

There are, indeed, critics who discover traces of an older picture, lying behind that which we possess, in the fact that there is only the genealogy of S. Joseph to justify vigorous assertions of Christ's Davidic descent;[1] that S. Joseph is referred to as "father," "parent," and included in Simeon's blessing; that both S. Joseph and S. Mary WONDER at Simeon's prophecies, and are AMAZED by the Child's mention of God's house as "My Father's home." But the miraculous conception is far more deeply woven into the narrative than at first sight appears. Not only must the annunciation be made to S. Joseph, we must tear out S. Elizabeth. For a correspondency between the two women is evidently intended—the one "$\sigma\tau\epsilon\hat{\iota}\rho\alpha$," the other "$\pi\alpha\rho\theta\epsilon\nu\sigma$." And in the genealogy itself the phrase "Adam, son of God," connected as it is with the idea of Christ being a second Adam, inheritor of no taint from the first (cf. Romans v.; 1 Cor. xv.), involves some break in the descent, some new act of creation. Hence, if older picture there is, at all events the later development is previous to S. Luke.

But there is no necessity for any older picture whatever, even allowing the utmost possible significance to the anomalies above-mentioned. The essence

[1] This point, however, may easily be overrated. There was a long interval during which our Lord was reputed "Son of Joseph," and in the genealogy of Luke iv. there is copy perhaps of the family register. Before the miraculous conception was published, it would naturally have been on Joseph that the Messiah's Davidic claim was rested. And afterwards, even if the Davidic descent of the Blessed Virgin had been ascertained as clearly as S. Joseph's, yet the subsequent prominence of Joseph's kin as descendants of David,—they and not the Virgin's were accused on account of their birth, under Domitian and Trajan,—would account for the accentuation of the ancestry of Joseph.

of the Jewish marriage was the betrothal, not the taking home. Before the latter ceremony had been accomplished, S. Joseph and S. Mary were already "husband" and "wife," and their relationship could only be dissolved by a regular "divorcement." The office of the Holy Ghost, as Alford points out, need not exclude S. Joseph altogether. Christ is nowhere styled son of the Holy Ghost, nor is the Holy Ghost ever spoken of as His father.[1] The title "son of God" is independent of the Incarnation, and there is no hint that the Incarnation intensified the relationship of the Son to the Father. The narrative simply states that Christ's birth was miraculous, was not attributable to any action or volition of His mother's husband. When the rib was taken from Adam's side, Adam was unconscious. It is at any rate easier to suppose that the author of the Preaching entertained such a view as this than to make any cleavage in the text.

Proof that the general historicity of Luke i. 5–ii. is not lower than a Petrine origin involves, will be attempted presently, in connection with the correspondent section of S. Matthew.

XIII.

Reasons for seeking the "Preaching" elsewhere than in "the Gospel according to S. Mark":—

1. "The Gospel according to S. Mark" is, as we shall endeavour to demonstrate presently, secondary to

---

[1] The looseness of language and idea in early times is shown by the allusion to the Holy Ghost as Christ's "Mother" in the Gospel according to the Hebrews.

other documents (whereas one would expect the record of S. Peter's Preaching to be primitive), and the documents to which it is secondary will be otherwise accounted for.

2. That S. Luke was in possession of "the Gospel according to S. Mark," critics are agreed. But if "the Gospel according to S. Mark" be the original Petrine document, S. Luke's attitude towards it becomes incomprehensible. Let S. Luke's other authorities have been what they may, yet at least one would expect deference to S. Mark's account of the denials. Who could have known better what actually occurred in the high priest's hall than S. Peter? Who have re-echoed S. Peter more accurately than his amanuensis? But S. Luke deviates from Mark xiv. very widely,[1] altering the words of warning, and the occasion of their utterance; substituting for the second maid, a man-servant; distinguishing one voice only in the third accusation; and excluding absolutely S. Peter's retreat into the porch.[2]

3. Between "the Gospel according to S. Mark" and the First Epistle of S. Peter there is not the slightest similarity of style and diction. They contain not a single word or phrase peculiar.

4. The title of the second gospel may not be much older than the middle of the second century. The fact that S. Mark was well known as the author of a gospel would account for the transference of his name to an

---

[1] It is similarly significant that the author of the fourth gospel, in his account of the denials, should follow Luke xxii. rather than Mark xiv.; and the author of 2 Peter, in his citation of the voice, "heard on the holy mount," Matt. xvii. rather than Mark ix.

[2] "The Lord turned and looked at Peter" implies Peter's presence in the hall. Once outside, he would not be likely to return. In Matt. xxvi. 73 the officers come out to him.

anonymous gospel, if the document of which he was actually the author had been merged in other documents. None of the early fathers cite the gospels by name. And the case of the Epistle to the Hebrews, variously assigned by second century titles to Paul or Barnabas, or neither, warns us against accepting the decision of second-century scribes as final.

Reasons for identifying the "Preaching" with the document peculiar to S. Matthew and S. Luke—

1. It agrees—and no other document forthcoming does—with John the Elder's description, being disorderly, perfectly independent, and containing likely subject-matter for an Apostle's discourses.

2. The great deference paid to it by S. Luke seems to involve its apostolic origin. Whenever S. Luke has to make his choice, he always prefers it to " the Gospel according to S. Mark." Thus he sacrifices the call of the four disciples, Mark i. 16–20; the murmuring at Nazareth, vi. 1–6; the Corban discourse, vii. 1–23; the divorce disputation, x. 1–12; the request of James and John, x. 35–45; the blasting of the fig-tree, xi. 12–25; the unction at Bethany, xiv. 3–9; the mockery by Pilate's soldiers, xv. 16–20; also Mark ii. 21, iii. 27.

3. It relates facts about S. Peter which are likely to have come from S. Peter's own lips: " Henceforth catch men;" " Simon, Simon, Satan hath desired to have thee;" " The Lord turned and looked on Peter."

And the part of the Acts with which it is most closely connected exhibits certain phenomena, which S. Mark's authorship would best explain. Thus the author of Acts xii. is well acquainted with the interior arrangement of S. Mark's mother's house. We hear what the inmates say and do while S. Peter stands at the door knocking. And then S. Peter's history comes to an abrupt termination just at the moment when we know that S. Peter and S. Mark parted company. It is resumed in xv., when S. Peter returns to the place where S. Mark is last heard of; then terminates altogether when S. Mark again starts on his journeys.[1] And it is worth noticing, just at this point, what a huge gap occurs in the history of S. Paul—after the rupture with S. Mark, before the meeting with S. Luke—the whole foundation of the churches of Galatia, one of the most important events of his life, shrunk in a single line!

4. It is closely related to the First Epistle of Peter.[2] The transience of mundane glory, the spiritual progeny of Abraham, the trial and stablishment of faith in temptations, love covering many sins, participation in Christ's glories as in His sufferings, Christ's submission to earthly ordinances, His patience under injury, His resignation on the Cross—these are among the thoughts common to both.

Among the words and phrases peculiar may be noticed:—καιρὸς ἐπισκόπης, ἡμέραι Νωέ, ὁ Ἐκλεκτός (of Christ), ἀντίδικος, ἐκτενής, ἐκτενῶς, ἀνάστασίς ἐκ νεκρῶν, ποίμνιον, ἀποδιδόναι λόγον (exc. Hebrews), ἐπηρεάζειν, ἐκζητεῖν (exc. Hebrews).

That the list of words peculiar, is not longer may be accounted for, partly by the fact that 1 Peter is

[1] The references to S. Mark's defection can scarcely come from S. Mark himself. They contain several of S. Luke's own favourite expressions, ὑποστρέφειν, ἀποχωρεῖν, συνέρχεσθαι, ἐκπλεῖν.

[2] Much more closely than to the epistles of S. Paul. It is perhaps worth noticing that the epistles of S. Paul, to which it is most nearly related, are his earliest ones—I. and II. Thessalonians, written while the influence of Barnabas was still fresh, Colossians, Philippians, Ephesians, written after the re-meeting with S. Mark.

"by the hand of Silas," not of Mark; partly by the fact that the disciples of S. Peter and S. Paul approximated—S. Mark and Silas attached to S. Peter and S. Paul almost equally! S. Luke their companion! How else can the Paulinism of 1 Peter be accounted for? The list of words and expressions common to the Preaching and 1 Peter, but not quite peculiar, is very long indeed.

5. The Epistle to the Hebrews was evidently written by some one who stood high in the sub-apostolic rank, deeply imbued with Pauline phraseology, nevertheless a *persona grata* to the Hebrews he addresses. No Gentile like S. Luke, no mere disciple of S. Paul, would have ventured to such an audience on a tone of such lofty remonstrance. "Ye have need that I teach you again the first rudiments of the faith." It appears from the use made of the epistle in 1 Clement and "Barnabas," that the writer's name was revered in Rome and Alexandria. He intends soon to visit the Church he addresses in the company of Timothy. May we not complement Heb. xiii. 23 with 2 Tim. iv. 11, and identify him with the man in whose company Timothy is last heard of? Moreover, S. Mark was a Levite,[1] and this fact would go to explain the sacerdotalism of the epistle, as also of Luke i. 5–ii., where we are reminded that Christ's parents attended feasts, revered the temple, and offered sacrifice.

XIV.

Critics are generally agreed that the last twelve verses of S. Mark stand by themselves, apart from the

---

[1] Acts iv. 36; Col. iv. 10. Tradition gives S. Mark the πέταλον.

rest of the gospel. They are omitted in many MSS., and contain no less than twenty-one words and expressions which elsewhere in the gospel occur never. I have assigned them to the Preaching for the following reasons:—

1. They are absolutely independent of the triple tradition.

2. They were known to S. Luke. In Luke xxiv. 11 "ἠπίστουν" (disbelieved) is a reflection of Mark xvi. 11. And, with a single exception,[1] every one of the details of the appearance to the two walking into the country is reproduced in the Emmaus history.

3. They are connected with Acts. In ver. 19, as in Acts i. 9, Christ is received up "when He had spoken;" and in Acts x. 42 allusion is made to the fact, peculiar to ver. 16, that He had spoken of the final judgment. The injunction in ver. 18, "Preach the Gospel," is alluded to in Acts i. 2 (D). And "Ye shall pick up serpents" suggests cognisance of the miracle recorded in Acts xxviii.

4. Ver. 9 depends on Luke viii. 2; and ver. 18 (immunity from things noxious) recalls Luke x. 19.

There is a remarkable coincidence between vers. 19, 20: "The Lord, after He had spoken (concerning salvation, and tongues, and healings), sat down at the right hand of God. And they went forth and preached everywhere, the Lord working with them, and confirming the word by the signs that followed;" and Hebrews ii. 3, 4: "Salvation, having been at first spoken through the Lord, was confirmed unto us by them that heard; God bearing witness with them by signs and

---

[1] That the two were disbelieved. S. Luke had reasons at this point for departing from the Preaching, which will be found in Chapter XXIV.

wonders, and by manifold powers, and by gifts of the Holy Ghost" (cf. Acts iv. 30; xiv. 3). The expression "sat down at the right hand of God" occurs in Hebrews frequently.

A coincidence of language, again, between ver. 10, "πένθειν καὶ κλαίειν," and Luke vi. 25; and between ver. 20, "ἐπακολούθειν," and 1 Pet. ii. 21.

In fine, nearly all the twenty-one words and expressions which occur in Mark xvi. 9–20, and nowhere else in the gospel, are found in the Preaching, 1 Peter, or Hebrews—πορεύεσθαι εἰς, ἀναλαμβάνειν (of the Ascension), ἐκβάλλειν ἀπό, ὁ κύριος, μετὰ ταῦτα, ὄφις, βεβαιοῦν, ὕστερον (adv.), ἐκεῖνος (absolute use of), θεᾶσθαι, ἀπιστεῖν.

XV.

And now let us temporarily dismiss the "Preaching" from our calculations, and proceed to the second of our theses—the duplicity of the lowest stratum of the triple tradition.

Two tables of doublets were exhibited at the beginning of this work, the consideration of which was deferred.

These tables, like the other two, may be supplemented by certain inconsistencies or textual incongruities.

Firstly, with regard to S. Matthew.

How strange it is to hear Christ enjoining secrecy on the leper, when great multitudes are present (viii. 1, 4); to have two announcements of the Passion almost simultaneous (xvii. 9, 22, 23); to find John's disciples captious (ix. 14) after John has so thoroughly recognised our Lord's prerogative (iii. 14); to hear of

THE FORMATION OF THE GOSPELS. 65

angels ministering to Christ, when He is no longer in the desert (iv. 11);[1] to hear the misgivings of the disciples, " Bread in a desert place ! " (xv. 33), after provision has been made in a similar contingency (xiv. 14–21); to find Herod's opinion cited (xvi. 14) so long after it is expressed (xiv. 2); to hear that the disciples are " exceeding sorry " (xvii. 23) at an announcement which they have already heard twice (xvi. 21 ; xvii. 9); to find the disciples repelling children (xix. 13) after our Lord's disposition towards children has just been expressed so freely (xviii. 1–5); to hear them contending for the first places (xx. 20–28), just after a similar contention has been quelled (xviii. 1–5); to find, after the climax to parabolic teaching (xiii. 33, 34, 35 ; cf. Mark iv. 33, 34), that the parables continue ; to hear Christ explaining why His disciples fast not (ix. 14, 15),[2] just after He has issued His regulations on the subject (vi. 16–18 ; cf. iv. 2; xvii. 21); to hear of Christ's sudden arrival in Cæsarea-Philippi (xvi. 13), just after He has left those parts (xv. 29); to find that it is on the occasion of their second interview with Christ, after His assumption of authority, that the priests ask whence His authority is derived (xxi. 12–23); to hear of Judas, " from that time he sought opportunity," when the opportunity is distant only a few hours (xxvi. 16); to hear of Pilate's scruples and his wife's intercession just before he sentences Christ to be scourged, and allows the soldiers to mock; to hear Christ saying, " When

---

[1] In Mark i. 13 the angels minister continuously (διηκόνουν) *during the forty days.*

[2] And also (if we may complement Matt. ix. 14, 15 out of the parallel passage, Luke v. 33), why they pray not, after a proper form of prayer has been given (vi. 5–15).

E

ye see these things beginning to come to pass, know that He is nigh" (xxiv. 33), when the actual advent has just been described; to hear Christ bidding certain women "*All* hail" when the context (xxviii. 1) only assures us of the presence of two; to hear Simon's surname used (iv. 18) before he receives it (xvi. 18); to hear of "the morrow, which is after the Preparation" (xxvii. 62) when the Preparation has not been mentioned" (cf. Mark xv. 42); to have the same place variously referred to by its proper name (viii. 5, &c.), and as "His own city" (ix. 1).

Secondly, with regard to S. Mark.

How strange to find prophecies of different prophets combined (i. 2, 3), and words of Malachi's attributed to Isaiah; to hear Christ enjoining secrecy on Jaïrus (v. 43) when a great throng is outside the house acquainted with the child's death; to hear of the call of "Levi" (ii. 14), and yet find no provision for "Levi" in the list of the Twelve (iii. 16–19);[1] to find such hesitation as to the name of the tenth apostle, "Lebbæus," or "Thaddæus" (iii. 18); to hear of the great amazement of the disciples at the storm stilling (vi. 51), after they have already witnessed a similar miracle (iv. 41); to hear the same district variously referred to as "Decapolis" (vii. 31) and "villages of Cæsarea-Philippi" (viii. 27); to hear of the disciples sailing for "Bethsaida" and arriving at "Gennesaret" (vi. 45, 53); to hear of the apostles seeking privacy (vi. 31), and mooring to the shore (vi. 53), and immediately afterwards of their being on circuit through "villages and cities" (vi. 56); to find the scene so

---

[1] The *v. r.* "Lebbæus," in the list of the Twelve, does not help us. "Levi" and "Lebbæus" are not likelier to have come from the same hand than "Alphæus" and "Cleopas" in S. Luke.

rapidly and abruptly shifting in iii. 9–19—to the boat, to the mountain, to the house in Capernaum;[1] to hear of Christ returning openly to Capernaum (iii. 19) so soon after His precipitate retreat from persecution (iii. 6, 7); to find the narrative harking back to the contention for the chief place (ix. 50) after the incident of the exorcist has intervened; to find that when Christ's second Sabbath cure excites such surprise and indignation (iii. 1–6), His first has been performed without protest (i. 21–28); to hear the disciples soliloquising, " What can He mean by bidding us beware of Pharisaic leaven ? we have no bread in the boat," just after it has been stated that they were disturbed at having " only one loaf " (viii. 14–21); to hear of Christ passing " through Sidon " on his way from Tyre to Decapolis (vii. 31);[2] to hear of Christ passing " thence through the midst of Galilee " when He is already in the midst of Galilee (ix. 30 ; cf. Matt. xvii. 22), and is about to arrive in Capernaum (Mark ix. 33); to hear at the crucifixion that it is only " the third hour " (xv. 25), when it was already morning before Christ left the high priest's palace (xv. 1); to find the soldiers offering vinegar in mockery after their compassionate offer of the anodyne " wine and myrrh ; " to find the same woman variously referred to as " mother of Joses " and " mother of James " (xv. 47 ; xvi. 1).

[1] That it is the house in Capernaum that is referred to in iii. 19 is shown by the context. It is in Capernaum that we should expect to find " His friends," " His mother and brethren." And there is an obvious connection between iii. 19, 20, and ii. 1, 2, and i. 33—at each visit to Capernaum, the crowd increasing !

[2] In Mark viii. 14–21 (cf. Matt. xvi. 5–12) there are two distinct lines of thought ; (*a.*) The disciples are anxious at having only one loaf. Christ reminds them of the previous miracle, and reproves them for want of faith, (*b.*) Christ bids the disciples beware of Pharisaic leaven. They take His remark literally, and reply that they have no bread on board. Christ reproves them for not understanding.

XVI.

Thus far we have collected upwards of a hundred doublets and inconsistencies, some striking, others questionable.

But if now, by one decisive test, all the doublets and inconsistencies classified under the symbol A, together with the paragraphs they involve, can be distinguished *en bloc* from the doublets and inconsistencies grouped under B, the argument will be fairly clenched. And this decisive test is forthcoming. *The extraordinary discrepancies between S. Matthew and S. Mark with regard to the order in which they arrange the events of the first half of our Lord's ministry, can all be conveniently explained by supposing that the compilers of S. Matthew and S. Mark dovetailed identical documents— C and D let us call them—at different points; and the matter of which C and D must severally consist, in order to make this operation feasible, exactly follows the lines of cleavage involved by the doublets and inconsistencies. C and D are A and B.*

Here is the present order:—

S. Matthew.	S. Mark.
John the Baptist.	John the Baptist.
Locusts and honey.	
Went out all Jerusalem.	Went out all Jerusalem.
	Locusts and honey.
Call of Peter.	Call of Peter.
⎧ Circuit of Galilee.	
⎨ On the mountain.	
	⎧ Demoniac.
	⎨ Peter's mother-in-law.
	⎨ Crowd at the door.
	⎩ Simon and others follow.
⎨ His disciples come unto Him.	
⎩ Sermon.	

THE FORMATION OF THE GOSPELS.

	Circuit of Galilee.
Leper.	Leper.
Centurion's servant.	
{ Peter's mother-in-law.	
{ Crowd at the door.	
{ His disciples follow.	
{ Storm.	
{ Gadara.	
{ Palsy.	{ Palsy.
{ Matthew.	{ Levi.
{ Feast.	{ Feast.
{ Fast.	{ Fast.
Jaïrus.	
{ Two blind men.	
{ Dumb devil.	
{ Beelzebub.	
{ Circuit of Galilee.	
{ Appointment and mission of the Twelve.	
{ Corn-plucking.	{ Corn-plucking.
{ Withered hand.	{ Withered hand.
{ Retirement.	{ Retirement.
	{ In a boat.
	{ On the mountain.
	{ Appointment and mission of the Twelve.
	{ His friends attempt to seize Him.
{ Blind and dumb devil.	
{ Beelzebub.	{ Beelzebub.
{ Mother and brethren.	{ Mother and brethren.
{ Sower.	{ Sower.
	{ Storm.
	{ Gadara.
	{ Jaïrus.
Nazareth.	Nazareth.
	{ Circuit of Galilee.
	{ Mission of the Twelve.
Death of John.	Death of John.
Five thousand fed.	Five thousand fed.
Corban.	
Well did Isaiah prophesy.	Well did Isaiah prophesy.
	Corban.
Draught of meats.	Draught of meats.

Here is the pedigree of the present order:—

S. MATTHEW.

A.	B.
John the Baptist.	John the Baptist.
Locusts and honey.	
	< Went out all Jerusalem.
Baptism.	Baptism.
Call of Peter.	
	Circuit of Galilee.
	On the mountain.
¹ <	His disciples come.
	Sermon.
	Centurion's servant.

(Demoniac.)²
Peter's mother-in-law.
Crowd at the door.
Simon and others follow.
³ Leper.

---

¹ Christ's authoritative discourse in the synagogue offers a rift for the insertion of this wedge.

² Omitted by the redactor, perhaps because of its similarity to the cure of the epileptic in B. Analogous reasons account for the omission of other matter bracketed.

³ The above is the order of A as given in S. Mark. In S. Matthew the order is different. We are obliged then to make our choice, and it is the order in S. Mark that has been chosen, because there are certain obvious reasons why it should have been changed in S. Matthew; but that the order in S. Mark could have developed out of the order in S. Matthew is inconceivable.

In S. Matthew the "Palsy, Matthew, Feast, Fast" group is inlaid in the middle of the "Storm, Gadara, Jaïrus." This arises thus—

"His friends" being strongly connected with "The sower," by the phrase "on that day" (Matt. xiii. 1), the redactor, who naturally identifies "His friends" with B's, "His mother and brethren," relegates "The sower" to an analagous position towards the latter. He is now left with the two groups, "Palsy, Matthew, Feast, Fast," and "Storm, Gadara, Jaïrus," disjointed. Moreover, the first of these seven events evidently requires that Christ should have just arrived in Capernaum (cf. Mark ii.1, 2). But the palsy cure of B has left Christ in Capernaum. Something then must be interposed. Christ must leave Capernaum to come back. In A the leaving takes place naturally enough—Christ goes forth at dawn to visit the neighbouring towns, His disciples follow, He heals a leper, and great crowds come to Him in desert places from

THE FORMATION OF THE GOSPELS. 71

    ⎧ Palsy.
    ⎪ Matthew.
    ⎨ Feast.
    ⎩ Fast.
    His friends.
3   Sower. In a boat.
    ⎧ Storm.
3 ⎨ Gadara.
    ⎩ Jaïrus.
    Two blind men.
    Dumb devil.
    Beelzebub.
    Circuit of Galilee.
    Appointment and mission of
       the Twelve.

                           Corn-plucking.
                           Withered hand.
                           Retirement.
                           (In a boat.)
                           (Appointment and mission of
                              the Twelve.)
                           Blind and dumb devil.
                           Beelzebub.
                           Sign of Jonah.
                           Mother and brethren.
                           Tares, &c.
    Nazareth.
                           Death of John.
                           Five thousand fed.
                           Walking on the sea.
    Gennesaret.
    Corban.
                           Well did Isaiah prophecy.
                           Draught of meats.

every quarter (cf. Mark i. 35-45). But the redactor is debarred from employing this section of A's by the fact that he has already reported from B, a circuit of Galilee, a coming of the disciples, and the congregation of great crowds (Matt. iv. 23, v. 1). He therefore transposes the leper cure, minus the crowds, as near to this B section as possible, relegates to shadow the following of the disciples (the true significance, however, of Matt. viii. 23 is unmistakably indicated by the Petrine interpolater's choosing this point for the insertion of the answers to worldly disciples), and breaks up the "Storm, Gadara, Jaïrus" group, as previously mentioned.

In Phœnicia.
Four thousand fed.
Sign of Jonah.

       Cæsarea-Philippi.
       Peter's confession.
       Transfiguration.
       Epileptic.

Announcement of Passion.

       < Temple rate.

Child in the midst.

       < The exorcist.

Offences.
Excommunication.

       Unmerciful servant.
       To Judæa.

Marriage.

       Blessing children.
       The ruler.
       The labourers.

Announcement of Passion.

       < Request of James and John.

Two blind men at Jericho.
Entry into Jerusalem.
Cleansing Temple.

       < Children's Hosannas.

Fig tree.
By what authority.

       The two sons.
       The husbandman.
       The wedding feast.

Seven brethren.
The great commandment.
David's Son and David's Lord.
Woe to the Pharisees.

       (Widow's mite.)

Eschatology.
       Eschatology.
       The virgins.
       The talents.
       Sheep and goats.

Meeting of Sanhedrim.

       < Supper at Bethany.

Judas' offer.
Supper in upper chamber.
To Mount of Olives.   To Gethsemane.

S. MARK.

John the Baptist.	John the Baptist.
Locusts and honey.	< Went out all Jerusalem.
Call of Peter.	
Demoniac.	
Peter's mother-in-law.	
Crowd at the door.	
Simon and others follow.	
	< Circuit of Galilee.
Leper.	
⎧ Palsy.	
⎪ Levi.	
⎨ Feast.	
⎩ Fast.	
	Corn-plucking.
	Withered hand.
	Retirement.
	In a boat.
	Appointment and mission of the Twelve.
His friends.	(Blind and dumb.)[1]
	Beelzebub.
	His mother and brethren.
Sower.	
⎧ Storm.	
⎨ Gadara.	
⎩ Jaïrus.	
(Two blind men.)[1]	
(Dumb devil.)[1]	
(Beelzebub.)	
Circuit of Galilee.	

---

[1] The redactor of S. Mark evidently had original information as to these cures, and more trustworthy than either A or B. The former has two blind men and a dumb (v. r., and deaf), the latter, a man blind and dumb (v.r., and deaf). For these in S. Mark are substituted the deaf stammerer in Decapolis and the blind man at Bethsaida. The later position they occupy agrees better with Christ's injunction of secrecy.

But it is not surprising that S. Luke, with all these conflicting accounts in his hands, should omit the cure of blindness and deafness altogether.

Mission of the Twelve.
Nazareth.[2]

Gennesaret.

Corban.

        ⟨ Death of John.
           Five thousand fed.

        < Well did Isaiah prophesy.

        < Draught of meats.

XVII.

Let us now consider whether the new sequences which this division of A and B establishes are such as to warrant the idea of original connection.

How naturally the circuit (Matt. xi. 1) leads up to Christ's visit to Nazareth (xiii. 53–58). It is a long leap, but it is encouraging to find in one of the cursives, the words with which the former breaks off, repeated at the beginning of the latter.

How natural, after Christ's evil reception at Nazareth, and inability to do any mighty work, to record the welcome in Gennesaret, and the manifestation of power at other places which He visited: "Wheresoever He entered—into villages, or into cities, or into the country—they laid the sick in the market-places!"

Let us consider A's eschatology. The surplusage in Matt. xxiv. exactly furnishes us with the matter of which we should expect A's eschatology to consist, making due allowance for the absence of the matter already reported in Matt. x., concerning apostolate and tribulation.

It is the second advent, and only the second advent,

---

[1] Preposed to the mission of the Twelve, because the disciples are mentioned as present with Christ; for the author of S. Mark attaches a far more definite character to the mission of the Twelve than attaches to it in A.

that is described. "False christs, false prophets;" "Nation against nation" (the analogy of B shows that the verses are to be thus inverted)—"These things are the beginning of travail throes," *i.e.*, of the travail throes of the Messiah. Then immediately follows the parable of the fig-tree, Christ describing His standing at the door, in the language of the bridegroom in the Song of Songs (ii. 9–13 ; v. 2).

The removal of Matt. iv. 23–viii. 13 brings the cure of Peter's wife's mother close to Peter's call, as in Mark i.; the removal of Matt. xiii. 31–35 brings together the explanation of a parable and the parable itself; the removal of Matt. xxvi. 6–13 allows the Blood-council and the offer of Judas to unite; the removal of Matt. xvi. 11–xvii. 21, allows "thence through Galilee" (cf. Mark ix. 30) to come into connection with the journey from Phœnicia and Decapolis.

The continuous exorcism in Mark iii. 11, 12, and the appointment of the Twelve, which it necessitates, adequately preface the cure of the blind and dumb demoniac which is introduced so abruptly in Matt. xii.

Mark iii. 19*b*–21, the return of Christ to Capernaum, follows equally well after the withdrawal of ii. 13 as after that of iii. 7—nay, better, A's design being this: Christ arrives in Capernaum; and the crowd gathers to the door. He arrives a second time and a greater crowd gathers,—there is no room even at the door. He arrives a third time and the crowd is greater than ever. The B section interrupts.

How naturally the command to avoid offence, to be at peace with one another, to resort to arbitration, and the extollation of the power of concord (Matt. xviii.

15–20; Mark ix. 43–50), follow after the contention who should be greatest.

The removal of the announcement of the Passion (Matt. xx. 17–19) brings the request of James and John for seats on the right hand and on the left into connection with xix. 28, where thrones are promised to the Twelve. Compare the parallel passage in the Preaching (Luke xxii. 24, 30).

The removal of the three parables (Matt. xxi. 28–xxii. 14), which are connected together by the thought of the Jewish rejection of God's message, restores the continuity of the disputations.

The removal of the Roman soldier's offer of vinegar on a reed allows the mockery, "He calleth Elias," to follow immediately after "Eli, Eli."

It may be added that the connections interrupted by the cleavage of A and B are all forced and artificial. For example, the link connecting the A and B sections of Matt. xviii. is formed only by "offence" and "little ones;"[1] only the word "widow" connects the denunciation of the Pharisees with the incident of the mite (Mark xii. 38–44).

Notice also, that some of the connections restored coincide with the connections in the Preaching. The centurion's servant follows the great sermon; "Beware of the leaven" follows the utterance concerning ablutions.

XVIII.

The accuracy of our distinction between A and B may be tested by certain peculiarities of style and tendency.

[1] Children, stray sheep.

The following words and expressions are peculiar to A :—διαφημίζειν, ἐμβριμᾶσθαι, ἀναχωρεῖν (absolute use of), τάφος, ἀθῶος, Ἰησοῦς ὁ λεγόμενος χριστός, συντάσσειν, ἀπέναντι, κράσπεδον, κατ'ὄναρ, ἐκτάζειν, θόρυβος, ἀργύρια, οἰκίακος, ἄσβεστος, παράγειν, ἐνθυμεῖσθαι, τὸ ῥηθὲν ὑπό, ὀψέ, ἕως τῆς σήμερον, σὺ ὄψει, προστάσσειν (exc. Acts).

Again, the pressing of prophecy in A is quite unique. For example, in Gen. xlix. 26 it is predicted of Joseph, Jacob's son, that he shall be *nezir*, *i.e.*, crowned. The author of Matt. ii. 23 actually applies Gen. xlix. 26 to our Lord's foster-father as a prophecy of his residence at Nazareth![1] The "children" for whom Rachel weeps, in Jer. xxxi. 15, are only children figuratively —her descendants. The "parables" also in which the author of Psalm lxxviii. opens his mouth are only such in quite other sense than those of Matt. xiii.[2] Again, in Matt. viii. 17, the whole point of the quotation depends on an ambiguity of the word "bare," which its original context in Isa. liii. 4 quite excludes; and in xxvii. 9, 10, alternate readings in Zech. xi. 13, *yozar* ("potter") and *aozar* ("treasury"), are combined.

Again, there seems to be some difference between A and B in apportioning the guilt of our Lord's death. A distinguishes himself from "the Jews" (xxviii. 15), and it is on them that he casts the main responsibility. The high priest's servants mock and spit; on the members of the Sanhedrim devolves the responsibility

[1] One may compare Saadiah's version, where "Nezir" is mistranslated "Nazirite." The reference of the prophecy to S. Joseph instead of our Lord would be doubtful ; but it evidently carries on a parallelism between the two Josephs—both sons of Jacob, both in Egypt. A new point is developed in Ignatius ad Ephes. xix.—Sun and moon and stars make obeisance to the Star of Bethlehem.

[2] "Parable" in Ps. lxxviii., &c., is rather "lesson from history."

of Judas; Pilate's wife intercedes; Pilate washes his hands; the people imprecate the curse on themselves and their children; the reproaches levelled at Christ on the cross are all from Jewish lips;[1] the centurion testifies to Christ's innocence, and to the marvellous rapidity of His death;[2] and finally, the members of the Sanhedrim stifle truth with a bribe. But B, on the other hand, calls attention to the Roman outrages —the scourge, the scarlet robe, the derisive title, the parted garments, the spear, the sponge.[3]

The following words and expressions are peculiar to B: τελεῖος, δικαιοσύνη, ἀφορίζειν, φράζειν, καταποντίζεσθαι, διστάζειν, μαθητεύειν, ἀνομία, ἁγία πόλις, θρόνος δόξης, ἕταιρε, συλλέγειν, Σίμων (vocative), συντέλεια τῆς αἰῶνος, ἀδελφοί μου (Christ speaking), ὡς ὁ ἥλιός, τὸ θέλημα τοῦ πατρός, ἀγανακτεῖν, σεληνιάζεσθαι.

In contradistinction to A, a "Book of Works," B may be fairly described as a "Book of Words." B contains the sermon on the mount and almost all the Matthæan parables. The narrative is only just sufficient to link the discourses together, sufficient to show to what period they belong. And when it is a miracle that is recounted, it is generally summed up in a single sentence, and manifestly recounted only for the sake of its inner significance or of the discourse with which it is connected. Never miracle for miracle's sake.

To account for the multitudes who congregate to hear the sermon on the mount, we are generally told that Christ "went about in all Galilee, preaching the

---

[1] Only Jews would be able to play on the word "Eli" as though it meant "Elias."

[2] Mark xv. 44, 45. Not as though anything unusual had been done to hasten it.

[3] Only a soldier would have "ὄξος."

gospel of the kingdom, healing all manner of disease, and all manner of sickness; and they brought unto Him all that were sick, holden with divers diseases and torments, possessed with devils, and epileptic, and palsied, and He healed them." It is a summary of events which the author does not intend to recount at length.

If "the blind and the lame" come into the Temple, and Jesus heals them there (Matt. xxi. 14), it is that we may contrast His disposition toward them with that of the Conqueror, whose successor He has just been acclaimed,—" And David took Zion, and said, 'Smite the blind and the lame, the hated of David's soul.' Wherefore they say, 'The blind and the lame shall not come into the house.'" Also by way of introduction to a parable in which the poor and miserable of this world, the blind and the lame (cf. Luke xiv. 21) are haled into God's great supper.

If Christ heals a blind mute, it is because of the utterances concerning Beelzebub which the cure occasions; He heals the centurion's servant, that many may come from the East and the West; heals the withered hand, to illustrate the new Sabbath doctrine; heals the epileptic, to emphasise the efficacy of faith and fasting; walks on the sea, to illustrate the danger of doubt.

The one miracle that remains, the feeding of the five thousand, may be accounted for by supposing that the author of B felt himself in a position to correct A. The number fed was larger, the material less.

Another distinction of B's is a similarity of language to that of the Apocalypse.

Thus it is not merely by doublets and incongruities and peculiarities of arrangement that A and B are distinguished from one another, but also by subject-matter and language. The former tests might be abandoned almost entirely. Taking any considerable section of A or B as a foundation-bone, an "*ossiculum Luz,*" one might rebuild almost the whole of A or B thereupon. The feeding of the five thousand, for example, connects itself with the preceding account of the death of John (Matt. xiv. 13); the account of the death of John connects itself with S. Peter's confession (Matt. xvi. 14), and with the Transfiguration (Matt. xvii. 14). From the feeding of the four thousand, one could proceed similarly.

This process would be applicable, too, in respect to the Preaching. For the three canonical gospels sometimes contain a true triple tradition. There are evidently three original documents behind the canonical —three, and three only. Take, for example, the salt metaphor. In Mark ix. 49, 50, it is connected somewhat mysteriously with "offences"; in Matt. v. 13 it is transferred to the preface of the new code which is to season the world; in Luke xiv. 33-35 it is connected with the idea of self-sacrifice. Take again the decision about divorce. In Matt. xix. 3-9 we have the disputation which leads up to this decision; in Matt. v. 32 the decision is extracted from its context, and inserted in the code of the new law; in Luke xvi. 17, 18, it reappears somewhat abruptly in a context analogous to that of Matt. xix. 3-9.

Thus, though the doublets and incongruities furnished us with a starting-point for our cleavage of the canonical gospels, that starting-point is only one of several that might have been chosen. The result gained by one process can be verified by another.

XIX.

In the preceding chapter the divisibility of S. Mark has been assumed. It is necessary now to justify this assumption; for at first sight, doublets and incongruities notwithstanding, S. Mark appears one and indivisible. Certain peculiarities of language and style run right through, binding the whole together—*e.g.*, περιβλέπεσθαι, συζητεῖν, θαμβεῖν, ἀλαλός, σπαράσσειν, ἐναγκαλίζεσθαι, διαστέλλεσθαι, εἰσπορεύεσθαι, ἐκθαμβεῖσθαι. It is clear, then, if our theory is to hold, that the original authorities in S. Mark have been subjected to some transformation process. Examination into the nature of this process resolves itself into a larger question—roughly speaking, the posteriority of S. Mark to S. Matthew.[1]

1. On the cases in which S. Matthew preserves a fuller text than S. Mark, it is not necessary to dwell at length. The fact that S. Mark preserves only half as many peculiar doublets and inconsistencies as S. Matthew, indicates the extent of S. Mark's omissions.

Examine Mark xiii. It will scarcely be questioned, comparing vers. 9–13 with Matt. x. 17–23, that in the former the text exhibits traces of clipping; and comparing vers. 14–27 with Matt. xxiv. 15–25, 29–31, that the differences are similarly significant: "Nor on a sabbath," "Sign of the Son of man in the heavens," "With the great sound of a trumpet," are less like after-touches, than original touches which an

---

[1] More exactly, the posteriority of S. Mark to A-B; of the shorter forms of A and B in S. Mark to the longer in S. Matthew, and (usually) of the longer in S. Mark to the shorter in S. Matthew.

Of course this leaves room for the passages relied on by those critics who advocate the priority of S. Mark to S. Matthew. Fragments of A and B, omitted, or obliterated in AB, are preserved in S. Mark.

after-writer might omit. Expressive of hope deferred is the change of "immediately after the tribulation of those days" into "in those days, after that tribulation."

Again, let us consider the omission of the two blind men of Matt. ix. 27–31. The reason why such an omission should have been made is obvious. The author of the second gospel was in possession of another account of the same event which he preferred (Mark viii. 22–26).[1] That his omission ought not to be attributed to ignorance of Matt. ix. 27–31 is clearly shown by the fact that he has retained the injunction of secrecy (Mark v. 43), applying it, however, to Jaïrus —to a case the publicity of which, as already pointed out, renders such an injunction quite inappropriate.

2. The short account of the raising of Jaïrus's daughter in Matt. ix. is obviously prior to S. Mark's. An abbreviator would never have left us in doubt whether the child was dead or in a swoon. And the strange introduction of "flute-players" does not look like an after-touch. But conversely, notice the confusion into which the expander fell, hesitating whether to date the cessation of the hæmorrhage from the moment of the woman's touch, or of Christ's address; and making the twelve years of the woman's sufferings also represent the age of the dead child.

3. Let us consider the case of S. Matthew's *pairs*— two Gadarene demoniacs, two blind men at Bethsaida, two at Jericho. It is easily conceivable that an evangelist, not an eye-witness, perplexed by contradictory traditions of miraculous cures, should have assumed

---

[1] That Mark viii. 22–26 is a post-addition appears from the awkwardness with which it fits its context. The "Bethsaida" mentioned cannot be Bethsaida Julias, for it is referred to as a "village." But the context requires Christ's presence on the other side of the Lake.

that the traditions referred to different men. Modern harmonists employ the same device. A later but better-informed evangelist might correct the error. But it is almost inconceivable that the author of the *pairs* should have been in possession of such circumstantial accounts of single cures as those given in Mark v., viii., x.

4. Similarly in the case of S. Matthew's account of the cure of the epileptic. It is more probable that xvii. 20 (cf. xxi. 21) should have been omitted by a later hand than added.

In this and the preceding cases it will be seen that the theory involves the classification as secondary of most of the picturesque detail with which S. Mark's miracles are surrounded. Other than an eye-witness might inform us that a mattress had four corners. "Borne of four" proves eye-witness no more than the "wild beasts" in Mark i. 13. It is in the nature of things that the later writer should dilate on the gravity of a demoniac's symptoms, the inveteracy of a hæmorrhage, the violence of an epileptic's paroxysm, should name for us the archisynagogos and the beggar of Jericho. Minute details would become valuable in proportion as the difficulty of obtaining them increased. When only a few fragments remained, they would all be carefully gathered up.

5. In the accounts of the attack on Christ for non-inculcation of fasting, one instinctively feels that the account which represents John's disciples themselves as captious is more likely to have been the original;[1] in the accounts of the murmuring of the disciples at the waste of the precious ointment, that the account which attributes the murmuring to all collectively is

[1] Besides the actual presence of John's disciples is certified by the independent Petrine narrative (Matt. xi. ; Luke vii.).

earlier than that which confines it to a few; that the "long robes" of Mark xii. 38 is explanatory of "enlarged hems and broad phylacteries" (Matt. xxiii. 5); and "unloose the latchet" explanatory of "bear the shoes" (Matt. iii. 11); that the "hired servants" (Mark i. 20) are meant to detract from the seeming unkindness of leaving old Zebedee to manage his boat alone; that "the time of figs was not yet" and "He would have passed them by" (Mark xi. 13; vi. 48) are embellishments not quite harmonious with their context; that the "cup of cold water to one of these little ones in the name of Christ" is a simplification of Matt. x. 42; that the reference to the "νόμος" in the lawyer's question (Matt. xxii.) has been designedly sponged out in Mark xii.;[1] that a later writer would not refer so simply to "the other Mary," whom an earlier had distinguished by her relationship to Joses (cf. Matt. xxvii. 61; Mark xv. 47), but conversely; that "when the Sabbath was passed, on the first day of the week," is a correction of "late on the Sabbath, as it drew on to the first day of the week" (Matt. xxviii. 1).

But the most striking example of posteriority is afforded by a comparison of Matt. xiv. 12, 13 with Mark vi. 30, 31. In S. Matthew the disciples (of the Baptist) come and tell Jesus what has been done (to John), and Jesus (for the sake of safety) withdraws into privacy. In S. Mark the Apostles, returning from their mission, come and tell Jesus what they themselves have done. And another reason for withdrawal into privacy is suggested—that they may rest after their fatigue. The brevity of the Matthæan

[1] The word "νόμος," so common in the first canonical gospel, does not occur at all in the second.

account makes the sense a little obscure. A very slight misapprehension accounts for the process by which Matt. xiv. 12, 13 develops into Mark vi. 30, 31. The reverse process is simply inconceivable.

6. Similar inferences may be drawn from S. Mark's account of the mission of the Twelve. "Shod with sandals" is explanatory of "no shoes;" "a staff only" mitigatory of "no staff;" "by two and two" inferred from the enumeration of the Apostles in couples.

But minute scrutiny carries us much further. It becomes obvious that Mark vi. is partly founded on a misunderstanding of Matt. x. Christ's charge in Matt. x. applies to a general lifelong mission. The Twelve are appointed, and then told what Apostleship implies. It is never stated that they go; never stated that they come back. And the context seems to show that they never quitted Christ at all. But in Mark vi. the Twelve are actually despatched on a temporary mission. They go; they return. And portions of the charge which are inapplicable to such a mission are transferred to another occasion (cf. Mark xiii. 9–13).[1]

On the whole, it would seem that the peculiar phenomena of the second canonical gospel may be best explained by supposing that the author had heard comments on A and B by an intermittent eyewitness.

XX.

The idiosyncrasies of A and B in S. Matthew appear too strongly marked to leave very much room

[1] Mark vi. is coloured by some dim tradition of the despatch of the Seventy. That the Twelve were included in the Seventy is shown by Luke ix. 52, 54; xxii. 35.

for the redactor. Such as is left, is left chiefly in those passages in which the leaning towards prophecy is most conspicuous. A comparison, for example, of Matt. xxvii. 34 with Mark xv. 23, suggests at first sight that the "myrrh" of the latter, the ordinary anodyne given to criminals, is prior to the "gall" of the former. And when one compares the passages in S. Matthew, in which the fulfilments of prophecy are chronicled, with those in S. Mark, where they are absent, it is tempting to regard these chronicles of fulfilment as after-thoughts, the text in which they are absent as prior. Just as in S. Mark the original A and B text has been disguised by the exaggeration of picturesque details, so also in S. Matthew has it not been developed in another direction? But the reverse process is conceivable. Prophetic analogies might have been excised by an evangelist who wrote for Gentiles.

The root of the whole matter lies in Matt. i., ii., and there the question must be fought out. Matt. i., ii. carries with it almost all the sections open to suspicion. Is Matt. i., ii., as so many critics claim, a redactor's post-addition? or is it, as printed at the end of this volume, part and parcel of A? Our reasons for adopting the latter alternative are as follows :—

1. The very peculiar usage of prophecy, previously alluded to, which is so distinctive of Matt. i., ii., is continued only in sections which on other grounds are assignable to A.[1] This may be simply a coincidence, but the chances are the other way.

So, too, as to language. The words distinctive of S. Matthew, above enumerated, which occur in Matt. i., ii., occur elsewhere only in A sections.

---

[1] The only possible exception being Matt. xii. 17-21.

These two characteristics unmistakably connect together as from the same hand Matt. i., ii., the removal from Nazareth to Capernaum, Pilate's ablution, his wife's dream, and the guard, xxvii. 62–66, xxviii. 11–15. To separate all these sections from the rest of A is difficult in the extreme.[1]

2. The frequent address to our Lord in A sections as "Son of David," seems to involve a genealogy in which Davidic descent is justified. This indeed is often admitted, but from the fact that the Davidic descent is traced through Joseph, an inference has been drawn hostile to the narrative of miraculous conception.

But the genealogy is indissolubly connected with the narrative that follows. The parallelism, already pointed out, between the two Josephs, begins in i. 16: "Joseph was begotten by Jacob." In i. 20 Joseph is addressed as "Son of David." That women should figure in the genealogy at all is of itself suggestive, and the character of the women chosen, not Sarah Rebecca, Leah, but four of foreign extraction, and not blameless life, produces impression that some striking antithesis is intended, that the genealogy is to terminate in a virgin "all holy," in the words of Justin and Irenæus, "the advocate of Eve."

And it has already been pointed out that the idea of miraculous conception need not altogether exclude S. Joseph.

3. The subjective arguments against Matt. i., ii.,

---

[1] Thus the guard section contains the distinctively A word, διαφημίζειν. Special reasons for identifying the guard as an integral part of A will be found in Chapter XXIV. Again, the removal to Capernaum is involved by the indisputably A passage ix. 1. Pilate's wife's dream (the only occasion, except in Matt. i., ii., where dreams are mentioned), his ablution, and Judas's repudiation of responsibility, attune thoroughly to A's direction of the onus of guilt.

sometimes discovered in the remainder of A, are far from decisive, *c.g.*, The sufficiency of the descent of the Holy Spirit at the baptism to account for the title "Son of God;" the confidence of the Nazarenes that they know all about Christ's origin; the readiness of "His friends," including apparently His mother, to charge Him with madness, and to attempt a forcible seizure. And, on the other hand, in the narrative of the woman taken in adultery, which, as will be presently shown, belongs to A, it almost seems as if some account of miraculous conception is involved; for if the reference to Moses having "commanded that such should be stoned" is to be sustained, the woman brought before our Lord must have been "a virgin betrothed;" and it is significant that this narrative of the woman taken in adultery should follow —this will be shown presently—the discussion concerning Messiah's descent from David.[1]

Whatever the objections above cited to the doctrine of the miraculous conception may be worth, they are by no means incompatible with the antiquity of Matt. i., ii. They point too far back altogether. For whether or not the miraculous conception was part of the primitive Christian creed, it is at any rate certain that it was widely accepted some time before the date which is here desiderated for A. It has been already pointed out that the Pauline doctrine of original sin involves a second Adam, sinless from the very first, conceived otherwise than the rest of Adam's descendants. And in the imagery of Revelation xii.

[1] So too in the fourth gospel the discussion concerning the Davidic descent (vii. 37–52) appears not unconnected with the innuendo (viii. 41, 48), "WE were not born in FORNICATION. Say we not rightly that thou art a Samaritan?"

one may discern in the woman "clothed with the sun," who brings forth the man child, an allusion to the unique glory of the virgin mother.[1] The relationship of Matt. i., ii. to Luke i. 5–ii. proves clearly that the idea of miraculous conception was anterior to both. And in Matt. i., ii. the stress laid on S. Joseph's non-repudiation of his wife, presupposes the existence of the slander, re-echoed by the Jew of Celsus, that he dismissed her with disgrace. Thus it was no new doctrine that Matt. i., ii. introduced, and the incongruity, if incongruity it is, of that section with the remainder of A is due, not to its being by a different hand, but to incongruity beneath.

4. The objection to Matt. i., ii., that the matter there contained was unknown to S. Luke, S. John, and the Hebrew evangelist will not bear close investigation.

a. The argument against S. Luke's acquaintance with Matt. i., ii., that knowing this account of Christ's birth he would never have given currency to another so diverse without indicating some method of reconciliation rests on the assumption that if S. Luke knew this account, he must also have recognised its apostolic origin and its absolute authority. Even so the argument becomes invalid when we discover that S. Luke's intention was only to harmonise our second canonical gospel to the Preaching, and that Luke i. 5–ii. belonged to the latter.

That there are, according to some authorities, interpolations in Luke ii. 39, iv. 31, from Matt. ii. 23; iv. 13, proves little—they may be due to some late copyist; but

---

[1] The imagery of Revelation is often reflective. For example, "Keep thy garments, lest thou walk naked," recalls the startling incident mentioned in Mark xiv. 51, 52. "Root and offspring of David," recalls the discussion about David's Son and David's Lord.

the context that S. Luke chooses for the riot at Nazareth (Luke iv.) is of real importance in this connection, for he evidently chooses it in consequence of the removal from Nazareth to Capernaum, recorded in Matt. iv. 13, a passage demonstrably by the same hand as Matt. i., ii.

b. The argument from S. John's omission to answer the objection, "Cometh not Christ of the seed of David from Bethlehem?" "Can any good thing come out of Nazareth?" becomes nugatory when we notice that it is his manner to leave such objections to answer themselves. No answer is deigned to the insinuation that Christ was born in fornication, and that His father was a Samaritan.

A most probable proof of the direct use of Matt. i., ii. is found in John ii. 20, " Forty and six years has this temple been in building," for Josephus informs us that the building was commenced nineteen years before Herod's death, so that twenty-seven years must have elapsed since his death when this remark was made; and our Lord, according to Luke iii. 23, being thirty years of age, it follows that Herod's life and our Lord's overlapped three years; which is exactly the implication in Matt. i., ii., where Christ is reckoned among the children of two years, and provision made for a sojourn in Egypt of about a year.

c. Reasons for supposing that Matt. i., ii.—as also Luke i. 5–ii.—were not unknown to the Hebrew evangelist, will be found in Chapter XXIII.

5. There is not less historicity in Matt. i., ii. or in Luke i., 5–ii.—for it will be convenient to examine the two accounts together—than our theory of their origin requires. The general effect of the pictures may be

THE FORMATION OF THE GOSPELS.

true or otherwise, but the colours are certainly not due to fancy or imagination. Thus—

a. For some strange appearance in the sky about the time of Christ's birth, Origen was able to cite the testimony of Hadrian's chronicler, Phlegon; and astronomers inform us that certain planets were in conjunction. Consequently it will not be altogether in favour of Luke i. 5–ii. if the star is there absent. But is the star really absent? Surely it is alluded to in

> "The Day-spring from on high,
> To guide our feet into the way of peace."

b. Matt. i., ii., Luke i. 5–ii., quite independent, agree in this, that some strangers visited the infant Christ. But the former brings them "from the East" ("from Arabia," Justin understands). The visitors in Matt. i., ii. appear to have developed out of the humbler shepherds under the influence of prophecy, "Kings from Arabia shall bring gifts," but even in this development there is nothing really untrue to history. Herod, in his last years, as Josephus informs us, was continually troubled by Arabian emissaries. In the Antipater conspiracy A.D., Arabian chieftains participated. And a later tradition, strangely enough, connects the visitors of Matt. ii. with Antipater.

c. For the murder of the Innocents, Origen was unable to obtain any corroboration, and it is certainly singular that other historians besides Josephus should be silent on the subject; but some allusion to a birth-peril which Christ escaped may perhaps be discovered in the imagery of Revelation,—often, as already said, reflective—the red dragon standing before the star-crowned woman, ready to devour her man-child. And in the "Assumption of Moses," written at the beginning of the first century A.D., Herod is denounced as a "slayer of the old and the YOUNG" ("juvenum,"—but this is a translation probably of "παίδων"), and compared to Pharaoh.[1]

d. Again, as to "the inn" and "the manger"— here probably is another feature common to both birth-scenes.

To the *south* of Bethlehem, in the time of Jeremiah, there existed a celebrated inn, named after one of David's followers, Chimham, which was used by travellers on their way to Egypt (Jer. xli. 17). And onwards from the second century A.D. a cave to the *south* of Bethlehem, in which traces of a manger might be discovered by those who searched, was in some way connected by local tradition with the nativity.[2]

This cave-stable may have been the sole relic of an inn that existed A.D. on the site of Chimham's.

In Luke i. 5–ii. inn and stable appear naturally enough. But at first sight they appear to have no place in Matt. i., ii., where the Blessed Virgin and S. Joseph are represented as residents at Bethlehem, not there merely for a temporary purpose. But may it not be that the inn and cave-stable have left traces in the flight into Egypt? In the manger, might not Christ have been temporarily concealed from Herod's emissaries.[3]

---

[1] *Vide* Fritzsche's "Pseudepigrapha," pp. 713, 714. The reason for the parallelism between Pharaoh and Herod, drawn in Matt. ii., is sufficiently obvious. Evil ever trying to strangle good in the cradle! Christ wonderfully preserved from Herod, as Moses from Pharaoh! But why should such a parallelism have been drawn by a pre-Christian writer, if the massacre at Bethlehem is quite mythical?

[2] Jerome.

[3] This is suggested in the Protevangel.

e. Matt. i., ii., Luke i. 5–ii. agree in describing S. Joseph as a rigorous observer of the Law, and they agree in their description of his relationship to the Blessed Virgin (*cf.* Matt. i. 25 ; Luke ii. 5).

f. Matt. i., ii., Luke i. 5–ii. agree that Christ was born at Bethlehem, though they bring it about very differently. But birth at Bethlehem was not an indispensable qualification of the Messiah. Micah had only predicted that the Messiah would come of a Bethlehemite family. One never hears that any claim to have been born in Bethlehem was advanced by Barcocheba, the Messiah coming in his own name, whom the Jews received. Jerusalem is the Messiah's birth-place according to "Enoch." In this case, then, the narrative is not weakened by the prophecy ; and in others, by the very weakness of the prophecies cited in illustration, it is really strengthened. It is so evident that events are not being invented to suit prophecies, but prophecies pressed to suit events.

Thus the materials of Matt. i., ii., Luke i. 5–ii. are historical. Whether or not they are rightly combined is another question.[1]

---

[1] The surrender of one or two details in Matt. i., ii., Luke i. 5–ii. does not necessarily entail the surrender of the whole. The visit of the Magi and the persecution of Herod might be separated. The mere fact of Davidic descent, apart from any other reason, would account for Herod's apprehensions. And again as to the celebrated enrolment undertaken by Quirinius, A.D. 7,—S. Joseph and the Blessed Virgin may have visited Bethlehem on this occasion, the name of Jesus may have been entered on the registers, but other reasons are discoverable which might have brought about the Blessed Virgin's visit to Bethlehem at an earlier period. Bethlehem was a Levite town, might be described as "in the hill country," and the Protevangel actually makes it the home of the Blessed Virgin's relatives, Zachariah and Elizabeth. Or when Joseph "took unto him his espoused wife," it may have been to his own home at Bethlehem from hers at Nazareth.

XXI.

The construction-theory adopted involves certain very definite conclusions as to the date and order of our canonical gospels, and the gospels anterior.

A and B and the Preaching, and their developments, must all have appeared at very short intervals. This, indeed, is only what *a priori* reasoning would lead us to expect. For in describing the second advent, the apostles reckon themselves among the quick (cf. 1 Thess. iv. 17). Why trouble to write? Taking then our Lord's age as an index of theirs, and threescore and ten as man's average, one might conclude that it was about the year 70 that written records of our Lord's life suddenly became a necessity. And when the last man was dead who could say, "I saw Jesus," it is natural to suppose that these written records suddenly acquired a new value, and lost their plasticity.

Not only A and B, but also AB, and "S. Mark," being quite independent of the Preaching, it follows that they must have appeared in rapid succession. And that no great interval elapsed between the publication of the first canonical gospel and of the third, follows from their independent treatment of the Preaching.[1]

---

[1] The rapidity with which the gospels followed one another, accounts too for the disappearance of the earlier forms. A and B, as we have seen, were unknown to John the Elder,—at any rate in their true character. And the evidence of their existence which we have been able to adduce is all internal. They were superseded by AB so quickly, and AB was so much better suited for general use. Remembering how widely Tatian's Harmony superseded our canonical gospels, it is not a matter for wonder that some eighty years earlier, a Harmony of A and B was more successful still.

Let us imagine a possessor of AB, contrasting it with our canonical S. Matthew. The absence of the Petrine sections would make it appear a less perfect document, and he would probably supply the deficiencies.

THE FORMATION OF THE GOSPELS. 95

No influence of the fourth gospel can be detected even in the latest of the redactions, but conversely. This, however, touches on a question which, for present purposes, it is needless to discuss.

Of the posteriority of S. Mark to A B we have already spoken, and the priority of S. Mark to the corresponding sections in S. Luke is generally admitted.[1]

The posteriority of B to A is shown by its supplementary character. What A has recorded, B generally omits. Where A has preserved just the shreds of parables, *c.g.*, "Every plant which my Father planted not shall be rooted up," "Whoso shall give to one of these little ones a cup of cold water shall have his reward," "To him that hath, shall be given," B restores the full original. But perhaps a better test is afforded by a comparison of A's eschatology with B's. In the former, the destruction of Jerusalem finds no place. But in the latter it is prominent.

The general counsel, "When they persecute you in this city, flee," has become a definite command that at a particular moment Christians are to quit Jerusalem.

It was revealed to the Christians that they were to fly—so states Eusebius, apparently on the authority of Hegesippus—whence it would seem that the command to fly was not written in letters plain and clear before the flight actually took place.

At a later date AB would be regarded as a mutilated S. Matthew. Probably the original manuscript received the Petrine interpolations, before many copies were taken.

[1] This priority is conclusively shown by the following fact, that sections of S. Mark incorporated in S. Luke involve sections omitted, *e.g.*, Luke iv. 38 involves Mark i. 16-20; Luke xviii. 35 involves Mark x. 1; Luke xxii. 71 involves Mark xiv. 57, &c. *Cf.* Chapter V. Luke xx. 39, 40 involves Mark xii. 28-34; Luke xxii. 52 involves Mark xiv. 43; Luke xxii. 47, 48 involves Mark xiv. 44; Luke ix. 45 involves Mark viii. 33.

In fact, the B document all through bears the impress of the great agony of A.D. 70; the days are being shortened; the king's messengers have all been slain; his armies draw near; the city of murderers shall be burned; overhead there is "a great star flaming like a sword"[1]—it is "the sign of the Son of Man."

But a later date than A.D. 70 is equally precluded, for the Evangelist plainly betrays his expectation that the fall of Jerusalem will be followed by the Second Advent "immediately."

Contrast the tendency of the redactors. When S. Luke took his gospel in hand, about a decade later, the references to the speedy coming of Christ were already an offence. "Some standing here shall see the Son of Man coming in His kingdom." "When ye see these things, know that the Son of Man is nigh, even at the doors." "He that endureth to the end shall be saved." These expressions S. Luke softens down, applying them to Christ's coming in an impersonal sense—in the extension of the Gospel—"Some here shall see the kingdom of God," "When ye see these things know that the kingdom of God is nigh," "In patience win your souls."

When S. Luke informs us that the Husbandman went away "for a long time" (ἱκανοὶ χρόνοι), and that the parable of Pounds was designed against a belief that the Messianic kingdom "was immediately to appear" (παραχρῆμα ἀναφαίνεσθαι), one remembers that ἱκανοὶ χρόνοι and παραχρῆμα and ἀναφαίνεσθαι, by the tests of Chapter XI., are proved to be expressions of S. Luke's own.

---

[1] Josephus, Wars, VI., v. 3. Similarly, in the Sibylline verses, "swords in the sky" are a sign of Messiah's approach.

To turn to the Preaching. That expression of John the Elder, "What he *remembered* of S. Peter's discourses," distinctly implies that S. Mark wrote after S. Peter's death.[1] And the Petrine eschatology corroborates this view. When S. Mark makes mention of the "palisade" which the Romans built round Jerusalem (Luke xix. 43; cf. Josephus), it may be inferred that his remembrance of S. Peter's words had been quickened by the events of A.D. 70.

But that year is not far past. "Lift up your heads, your redemption draweth nigh."

XXII.

The "Gospel according to S. John," in the opinion of most critics, was written considerably later than the synoptic gospels. Its exact relation to them, however, is, by general admission, extremely difficult to determine. The object of the following chapter is to show that, by the foregoing construction-theory, the unexpected in S. John, in the historical portions, is greatly diminished. Into the vexed question of the authorship and authenticity of the fourth gospel it is not

[1] In 2 Peter i. 15 a design of perpetuating his preaching is imputed to S. Peter himself. But it is only a design, and, except on the hypothesis that the second epistle of Peter's is actually his, it is by no means certain that this passage refers to the document of which we are speaking at all. Lactantius (iv. 21) apparently connects it with the "Prædicatio Petri et Pauli," and certainly the promise of its contents (2 Peter i. 14), incitations to godliness, virtue, and knowledge, accord better with what is known of this apocryphal document.

Irenæus follows Papias in dating the Preaching after S. Peter's death. The writers who date it before, Clement of Alexandria, &c., appear to have misunderstood John the Elder's statement, as though he had said that S. Peter discoursed to meet the wants of S. Mark. And they deprive themselves of credit by dating it in the forties, adopting the Clementine figment of S. Peter's arrival in Rome in the reign of Claudius.

necessary to enter. For in any case the argument for the existence of the original gospels, A and B and the Preaching, will hold good, if it can be shown that they offer greater scope than their canonical developments for certain statements of the fourth evangelist.[1]

One of the chief discrepancies between the fourth evangelist and the synoptists, is in respect to the duration of our Lord's ministry, and the number of His visits to Jerusalem. From the canonical S. Matthew, S. Mark, S. Luke, one would gather that He only visited Jerusalem once (cf. Mark xi. 11).

But when once the great Petrine section (Luke ix.–xix.) is released from its present cramped position, its evidence strongly favours the view taken by the fourth evangelist. It is the most natural inference from Luke ix.–xix., that our Lord visited Jerusalem several times.[2] S. Luke's original knowledge was slight, and he had to reconcile a document which exhibited a constant tendency "towards Jerusalem" with another which mentioned a single journey.

Similarly, as to A and B, the appearance of chronological arrangement is much fainter there than in the redactions. Comparing A and B with the Preaching, one is compelled to the conclusion that in A and B the arrangement is to a large extent subjective. All that Christ ever said about apostleship

---

[1] If, indeed, the author of the fourth gospel is not John the Apostle, but John the Elder, he cannot have possessed A and B (see Chapter I.). But he possessed another redaction of A and B, besides the canonical redactions—for we shall endeavour to show in the next chapter that the "Gospel according to the Hebrews" was of this character.

[2] Of course there is this alternative, but it commends itself less, that our Lord's last visit to Jerusalem was of considerable duration, and that the appearance of previous visits is due to the "disorder" of the Petrine document.

THE FORMATION OF THE GOSPELS. 99

is worked into one grand missionary charge. His various decisions on the legal points submitted to Him from time to time are gathered into the tables of a new Sinaitic code. The various invectives, called forth by different exhibitions of Pharisaic hypocrisy, are pressed into one railing accusation. All His scattered prophecies of the future, immediate or remote, converge,—prophecies of the end of Jerusalem and of the end of the world, prophecies of His own advent, in the extension of the gospel, or to the individual, or on the clouds of heaven.

So too with regard to the special matter in point. It would be quite in accordance with the spirit of A and B to combine various visits to Jerusalem in one. The ministry climaxes with Christ's testimony at headquarters, and the events of months and years—events which in the Preaching lie strewn up and down the ministry—are pressed as it seems into one short week.

Thus the fourth evangelist assigns the cleansing of the temple and the challenge " By what authority ? " to one visit, ii. 13, &c.; the " gathering together " of the Pharisees, David's Son and David's Lord, the widow's mite,[1] the lawyer's question,[2] " I am the God of Abraham " to another, vii. 41–52, viii. 20, 48, 56, 58; the council in the house of Caiaphas to a third, and that not the last, xi. 47–53.[3]

---

[1] John vii. 32, 42, 45, corresponds to Matt. xxii. 34, 41–46. The woman taken in adultery properly belongs, as will be shown presently, after Matt. xxii. 46; and that it is followed in the fourth gospel by a reference to Christ's presence "in the treasury" shows perhaps that the author of the fourth gospel assigns the mite (Mark xii. 41) to the same occasion.

[2] " Say we not rightly that thou art a Samaritan ? " connects itself with the answer to the lawyer, in which Christ describes Himself under the figure of a Samaritan.

[3] Attention has already been drawn to the expression used in Matt.

Now let us examine the Johannine visits to Jerusalem in detail. It will perhaps be best to start in the middle.

1. In John vii. we hear that Christ went up to the Feast of Tabernacles[1] "in secret." This journey corresponds with that recorded in A, Mark ix. 30, "He passed through Galilee, and would not that any man should know it,"[2] and in B, Matt. xix. 1; Mark x. 1, "He departed from Galilee and came into the borders of Judæa." Thus a new dovetailing of A and B is involved, different from that either of AB, or S. Mark (cf. Matt. xvii. 24; Mark ix. 33), for after this journey to the Feast of Tabernacles, Christ, according to the fourth gospel, returns to Galilee no more.

2. Then, after the parable of the Good Shepherd, the reference to "other sheep, not of this fold," Christ, according to the fourth gospel, "went away into the place where John was at the first baptizing"—a statement correspondent to that in Matt. xix. 1; Mark x. 1, after the incident of the independent exorcist, the parable of the sheep astray, "He came beyond Jordan."

xxvi. 16, "From that time he sought opportunity," as indicative of some interval between the conspiracy and its success.

It is perhaps worth noticing that these identifications of Johannine matter and synoptic, and others to be mentioned presently, are all, or nearly all, implied in the Diatessaron.

[1] That Christ did attend a celebration of the Feast of Tabernacles has already been inferred from the Preaching (Luke xvi. 9). With this passage may be compared S. Peter's remark at the Transfiguration, "Let us build here three tabernacles,"—for the remark is meaningless unless we suppose that a celebration of the feast was at hand. And it is noteworthy that S. Peter made this remark just after his great confession—"six days after"—for in the fourth gospel his confession just precedes Christ's journey to the Feast.

[2] Any lingering doubt as to the accuracy of this identification of the journey of Mark ix. 30 with that described in John vii., is taken away when we notice that Matt. xvii. 22 also, the passage correspondent in AB, "While they abode (ἀναστρεφομένων αὐτῶν) in Galilee," is reflected in John vii. 9, "He *abode* in Galilee" (after the feast had begun).

3. From Bethany, beyond Jordan, Christ, according to the fourth gospel, journeys to Bethany, near Jerusalem, and the despondent remark of Thomas enables us to identify this journey with that recorded in A, Mark x. 32, "They were in the way going up to Jerusalem, and they that followed were afraid." In B, Matt. xix. 15; Mark x. 17, this journey is alluded to more vaguely, "He departed thence," *i.e.*, from beyond Jordan.

4. From Bethany, near Jerusalem, Christ, according to the fourth gospel, retires to "a city near the wilderness." Here we seem at fault. One searches the synoptic gospels in vain for something correspondent; but now the Diatessaron informs us that the Preaching, in its original form, supplied exactly what is required, viz., that Christ's withdrawal to some place apart, Luke ix. 11—"a desert place," we may infer from the new context for it which S. Luke felt justified in finding— followed after the parable of the Pharisee and the publican.

5. Having now fixed the journey of John vii.; Mark ix. 30; Matt. xix. 1 as a starting-point, let us work backwards. According to the fourth gospel, when the feeding of the five thousand took place, " the Passover was at hand." The only possible justification in the synoptic gospels for this statement is furnished in Matt. xiv. 1 (B), where the feeding is described as taking place " at that season." Let us assume that the fourth evangelist understood this expression as equivalent to " at that feast-tide."

6. If the fourth evangelist understood " at that season," Matt. xiv. 1 (B), as equivalent to " at that feast-tide," then the previous passage in which this expression is used, Matt. xii. 1 (B), he must have inter-

preted similarly. And how reasonably this works! In John v. we have a feast to which Christ went up, and a Sabbath cure. It is a Sabbath cure that Matt. xii. 1 introduces.[1] It may be added that Christ's words in Matt. xii., "The priests profane the Sabbath," "One greater than the temple is here," are suggestive of presence in Jerusalem; and in the opinion of most critics the *v. r.* in Luke vi. 1, "$\delta\epsilon\upsilon\tau\epsilon\rho o\pi\rho\omega\tau\omega$," if to be retained, indicates the proximity of a Passover.

7. We have one more journey to consider. In John ii. 13; iii. 22, Christ journeys to Jerusalem, and then comes into Judea and to the Jordan. Here again the only possible justification is furnished in B,—Matt. iv. 25, "Multitudes *followed Him from* Jerusalem, Judea, and beyond Jordan."[2]

Now the result of connecting these three Johannine feasts with Matt. xiv. 1; xii. 1; iv. 25, is this, that it involves a new dovetailing of A and B on the part of the fourth evangelist, different from that either of AB, or S. Mark. It involves our preposing a considerable amount of B (viz., circuit, sermon, centurion's servant, corn-plucking, withered hand) to the arrest of John (A, Matt. iv. 12; Mark i. 14). For in John iv. we are expressly told that the cure of the nobleman's son (*i.e.*, the centurion's servant) was Christ's *second* after the withdrawal into Galilee, and hence one may see that the fourth evangelist reckoned it previous to A's cure of the demoniac in Capernaum, Peter's mother-in-law, the leper, &c.

---

[1] The concomitant circumstances of both Sabbath cures are the same. The Jews attempt to kill Jesus. Jesus withdraws to the sea. Great multitudes follow. Jesus goes up into the mountain. Matt. xii. 14, 15; Mark iii. 6, 7, 13; John v. 18, vi. 1-3.

[2] Hence the *v. r.* in Luke iv. 44, "Preached in Judea."

There are many miscellaneous points that might be noticed, bearing out the view above-taken of the relationship of the Johannine tradition to the Synoptic.

Sometimes the fourth gospel recalls the original order of A and B. Thus we have the withered hand (= John v.) immediately after the centurion's servant, and S. Peter's confession almost immediately after the walking on the sea, only the discourse about the Bread of Life intervening, thus in a position analogous to that of the parable of the Draught of Meats.[1]

Then, again, the celebrated discrepancy between the Synoptists and the fourth gospel as to whether the Passover was eaten on the Thursday or the Friday, is lessened by the following fact, that the identification of "the first day of unleavened bread" with "the day on which the Passover must be slain" now rests only on the authority of a redactor. Rabbinical literature distinguishes the two, and indeed this seems most natural in face of the Mosaic regulation—"Even the day previous shall ye cast all leaven out of your houses."

XXIII.

The aim of the following chapter is to show, from the fragments which survive of the "Gospel according to the Hebrews," additional proof of the existence of the three original documents desiderated—our hypothesis being that out of these the "Gospel according to the Hebrews" arose, in much the same way as the canonical redactions; later, however, as shown by certain meretricious after-touches.

[1] The food that kills! the food that quickens!

THE FORMATION OF THE GOSPELS.

The Hebrew evangelist blends the rich young ruler's inquiry with the scoffs of the Pharisees, lovers of money, reported in Luke xvi.;[1] *i.e.*, he assigns to the same occasion passages in the triple tradition and the Preaching, between which S. Luke has distinguished.

He reports Christ's challenge, "Handle me and see," which is peculiar to our third canonical gospel. All we know of the sect, or sects, which employed the "Gospel according to the Hebrews," goes to show the unlikelihood of the direct indebtedness of their evangelist to the most prominent disciple of S. Paul.

Another instance of his indebtedness to S. Luke is probably preserved for us in the Gospel of Nicodemus, viz., "*Baddach aphkid ruel.*"[2] And when the same authority that supplies this last fragment proceeds to inform us that the soldiers girded Christ for crucifixion with a "tattered scarlet robe," it is at least a plausible guess that the Hebrew evangelist transferred to Calvary the mockery by Roman soldiers, in order to make room for the mockery by Herod's.[3]

The Hebrew evangelist also preserves a fragment of A, viz., the history of the woman taken in adultery, which the canonical redactors omit.[4]

---

[1] "The other of the rich men said, I have performed the law and the prophets. And the Lord said unto him, How sayest thou? Behold many of thy brethren, sons of Abraham, are dying of hunger, and thy house is full of much goods, and there goeth out nothing unto them." The allusion here to the parable of Dives, which in Luke xvi. follows the scoff of the Pharisees, is obvious.

[2] Heb., *Beyadcha aphkid ruchi* ("Into thy hands I commend my Spirit"). The Gospel of Nicodemus probably assumed its present shape just at the time when Jerome had brought the "Gospel according to the Hebrews" into notoriety. The other Hebrew phrase which it contains is expressly assigned to the "Gospel according to the Hebrews" by Jerome—"*Hosanna barrama.*"

[3] Cf. the *v. r.* supplied by D in Luke xxiii. 37, "περιθέντες στέφανον."

[4] Eusebius only states that the "Gospel according to the Hebrews"

Perhaps also a fragment of B. "Be ye wise usurers" is quoted again and again by authorities whose occasional use of the "Gospel according to the Hebrews" is indisputable. It would follow well the parable of the talents, the original termination of which seems in Matt. xxv. to have been slightly superseded by the Preaching.

Direct use of A may be inferred from, "There was a certain man, Jesus by name, about thirty years of age (matter peculiar to S. Luke again), who chose us out. And He came to Capernaum, and entered into the house of Simon, and said, Passing by the lake of Tiberias, I chose out James and John, and Simon, and Andrew . . . and Thaddæus, and Simon Zelotes, and Judas Iscariot; and thee, Matthew, sitting at the receipt of custom. I will that ye be twelve apostles unto Israel." For here its original force is given to Mark i. 36.

And direct use of the Preaching may be inferred from, "Just now my Mother, the Spirit carried me up to the great mountain Tabor," for these words, if they refer to the Temptation,[1] show that the Hebrew evan-

contained the history of "a woman accused of many sins before our Lord," and the identity of this history with that contained in John vii. 53-viii. 11 is sometimes questioned. But answer has been made that this identity is distinctly implied by Rufinus, to whom the exact facts of the case must have been well known.

That this history belongs to A is shown by its style: and that its proper position is after Matt. xxii. 46*a*, by its occupying an analogous position in the fourth gospel; by its position after Luke xxi. in certain cursives; and by the complementariness of "Every one to his own home" to the gathering of the Pharisees described in Matt. xxii. 34, 41. Cf. John vii. 32-52.

[1] The alternative is to apply them to the Transfiguration. But conveyance by the Spirit rather recalls the Temptation. And they evidently introduce an event at which no witnesses were present. It should be noted that the author of the Clementines, whose indebtedness, direct or indirect, to the "Gospel according to the Hebrews" is generally admitted, twice puts an account of the Temptation into Christ's own mouth (Ante-Nicene Library, pp. 190, 290, cf. p. 146).

gelist put the one Petrine temptation, the third in Matt. iv., the second in Luke iv., in a place by itself.

Use of Matt. i., ii., Luke i. 5–ii. (of importance in connection with our affiliation of these sections), may be inferred from the persistency with which certain uncanonical details—related, sometimes to the former narrative, sometimes to the latter, and sometimes pointing to a compromise between the two—are added to the Birth-scene by writers whose occasional use of the "Gospel according to the Hebrews" is on other grounds probable. That the "Gospel according to the Hebrews" contained any account of the Nativity at all has sometimes been questioned, but a majority of critics are now in favour of interpreting certain expressions of Jerome's as implying the presence of "Thou Bethlehem," "out of Egypt," "called Nazarene."

The "yokes and ploughshares," made by our Lord in boyhood, are mentioned in the second century by Justin [1] and the author of the Gospel of Thomas. It is most unlikely that either copied from the other.

The distaff, the skeius, at which the Blessed Virgin worked, are mentioned in one of the authorities which the Jew of Celsus employs (Origen v. Cels., Ante-Nicene Library, p. 457), and in the Protevangel of James.

The marvellous magnitude of the star of Bethlehem "dimming all others" is mentioned in the Protevangel and the Ignatian Epistles.[2] Here again the chances of either drawing from the other are small.

---

[1] Justin, in common with the "Gospel according to the Hebrews," mentions the lightning-flash on the Jordan, at the time of the Baptism, and speaks of the Holy Spirit as having waited for Christ in all the prophets, and ultimately finding complete rest in Him.

[2] The author of the epistles quotes our Lord as saying, "Handle me and see, that I am not a bodiless *demon*"—words found in the "Gospel according to the Hebrews."

"Arabia," as the home of the Magi, is mentioned by Justin, and so often, that it scarcely looks like a mere fancy of his own.

A "cave" as the scene of the Nativity, is mentioned by Justin and the author of the Protevangel,—but neither is likely to have drawn from the other, for they introduce it in quite a different manner,—before the arrival at Bethlehem, or after the failure to find room there. It may be added that the idea of birth in a cave inevitably implies presence at Bethlehem for some purpose purely temporary, *i.e.*, involves the taxation, or something analogous.

The "Magi in the cave." This, too, is common to Justin and the Protevangel. It is the first night that the Magi arrive, usurping the place of the shepherds. Thus shepherds and Magi are partially identified,—otherwise, the former are sacrificed.

XXIV.

Let us now examine minutely the records of the Resurrection.

Partly owing to the presence of a foreign termination in S. Mark and loss of the original, partly owing to the extra information furnished in 1 Cor. xv. 5–7, it comes to pass that harmonistic difficulties here climax. But a minute examination of this portion of the sacred narrative will result in a most striking corroboration of the foregoing construction-scheme.

Here, then, is a reconstruction of the original text of A and B.

A.

Mark xv. 39, 42-46.

And He yielded up His spirit. And when the centurion, which stood by over against Him, saw that He so yielded up His spirit, he said, Certainly this was a righteous man.

And when even was now come, because it was the Preparation, there came Joseph of Arimathæa, a councillor of honourable estate, who also himself was looking for the kingdom of God: and he boldly went in unto Pilate, and asked for the body of Jesus. And Pilate marvelled if He were already dead: and calling unto him the centurion, he asked him whether He had been any while dead. And when he learned it of the centurion, he granted the corpse to Joseph. And he bought spices, and taking Him down, wound Him in linen cloths, with the spices, and laid Him in a tomb which had been hewn out of a rock. And he rolled a great stone to the door of the tomb, and departed. And

Matt. xxvii. 61-xxviii. 8, 11-15.

Mary Magdalene was there, and the other Mary, sitting over against the sepulchre.

Now on the morrow, which is the day after the Preparation, the chief priests and the Pharisees were gathered together unto Pilate, saying, Sir, we remember that that Deceiver said, while He was yet alive, After three days I rise again. Command therefore that the sepulchre be made sure until the third day, lest haply His disciples come and steal Him away, and say unto the people, He is risen from the dead; and the last error will be worse than the first. Pilate said unto them, Ye have a guard: go your way, make it as sure as ye can. So they went and made the sepulchre sure, sealing the stone, the guard being with them.

Now late on the sabbath day, as it began to dawn towards the first day of the week, came Mary Magdalene and the other Mary to see the sepulchre. And behold, there was a great earthquake; for an angel of the Lord descended from heaven, and came and rolled away the stone, and sat on it. His appearance was as lightning, and his raiment white as snow: and for fear of him the watchers did quake, and became as dead men. And the angel answered and said to the women, Fear not ye: for I know that ye seek Jesus, the Nazarene, which hath been crucified. He is not here; for He is risen, even as He said. Come, see the place where He lay. And go quickly, and tell His disciples and Peter He is risen from the dead; and lo, He goeth before you into Galilee; there shall ye see Him as He told you. And they went quickly from the tomb with fear and great joy, and ran to bring His disciples word.

Now while they were going, behold, some of the guards came into the city, and told unto the

THE FORMATION OF THE GOSPELS.

chief priests all the things that were come to pass. And when they were assembled with the elders, and had taken counsel, they gave large money unto the soldiers, saying, Say ye, His disciples came by night, and stole Him away while we slept. And if this come to the governor's ears, we will persuade him, and rid you of care. So they took the money, and did as they were taught: and this saying was spread abroad among the Jews, and continueth until this day.

Luke xxiv. 12.

But Peter arose, and ran unto the tomb, and stooping, and looking in, he seeth the linen cloths by themselves. And he departed to his home, wondering at that which was come to pass.

. . . .

Luke xxiv. 34, 36–53.

The eleven gathered together, and them that were with them, saying, The Lord is risen indeed, and hath appeared to Simon.

And as they spake these things, He Himself stood in the midst of them, and saith unto them, Peace be unto you. But they were terrified and affrighted, and supposed that they beheld a spirit. And He said unto them, Why are ye troubled? and wherefore do reasonings arise in your heart? See My hands and My feet, that it is I Myself; handle Me, and see; for a spirit hath not flesh and bones, as ye behold Me having. And when He had said this He showed them His hands and His feet. And while they still disbelieved for joy, and wondered, He said unto them, Have ye here anything to eat? And they gave Him a piece of a broiled fish. And He took it, and did eat before them.

And He said unto them, These are My words which I spake unto you, while I was yet with you, how that all things must needs be fulfilled, which are written in the law of Moses, and the prophets, and the psalms, concerning Me. Then opened He their mind, that they might understand the scriptures; and He said unto them, Thus it is written, that the Christ should suffer, and rise again from the dead the third day; and that repentance and remission of sins should be preached in His name unto all the nations, beginning from Jerusalem. Ye are witnesses of these things. And behold, I send forth the promise of My Father upon you: but tarry ye in the city, until ye be clothed with power from on high.

And He led them until they were over against Bethany: and He lifted up His hands, and blessed them. And it came to pass, while He blessed them, He parted from them, and was carried up into heaven. And they worshipped Him, and returned to Jerusalem with great joy: and were continually in the temple, blessing God.

B.

<small>Matt. xxvii. 50–60.</small>

And He yielded up His spirit.

And, behold, the veil of the temple was rent in twain from the top to the bottom; and the earth did quake, and the rocks were rent; and the tombs were opened; and many bodies of the saints that had fallen asleep were raised; and coming forth out of the tombs after His resurrection they entered the holy city, and appeared unto many.

And they that were watching Jesus, when they saw the earthquake, and the things that were done, feared exceedingly. And many women were there beholding from afar, which had followed Jesus from Galilee, ministering unto Him: among whom was Mary Magdalene, and Mary the mother of James and Joses, and the mother of the sons of Zebedee.

And when even was come, there came a rich man from Arimathæa, named Joseph, who also himself was Jesus' disciple. And Joseph took the body, and wrapped it in a clean linen cloth, and laid it in his own new tomb, which he had hewn out in the rock. And Mary Magdalene, and Mary the mother of James and Joses, and the mother of the sons of Zebedee beheld where He was laid. And they bought

<small>Mark xvi. 1–4.</small>

spices that they might come and anoint Him. And very early on the first day of the week, they come to the tomb, when the sun was risen. And they were saying among themselves, Who shall roll us away the stone from the door of the tomb? And looking up, they see that the stone is rolled back: for it was exceeding great.

And, behold, Jesus met them, saying, All hail! And they came and took hold of His feet, and worshipped Him. Then saith Jesus unto them, Fear not; go tell My brethren that they depart into Galilee, and there shall they see Me.

<small>Matt. xxviii 9, 10, 16–20.</small>

And the eleven disciples went into Galilee, unto the mountain where Jesus had appointed them. And when they saw Him, they worshipped Him: but some doubted. And Jesus came to them and spake unto them, saying, All authority hath been given unto Me in heaven and on earth. Go ye therefore, and make disciples of all the nations, baptizing them in the name of the Father, and of the Son, and of the Holy Ghost: teaching them to observe all things whatsoever I commanded you: and lo, I am with you alway, even unto the end of the world.

In piecing together the two foregoing narratives certain special tests and principles, besides the general ones already mentioned, come into play.

1. As to the visits of the women.

a. There is the division according to the *number* of women who come to the tomb. "*All* hail," and "saying *among themselves*," imply the presence of more than two.

b. There is the division according to the *purpose* with which the women come—whether to open the tomb and embalm the sacred body, or merely "to see" the tomb, which is sealed and guarded, the embalming presumably being already performed. With regard to this last point it may be noticed that "ὀθόνια" (Luke xxiv. 12—a word indicative of more careful wrappage than "σίνδων") probably points back to an account of the entombment, which has perished from the synoptic record, but left its traces in John xix. 40.

c. There is the division according to the *distance* the women come. The writer who has told us that the saints came out of their tombs after Christ, and went into the holy city, will scarcely bring the women quite as far as the sepulchre. Christ will meet them before they arrive. Moreover, the command "Go" (Matt. xxviii. 10) can scarcely be addressed to women who are already going quickly in the direction intended.

d. There is the division according to *the hour* at which the women come. In Mark xvi. 2 "the sun has risen" (or, "is rising," D). This would be after six o'clock. If it is embalmment that the women intend, light would be necessary, and it is involved in their perceiving the derangement of the sepulchre from a distance. But in Matt. xxviii. 1 the arrival is timed "late on the Sabbath, as it drew on to the first day of the week," an expression which can only imply six o'clock on Saturday evening, or midnight; and the context, the whole story of the guard, precludes the former interpretation.

Or perhaps this division might be better expressed as a division according to the hour at which the Resurrection took place—whether a moment after midnight or at sunrise—for in both cases it is immediately after the Resurrection has taken place that the women arrive on the scene. Christ has only walked a little way from the tomb when they meet Him (Mark xvi. 4; Matt. xxviii. 9). They and the soldiers carry back the intelligence almost simultaneously (Matt. xxviii. 11). Moreover, it is a natural inference from Matt. xxvii. 55,[1] xxviii. 5, that in both cases the women partially witness the phenomena by which the Resurrection was accompanied—an inference slightly supported by the curious reading of the old Latin in Mark xvi. 4,[2] where Matt. xxvii. 52, 53 is transferred to its chronological position, and the saints rise with Christ just as the women approach.

2. That the termination of A is preserved in Luke xxiv. may be deduced from the previous tendency of A. The visit of S. Peter to the tomb, and his special vision (vers. 12, 34), follow naturally after his special address (Matt. xxvi. 31–35), and his particularisation in the angelic message (Mark xvi. 7). Besides, the reference in vers. 44–46, "These are My

---

[1] "Women afar off seeing these things"—the same things, one infers, as "those with the centurion watching Jesus." But the things which those with the centurion "saw done," can only be the phenomena of the earthquake. Of the rent veil they would, of course, know nothing; and the darkness had already lasted too long to produce their panic, evidently sudden. Now the earthquake, or at any rate an effect which common sense requires that we should consider as following immediately, is distinctly timed "after His resurrection."

[2] A reading apparently known to the author of the "*Ascensio Isaiæ*" (ed. Dillman, p. 13), and to Tatian.

words which I spake unto you, while I was yet with you, how that all things must needs be fulfilled. Then opened He their mind that they might understand," is to the not-understood prophecy of xviii. 31–34, which belongs to A indubitably.

Again, there is the argument from remainder. Except A, there is no other authority to which this section of Luke xxiv. can be tacked, and that S. Luke originated it is rendered improbable by the fact, already mentioned, that a certain portion—the challenge to feel—was present in the "Gospel according to the Hebrews."[1]

But it is unfortunate that we are obliged to reach A in this roundabout way, for the tests suggested in Chapter XI. show that S. Luke has paraphrased A considerably.

3. It has been borne in mind, in unravelling A and B, and distinguishing them from the Preaching, that the three original accounts of the Resurrection must be of such a kind that out of them the canonical accounts, in the order prescribed, can legitimately have arisen.

Firstly, that the account in the first canonical gospel is prior to that in the second. Subjective considerations have led many critics to prefer the latter, simpler as it is, and less inevitably miraculous, and to brand

---

[1] And probably more: for in dealing with this section of the sacred narrative, Justin, whose occasional use of the "Gospel according to the Hebrews" has already been referred to, adds certain details, of which the "Gospel according to the Hebrews" seems the likeliest source, *e.g.*, that Christ showed the disciples how it had been foretold that He would rise *and again appear in Jerusalem*; asked them, "*Have ye not yet faith?*" ate and drank with them *by their request;* and that *they* (not Thomas merely) touched and handled Him (de Resurrectione, ix.). This last detail is especially noteworthy, for it accords with the fragment of the "Gospel according to the Hebrews" above referred to, "THEY touched Him and believed" (Jerome—Catal. Script. Eccl. 16).

the guard as a comparatively late introduction. But against this may be urged the verbal similarity of the guard section to the rest of A, and the decided doublet of Matt. xxviii. 2–4 with xxvii. 21–54, the doublets being, *ex hypothesi*, deep and structural, and not attributable to embellishment. For omitting the guard in Mark xvi. there was an obvious reason, the difficulty of reconciling its presence with B's account of the intended embalmment.[1]

Then, again, there is the description of the women's action on leaving the tomb, "With great joy they ran to bring the disciples word," in Matt. xxviii. 8. But in Mark xvi. 8, "Trembling and astonishment (ἔκστασις)[2] had come upon them, and they said nothing to any one, for they were afraid." Which is prior? I think close scrutiny will show the former. The "trembling" and the "silence" are preparations for Christ's appearance to the women. The author of the second canonical gospel endeavours to improve on the first, and alters the attitude of the women in order to account for a repetition of the command, "Go, tell," a repetition of the exhortation, "Fear not."

It is a little strange to find the aspect of the angel changed; but this, the omission of the guard really necessitates. The appearance, terrific to the soldiers, is for the women alone beautifully softened.

Secondly, that the account in the third canonical gospel is posterior to the accounts in the first and second.

---

[1] Origen was able to avail himself of the testimony of Phlegon (Hadrian's chronicler) as to an earthquake just about the time of the Resurrection. Nor can the guard be dismissed as a late embellishment. The current Jewish slander, reported Matt. xxviii. 13–15, is not merely that the disciples stole the sacred Body, but that they did so *while the soldiers slept*.

[2] ἔκστασις is a word of the redactor's. Cf. Mark v. 43.

There are two angels,—but are the descriptions of the angel in Matt. xxviii. and of the angel in Mark xvi. so similar, that the angel here and the angel there could not fail to be identified? (For instances of similar duplication, see Chapter XIX.) The "lightning-like" apparel of these two (cf. Matt. xxviii. 3) warns us against inferring, from S. Luke's omission of the guard, that he was therefore ignorant of the document in which the guard found place. So, too, the attribution of the centurion's reverence, to his "seeing what was done," against a similar inference from S. Luke's omission of the earthquake,—for, as already pointed out, there was nothing but the earthquake for the centurion to see. Again, the peculiar phrase in ver. 24—S. Luke's own, be it remembered—" Him they saw not," by which it would almost seem as if the experiences of the Apostle or Apostles who visited the tomb are distinguished from those of the women, warns us against assuming ignorance on S. Luke's part of the appearance recounted in Matt. xxviii. 9, 10; Mark xvi. 9. The absence of more detailed reference is indeed rather an evidence of S. Luke's knowing more about the matter than he knew how to digest. That S. Luke assigns the purchase of the unguents by the women to Friday evening, whereas in Mark xvi. 1 the purchase takes place "after the Sabbath," is to be explained by the fact that this governing clause "after the Sabbath" belongs to A, and that in B's account of the purchase no note of time is given at all.[1] There is again a very probable proof in ver. 10 (if the reading of the R.V. be adopted) of S. Luke's usage of our second canonical gospel—of a copy imperfect as at present—an escape from the

[1] In D this governing clause "after the Sabbath" is omitted.

apparent *impasse* of Mark xvi. 8, " they told nothing to any one," thus—" the *other* women with them told."

But now we are confronted by a difficulty very much more serious—S. Luke's apparent suggestion of an ascension on Easter Day, and the conspicuous absence of any indication of an appearance in Galilee. The first point need not detain us. As in the case of the eschatological discourse (xxi.), S. Luke, who has his own ideas of artistic effect, avoids reproducing the breaks of time and scenery exhibited by his authorities, so here;—but the lateness of the hour at which the two return from Emmaus, the length of time necessary for explaining the Messianic prophecies and for the opening of the Apostles' hearts, the closed city gates, the visibility of the ascension, these are so many indications that he did not intend to imply immediate sequence of events. It may be added that of an ascension on Easter Day there is elsewhere not the slightest trace.[1]

But the second point, the omission of appearances in Galilee, cannot be dismissed so summarily. A and B and the Preaching, as will be shown presently, all involve Galilæan manifestations; but the portion of the Preaching doing so belongs to the second part of the Preaching, which probably did not come into S. Luke's hands until after the completion of his gospel. And, as before stated, S. Luke generally sacrifices his other authorities to the Preaching. Moreover, in A the departure to Galilee and the return are not very clearly marked. In B the return is omitted altogether. S. Luke, then, perceiving an apparent discrepancy between A and B as to the scene of the ascension, a mountain in Galilee, or a mountain near Jerusalem, not unac-

---

[1] Except possibly in the Epistle of Barnabas. But cf. Chapter X.

THE FORMATION OF THE GOSPELS. 117

quainted (for he had spent nearly a week in Jerusalem, Acts xxi. 17, 26) with the local traditions respecting the latter, determines to exclude a cross-light. He paraphrases the angelic message, "Go into Galilee," thus, "Remember how He told you while yet in Galilee," and allows it to appear that the manifestation to S. Peter and the first to the eleven, took place in Jerusalem, and on Easter day.

4. It has been borne in mind in separating A and B, and distinguishing them from the Preaching, that the result must be such as will give us a clearer idea of what actually happened. Let us then examine each document separately, and the authorities outside.

a. In A Christ declares that Peter and the other apostles will all be scattered abroad when He is smitten, but that after rising He will go before them into Galilee. Then again the angel bids to remind the apostles and Peter of this declaration, "There in Galilee shall ye see Him, as He told you." Consequently, when we hear that S. Peter "went to his own home," it is natural to suppose that it is his home in Galilee that is intended; indeed a home of his own in Jerusalem is quite inconceivable, when we remember the obligation incurred towards the man with the pitcher; and a lodging shared with the others would suit very ill with the fact of a special vision accorded to him. Moreover, Christ's declaration about the flock conveys the impression of a real scattering, enduring for more than a few hours—a scattering not only from the Shepherd but also from one another—and accordingly we hear of a *re-gathering*, Luke xxiv. 33. But in Jerusalem the apostles would all naturally have been together "in the upper chamber where they abode"

(Acts i. 13). Doubly inconceivable is it that they scattered after any convincing manifestation, any appearance to the whole college on the evening of Easter Day.[1]

When therefore Christ gives the commandment, "*Settle* (καθίσατε) in the city till ye be endued with power from on high," "Beginning from Jerusalem, ye are witnesses of these things," we must take this commandment as given in Galilee. It is "Settle *there*," "Begin from *there*," "Return to the capital, and make it your future head-quarters."[2]

And when we read "He led them to Bethany," we must understand that it is "from Galilee;" and "they returned to Jerusalem," that it is after several weeks' absence.

b. Similarly in B, Christ sends to the apostles, "Tell them that they depart into Galilee: there shall they see Me;" and then we hear that "they went into Galilee unto the mountain." It may be added, *à propos*

---

[1] Lactantius (iv. 20) has no doubt that Christ's first appearance to the Eleven took place in Galilee, and that it was in Galilee that "He opened their mind that they might understand the Scriptures." Possibly a truer impression of A than is preserved in Luke xxiv. reached Lactantius through some apocryphal medium. There are reasons for believing that some things from the "Gospel according to the Hebrews" have filtered into his works through the "*Prædicatio Petri et Pauli.*"

[2] The interpretation of this command which S. Luke gives in Acts i. 4, 5 (for the first five verses of Acts, as pointed out presently, are S. Luke's own), is evidently incorrect. "Remain here in Jerusalem (μὴ χωρίζεσθαι ἀπὸ), for ye shall be baptized with the Spirit, not many days hence," could not be addressed to men who were either under orders to go into Galilee, or had just arrived from Galilee for some special purpose and with no immediate intention of returning thither. Besides, the apostles were being "endued with power," long after Pentecost (cf. Acts iv. 29–31).

A very early tradition, perhaps derived from the "Gospel according to the Hebrews," fixes the term of residence enjoined for witness in Jerusalem at twelve years.

of this appearance on the mountain, that the little note "some doubted" points to a considerable number of spectators.

c. In the Preaching (Mark xvi. 9–20) the marks of time are very vague; but the "disbelief" in the report of the two from Emmaus requires some time for its display, more than a few minutes, and the "hardness of heart" with which Christ reproaches the Apostles produces the impression that their stubbornness was somewhat protracted. The fact, too, that there is a ceiling overhead when Christ is speaking precludes an interpretation of "When He had spoken, He was received up," as indicative of ascension there and then. In fine, one certainly gathers from the form of this appearance to the eleven as they sit at meat, as compared with the appearances to the eleven in A and B, that in all three cases several appearances to the Apostolic college are compressed, the scenery of one being allowed to predominate.

But we are not confined to Mark xvi. 9–20 for our knowledge of the intention of the author of the Preaching. As before stated, the Preaching is continued in the Acts.

In Acts i. 1–5 the thread of the narrative is taken up from Luke xxiv. 49, *i.e.*, S. Luke reminds us of the occasion when Christ was assembled with the Apostles, under the same roof and at the same board (συναλιζό-μενος), and convinced them of His real presence by certain proofs. But in ver. 6 where, as already mentioned (Chapter XI.), the Preaching recommences,[1] it is a new appearance that is described, introduced by "They therefore when they were come together," *i.e.*,

[1] It is, perhaps, worth noticing that some of Jerome's MSS. interpolated "Reveal Thy justice," a partial equivalent to "Restore the kingdom to Israel," into the appendix to S. Mark.

a larger circle of Apostles than the Eleven—the Seventy—for witness of this appearance, as we find subsequently, combined with long discipleship, was the indispensable qualification of the candidates for the office of Judas, and a considerable number were eligible.

Additional particulars concerning Christ's appearances are supplied by the Preaching, in Acts x. 41, 42, "He ate and drank with us" (D adds "for many days");[1] and in xiii. 31, "He was seen for many days of them which came up with Him from Galilee to Jerusalem," these last words containing an allusion, though not quite inevitably, to the manner of the journey summarised in Luke xxiv. 50; and to be considered in connection with Acts i. 12, 13, "Then returned they to Jerusalem, and when they were come in, they went up into the upper chamber where they usually abode,"—a strange expression surely if their absence had only been for a few hours.

d. In S. Paul's list of the appearances (1 Cor. xv. 5–7), there are many things to be noted.

His omission of the appearance to the women, if not due to his instinctive undervaluation of feminine testimony, would seem to point to the existence, even so early, of contradictory accounts. Here, as already pointed out (to account for a similar omission on the part of S. Luke), A and B and the Preaching are far from being harmonious, and *a priori* reasons render it

---

[1] Some grounds, afforded by the Diatessaron, for supposing that the Petrine narrative behind Acts i. spread Christ's appearances over *fifty* days have been noticed in Chapter X. That the Diatessaron extended into Acts i. is evident from Moesinger, pp. 240, 273–275. It is a slight objection that this notion of the Day of Pentecost being a Sunday, involves the Johannine date of the Passover, for the Preaching (Luke xxii. 15), is not incompatible with the Johannine date.

probable that they only reproduce discrepancies current on the first Easter Day,—that women so overwrought, after an experience so startling, uttered inconsistencies which nothing short of an immediate rigorous cross-examination would have sufficed to dispel. Admitted the *bona fides* of the women, yet for purposes polemical and apologetic—and such were S. Paul's—their evidence would have little force.

His assignment of the first appearance to S. Peter and to the Eleven is in exact accordance with A.

The appearance to the five hundred implies Galilee, for the whole number of disciples in Jerusalem did not exceed "a hundred and twenty."

And the appearance "to ALL the Apostles," as distinguished from the previously mentioned Eleven, is in exact accordance with what we have shown to be an inference from the Preaching (Acts i. 6, 21, 22).

But how are we to account for S. Paul's omission of the appearance at Emmaus? and, conversely, for the omission by A and B and the Preaching, of the appearance to S. James? Now S. James, according to the trustworthy testimony of Hegesippus, was the nephew of Cleopas. Was he his companion at Emmaus? It is noteworthy in this connection, that the "Gospel according to the Hebrews" fixes the appearance to S. James on Easter-Day, and associates it with a Eucharistic meal. Also noteworthy is the various reading for "Emmaus" in the Codex Bezæ, "Oulammaus," for "Oulammaus," according to the LXX. (Gen. xxviii. 19), had been the scene of a theophany to an earlier Jacob. Noteworthy, too, the strange periphrase (Luke xxiv. 33, 34; contrast Mark xvi. 13, 14) by which S. Luke avoids informing us whether the appearance to S. Peter was prior to that at Emmaus, or *vice versâ*, remembering that whether the glory of the first vision belonged to S. Peter or S. James was very early a matter of question (*vide* 1 Cor. xv. 5; contrast "Gospel according to the Hebrews").

e. The fourth gospel throws very little light on the points which the earlier documents leave obscure. Incidentally, however, it may be remarked—

That although at first sight the author appears to agree with S. Luke in fixing in Jerusalem, and on Easter Day, the first appearance to the apostolic college, yet that closer scrutiny renders this very doubtful. He has told us previously that "the disciples" (perhaps referring to others besides S. Peter and S. John) "went away to their own homes," and this must be taken in connection with the strong and clear declaration which it complements, "Ye shall be scattered, every one to his own" (xvi. 32). What he lays stress on is not that the appearance to the ten took place on the actual day of the resurrection, but on the same sort of day, the first of the week (cf. Epistle of Barnabas). Besides, if this appearance and the following one be assigned to Jerusalem, the sudden transition to Galilee in xxi. is left unaccounted for.

That a portion of xxi., our Lord's conversation with Peter and John, comes almost as a sequel to their joint visit to the tomb. The fire of coals, the threefold assertion of love, further connect it with the scene in the high priest's hall. And so it would seem that this appearance on the shores of the Sea of Galilee partly corresponds with that which in A and 1 Corinthians belongs to S. Peter alone.

Putting together all these authorities, A and B and

the Preaching, and S. Paul, and S. John, one gathers that the actual order of events was as follows:—

On Easter morning the women appeared, probably in two detachments, with contradictory accounts of what they had seen; one at least averring that she had actually seen Christ. They were disbelieved.

In the evening, James and Cleopas came in with an account of their experience at Emmaus. They too were disbelieved.

And then the Apostles scattered, every one to his own Galilean home, wondering at the strange termination of their dream, wondering and despondent. "We hoped that it was He who should redeem Israel." Peter resumed his fishing,—yet the task of stablishing faith was his.

Suddenly the startling intelligence was bruited abroad that Christ was risen indeed, had appeared to Peter.

In Capernaum,[1] the eleven again met together, and Christ showed Himself in their midst by certain proofs, showed them His hands and feet, ate and drank in their presence.

Again on the well-known mountain of the Beatitudes and the loaves, perhaps in the dim distance, for doubt was not precluded, to a larger circle of spectators —the five hundred.

Then, with their hearts high, anticipating an immediate restoration of the kingdom to Israel, a trumpet-blast proclaiming Messiah's triumph to the world, the Apostles all journeyed back to the capital—some hundred in company.

---

[1] "Fittingly at Capernaum," exclaims Ephraem, commenting on Tatian's text, "the city of consolation" (Moesinger, p. 272).

Past the familiar scenery, with all its memories and associations,—and they felt that again the Master was going before as their Guide.

He led them as far as the Mount of Olives, and there in the still morning twilight—it is always in the twilight—He was once more with them visibly, but far otherwise than they had expected. They alone were to be His witnesses (Luke xxiv. 48; Acts x. 41, cf. John xiv. 22). As day broke, He lifted up His hands in blessing, was lifted up and parted from them.

And the gifts which He received from the Father, and poured down upon the Church, came as proofs of His reception into Heaven.

THE GOSPELS WITHIN THE GOSPELS.

A is printed in ordinary type, B in italics, and the independent Petrine document in red.

The brackets denote transpositions or additions by the redactors.

The distinction of A and B is not continued in S. Luke, since the non-Petrine sections of that gospel are merely a reflection of S. Mark.

THE GOSPEL ACCORDING TO

S. MATTHEW.

1 THE book of the generation of Jesus Christ, the son of David, the son of Abraham.
2 Abraham begat Isaac ; and Isaac begat Jacob ; and Jacob begat Judas and his
3 brethren ; and Judas begat Phares and Zara of Thamar ; and Phares begat
4 Esrom ; and Esrom begat Aram ; and Aram begat Aminadab ; and Aminadab begat Naasson ; and Naasson begat Sal-
5 mon ; and Salmon begat Booz of Rachab ; and Booz begat Obed of Ruth ; and Obed
6 begat Jesse ; and Jesse begat David the king.
And David the king begat Solomon of
7 her that had been the wife of Urias ; and Solomon begat Roboam ; and Roboam
8 begat Abia ; and Abia begat Asa ; and Asa begat Josaphat ; and Josaphat begat
9 Joram ; and Joram begat Ozias ; and Ozias begat Joatham ; and Joatham be-
10 gat Achaz ; and Achaz begat Ezekias ; and Ezekias begat Manasses ; and Manasses begat Amon ; and Amon begat
11 Josias ; and Josias begat Jechonias and his brethren, about the time they were carried away to Babylon.
12 And after they were brought to Babylon, Jechonias begat Salathiel ; and
13 Salathiel begat Zorobabel ; and Zorobabel begat Abiud ; and Abiud begat
14 Eliakim ; and Eliakim begat Azor ; and Azor begat Sadoc ; and Sadoc begat
15 Achim ; and Achim begat Eliud ; and Eliud begat Eleazar ; and Eleazar begat Matthan ; and Matthan begat Jacob ;
16 and Jacob begat Joseph the husband of Mary, of whom was born Jesus, who is called Christ.
17 So all the generations from Abraham to David are fourteen generations ; and from David until the carrying away into Babylon are fourteen generations ; and from the carrying away into Babylon unto Christ are fourteen generations.
18 Now the birth of Jesus Christ was on this wise : When as his mother Mary was espoused to Joseph, before they came together, she was found with child
19 of the Holy Ghost. Then Joseph her husband, being a just man, and not willing to make her a publick example, was minded to put her away privily.
20 But while he thought on these things, behold, the angel of the Lord appeared unto him in a dream, saying, Joseph, thou son of David, fear not to take unto

thee Mary thy wife : for that which is conceived in her is of the Holy Ghost.
21 And she shall bring forth a son, and thou shalt call his name JESUS : for he shall save his people from their sins.
22 Now all this was done, that it might be fulfilled which was spoken of the Lord by the prophet, saying,
23 Behold, a virgin shall be with child, and shall bring forth a son,
And they shall call his name Emmanuel,
which being interpreted is, God with us.
24 Then Joseph being raised from sleep did as the angel of the Lord had bidden him,
25 and took unto him his wife : and knew her not till she had brought forth her first-born [a] son : and he called his name JESUS. [a] R. V. omits.

2 Now when Jesus was born in Bethlehem of Judea in the days of Herod the king, behold, there came wise men from
2 the east to Jerusalem, saying, Where is he that is born King of the Jews ? for we have seen his star in the east, and are
3 come to worship him. When Herod the king had heard these things, he was troubled, and all Jerusalem with him.
4 And when he had gathered all the chief priests and scribes of the people together, he demanded of them where Christ
5 should be born. And they said unto him, In Bethlehem of Judea ; for thus it is written by the prophet,
6 And thou Bethlehem, in the land of Juda,
Art not the least among the princes of Juda :
For out of thee shall come a Governor, That shall rule my people Israel.
7 Then Herod, when he had privily called the wise men, enquired of them diligently
8 what time the star appeared. And he sent them to Bethlehem, and said, Go and search diligently for the young child ; and when ye have found him bring me word again, that I may come
9 and worship him also. When they had heard the king, they departed ; and, lo, the star, which they saw in the east, went before them, till it came and stood
10 over where the young child was. When they saw the star, they rejoiced with exceeding great joy.
11 And when they were come into the house, they saw the young child with Mary his mother, and fell down, and worshipped him : and when

they had opened their treasures, they presented unto him gifts; gold, and
12 frankincense, and myrrh. And being warned of God in a dream that they should not return to Herod, they departed into their own country another way.
13 And when they were departed, behold, the angel of the Lord appeareth to Joseph in a dream, saying, Arise, and take the young child and his mother, and flee into Egypt, and be thou there until I bring thee word: for Herod will seek
14 the young child to destroy him. When he arose, he took the young child and his mother by night, and departed into
15 Egypt: and was there until the death of Herod: that it might be fulfilled which was spoken of the Lord by the prophet, saying, Out of Egypt have I called my
16 son. Then Herod, when he saw that he was mocked of the wise men, was exceeding wroth, and sent forth, and slew all the children that were in Bethlehem, and in all the coasts thereof, from two years old and under, according to the time which he had diligently enquired of
17 the wise men. Then was fulfilled that which was spoken by Jeremy the prophet, saying,
18 In Rama was there a voice heard, Lamentation, and weeping, and great mourning,
Rachel weeping for her children,
And would not be comforted, because they are not.
19 But when Herod was dead, behold, an angel of the Lord appeareth in a dream
20 to Joseph in Egypt, saying, Arise, and take the young child and his mother, and go into the land of Israel: for they are dead which sought the young child's life.
21 And he arose, and took the young child and his mother, and came into the land
22 of Israel. But when he heard that Archelaus did reign in Judea in the room of his father Herod, he was afraid to go thither: notwithstanding, being warned of God in a dream, he turned aside into
23 the parts of Galilee: and he came and dwelt in a city called Nazareth: that it might be fulfilled which was spoken by the prophets, He shall be called a Nazarene.

3 In those days came John the Baptist, preaching in the wilderness of Judea,
2 and saying, Repent ye: for the kingdom
3 of heaven is at hand. For this is he that was spoken of by the prophet Esaias, saying,
The voice of one crying in the wilderness,
Prepare ye the way of the Lord,
Make his paths straight.
4 And the same John had his raiment of camel's hair, and a leathern girdle about his loins; and his meat was locusts and
5 wild honey. Then went out to him Jerusalem, and all Judea, and all the
6 region round about Jordan, and were baptized of him in Jordan, confessing
7 their sins. But when he saw many of the Pharisees and Sadducees come to his baptism, he said unto them, O generation of vipers, who hath warned you to
8 flee from the wrath to come? Bring forth therefore fruits meet for repent-
9 ance: and think not to say within yourselves, We have Abraham to our father: for I say unto you, that God is able of these stones to raise up children unto
10 Abraham. And now also the axe is laid unto the root of the trees: therefore every tree which bringeth not forth good fruit
11 is hewn down, and cast into the fire. I indeed baptize you with water unto repentance: but he that cometh after me is mightier than I, whose shoes I am not worthy to bear: he shall baptize you with the Holy Ghost, and with fire:
12 whose fan is in his hand, and he will throughly purge his floor, and gather his wheat into the garner; but he will burn up the chaff with unquenchable fire.
13 Then cometh Jesus from Galilee to Jordan unto John, to be baptized of him.
14 But John forbade him, saying, I have need to be baptized of thee, and comest
15 thou to me? And Jesus answering, said unto him, Suffer it to be so now: for thus it becometh us to fulfil all righteousness.
16 Then he suffered him. And Jesus, when he was baptized, went up straightway out of the water: and, lo, the heavens were opened unto him, and he saw the Spirit of God descending like a dove,
17 and lighting upon him: and lo a voice from heaven, saying, This is my beloved Son, in whom I am well pleased.

4 Then was Jesus led up of the Spirit into the wilderness to be tempted of the
2 devil. And when he had fasted forty days and forty nights, he was afterward
3 an hungered. And when the tempter came to him, he said, If thou be the Son of God, command that these stones be
4 made bread. But he answered and said, It is written, Man shall not live by bread alone, but by every word that proceedeth
5 out of the mouth of God. Then the devil taketh him up into the holy city, and setteth him on a pinnacle of the temple,
6 and saith unto him, If thou be the Son of God, cast thyself down: for it is written,
He shall give his angels charge concerning thee:
And in their hands they shall bear thee up,
Lest at any time thou dash thy foot against a stone.
7 Jesus said unto him, It is written again, Thou shalt not tempt the Lord thy God.

S. MATTHEW.

Luke iii.
6-8, 13.

8 Again, the devil taketh him up into an exceeding high mountain, and sheweth him all the kingdoms of the world, and
9 the glory of them ; and saith unto him, All these things will I give thee, if thou
10 wilt fall down and worship me. Then saith Jesus unto him, Get thee hence, Satan : for it is written, Thou shalt worship the Lord thy God, and him only
11 shalt thou serve. Then the devil leaveth him, and, behold, angels came and ministered unto him.
12 Now when Jesus had heard that John was cast into prison, he departed into
13 Galilee ; and leaving Nazareth, he came and dwelt in Capernaum, which is upon the sea coast, in the borders of Zabulon
14 and Nephthalim : that it might be fulfilled which was spoken by Esaias the prophet, saying,
15   The land of Zabulon, and the land of Nephthalim,
   By the way of the sea, beyond Jordan, Galilee of the Gentiles ;
16 The people which sat in darkness Saw great light ;
   And to them which sat in the region and shadow of death
   Light is sprung up.
17 From that time Jesus began to preach, and to say, Repent : for the kingdom of heaven is at hand.
18 And Jesus, walking by the sea of Galilee, saw two brethren, Simon called Peter, and Andrew his brother, casting a net
19 into the sea : for they were fishers. And he saith unto them, Follow me, and I
20 will make you fishers of men. And they straightway left their nets, and followed
21 him. And going on from thence, he saw other two brethren, James the son of Zebedee, and John his brother, in a ship with Zebedee their father, mending their
22 nets ; and he called them. And they immediately left the ship and their father, and followed him.
23 *And Jesus went about all Galilee, teaching in their synagogues, and preaching the gospel of the kingdom, and healing all manner of sickness and all manner of*
24 *disease among the people. And his fame went throughout all Syria : and they brought unto him all sick people that were taken with divers diseases and torments, and those which were possessed with devils, and those which were lunatick, and those that had the palsy ; and he healed them.*
25 *And there followed him great multitudes of people from Galilee, and from Decapolis, and from Jerusalem, and from Judea, and from beyond Jordan.*

5   *And seeing the multitudes, he went up into a mountain : and when he was set,*
2 *his disciples came unto him : and he opened his mouth, and taught them, saying,*

3 *Blessed are the poor in spirit : for theirs is the kingdom of heaven.*
4 *Blessed are they that mourn : for they shall be comforted.*
5 *Blessed are the meek : for they shall inherit the earth.*
6 *Blessed are they which do hunger and thirst after righteousness : for they shall be filled.*
7 *Blessed are the merciful : for they shall obtain mercy.*
8 *Blessed are the pure in heart : for they shall see God.*
9 *Blessed are the peace-makers : for they shall be called the children of God.*
10 *Blessed are they which are persecuted for righteousness' sake : for theirs is the*
11 *kingdom of heaven. Blessed are ye, when men shall revile you, and persecute you, and shall say all manner of evil against*
12 *you falsely, for my sake. Rejoice, and be exceeding glad : for great is your reward in heaven : for so persecuted they the prophets which were before you.*
13 *Ye are the salt of the earth : but if the salt have lost his savour, wherewith shall it be salted ? it is thenceforth good for nothing, but to be cast out, and to be*
14 *trodden under foot of men. Ye are the light of the world. A city that is set on*
15 *an hill cannot be hid. Neither do men light a candle, and put it under a bushel, but on a candlestick ; and it giveth light*
16 *unto all that are in the house. Let your light so shine before men, that they may see your good works, and glorify your Father which is in heaven.*
17 *Think not that I am come to destroy the law, or the prophets : I am not come*
18 *to destroy, but to fulfil. For verily I say unto you, Till heaven and earth pass, one jot or one tittle shall in no wise pass*
19 *from the law, till all be fulfilled. Whosoever therefore shall break one of these least commandments, and shall teach men so, he shall be called the least in the kingdom of heaven : but whosoever shall do and teach them, the same shall be called great in the kingdom of heaven.*
20 *For I say unto you, That except your righteousness shall exceed the righteousness of the scribes and Pharisees, ye shall in no case enter into the kingdom of heaven.*
21 *Ye have heard that it was said by them of old time, Thou shalt not kill ; and whosoever shall kill shall be in danger of*
22 *the judgment : but I say unto you, That whosoever is angry with his brother without a cause, shall be in danger of the judgment : and whosoever shall say to his brother, Raca, shall be in danger of the council : but whosoever shall say, Thou*
23 *fool, shall be in danger of hell fire. Therefore if thou bring thy gift to the altar, and there rememberest that thy brother*

I

24 hath ought against thee; leave there thy gift before the altar, and go thy way; first be reconciled to thy brother, and then
25 come and offer thy gift. Agree with thine adversary quickly, whiles thou art in the way with him; lest at any time the adversary deliver thee to the judge, and the judge deliver thee to the officer,
26 and thou be cast into prison. Verily I say unto thee, Thou shalt by no means come out thence, till thou hast paid the uttermost farthing.
27 *Ye have heard that it was said by them of old time, Thou shalt not commit*
28 *adultery: but I say unto you, That whosoever looketh on a woman to lust after her hath committed adultery with her*
29 *already in his heart. And if thy right eye offend thee, pluck it out, and cast it from thee: for it is profitable for thee that one of thy members should perish, and not that thy whole body should be cast*
30 *into hell. And if thy right hand offend thee, cut it off, and cast it from thee: for it is profitable for thee that one of thy members should perish, and not that thy*
31 *whole body should be cast into hell. It hath been said, Whosoever shall put away his wife, let him give her a writing of*
32 *divorcement: but I say unto you, That whosoever shall put away his wife, saving for the cause of fornication, causeth her to commit adultery: and whosoever shall marry her that is divorced committeth adultery.*
33 *Again, ye have heard that it hath been said by them of old time, Thou shalt not forswear thyself, but shalt perform unto*
34 *the Lord thine oaths: but I say unto you, Swear not at all; neither by heaven;*
35 *for it is God's throne; nor by the earth; for it is his footstool: neither by Jerusalem; for it is the city of the great King.*
36 *Neither shalt thou swear by thy head, because thou canst not make one hair*
37 *white or black. But let your communication be, Yea, yea; Nay, nay: for whatsoever is more than these cometh of evil.*
38 *Ye have heard that it hath been said, An eye for an eye, and a tooth for a*
39 *tooth: but I say unto you, That ye resist not evil: but whosoever shall smite thee on thy right cheek, turn to him the other*
40 *also. And if any man will sue thee at the law, and take away thy coat, let him*
41 *have thy cloak also. And whosoever shall compel thee to go a mile, go with him*
42 *twain. Give to him that asketh thee, and from him that would borrow of thee turn not thou away.*
43 *Ye have heard that it hath been said, Thou shalt love thy neighbour, and hate*
44 *thine enemy. But I say unto you, Love your enemies, bless them that curse you, do good to them that hate you, and pray for them which despitefully use you, and*
45 *persecute you; that ye may be the children of your Father which is in heaven: for he maketh his sun to rise on the evil and on the good, and sendeth rain on the just*
46 *and on the unjust. For if ye love them which love you, what reward have ye?*
47 *do not even the publicans the same? And if ye salute your brethren only, what do ye more than others? do not even the*
48 *publicans so? Be ye therefore perfect, even as your Father which is in heaven is perfect.*

6 Take heed that ye do not your alms before men, to be seen of them: otherwise ye have no reward of your Father which is in heaven.
2 Therefore when thou doest thine alms, do not sound a trumpet before thee, as the hypocrites do in the synagogues and in the streets, that they may have glory of men. Verily I say unto you, They
3 have their reward. But when thou doest alms, let not thy left hand know what thy
4 right hand doeth: that thine alms may be in secret: and thy Father which seeth in secret himself shall reward thee openly.
5 And when thou prayest, thou shalt not be as the hypocrites are: for they love to pray standing in the synagogues and in the corners of the streets, that they may be seen of men. Verily I say unto you,
6 They have their reward. But thou, when thou prayest, enter into thy closet, and when thou hast shut thy door, pray to thy Father which is in secret: and thy Father which seeth in secret shall reward
7 thee openly. But when ye pray, use not vain repetitions, as the heathen do: for they think that they shall be heard for
8 their much speaking. Be not ye therefore like unto them: for your Father knoweth what things ye have need of,
9 before ye ask him. After this manner therefore pray ye: Our Father which art
10 in heaven, Hallowed be thy name. Thy kingdom come. Thy will be done in
11 earth, as it is in heaven. Give us this
12 day our daily bread. And forgive us our
13 debts, as we forgive our debtors. And lead us not into temptation, but deliver us from evil: For thine is the kingdom, and the power, and the glory, for ever.
14 Amen. For if ye forgive men their trespasses, your heavenly Father will also
15 forgive you: but if ye forgive not men their trespasses, neither will your Father forgive your trespasses.
16 Moreover when ye fast, be not, as the hypocrites, of a sad countenance: for they disfigure their faces, that they may appear unto men to fast. Verily I say
17 unto you, They have their reward. But thou, when thou fastest, anoint thine
18 head, and wash thy face; that thou appear not unto men to fast, but unto

S. MATTHEW.   131

thy Father which is in secret: and thy Father, which seeth in secret, shall reward thee openly.

19 Lay not up for yourselves treasures upon earth, where moth and rust doth corrupt, and where thieves break through
20 and steal: but lay up for yourselves treasures in heaven, where neither moth nor rust doth corrupt, and where thieves
21 do not break through nor steal: for where your treasure is, there will your
22 heart be also. The light of the body is the eye: if therefore thine eye be
23 single, thy whole body shall be full of light. But if thine eye be evil, thy whole body shall be full of darkness. If therefore the light that is in thee be darkness, how great is that darkness!
24 No man can serve two masters: for either he will hate the one, and love the other; or else he will hold to the one, and despise the other. Ye cannot serve
25 God and mammon. Therefore I say unto you, Take no thought for your life, what ye shall eat, or what ye shall drink; nor yet for your body, what ye shall put on. Is not the life more than meat, and the
26 body than raiment? Behold the fowls of the air: for they sow not, neither do they reap, nor gather into barns; yet your heavenly Father feedeth them. Are ye
27 not much better than they? Which of you by taking thought can add one cubit
28 unto his stature? And why take ye thought for raiment? Consider the lilies of the field, how they grow; they toil
29 not, neither do they spin: and yet I say unto you, That even Solomon in all his glory was not arrayed like one of these.
30 Wherefore, if God so clothe the grass of the field, which to-day is, and to-morrow is cast into the oven, shall he not much more clothe you, O ye of little faith?
31 Therefore take no thought, saying, What shall we eat? or, What shall we drink? or, Wherewithal shall we be clothed?
32 (For after all these things do the Gentiles seek:) for your heavenly Father knoweth that ye have need of all these things.
33 But seek ye first the kingdom of God, and his righteousness; and all these
34 things shall be added unto you. Take therefore no thought for the morrow: for the morrow shall take thought for the things of itself. Sufficient unto the day is the evil thereof.

7 Judge not, that ye be not judged. For
2 with what judgment ye judge, ye shall be judged: and with what measure ye mete,
3 it shall be measured to you again. And why beholdest thou the mote that is in thy brother's eye, but considerest not the
4 beam that is in thine own eye? Or how wilt thou say to thy brother, Let me pull out the mote out of thine eye; and, be-
5 hold, a beam is in thine own eye? Thou hypocrite, first cast out the beam out of thine own eye; and then shalt thou see clearly to cast out the mote out of thy brother's eye.
6 Give not that which is holy unto the dogs, neither cast ye your pearls before swine, lest they trample them under their feet, and turn again and rend you.
7 Ask, and it shall be given you; seek, and ye shall find; knock, and it shall be
8 opened unto you: for every one that asketh receiveth; and he that seeketh findeth; and to him that knocketh it
9 shall be opened. Or what man is there of you, whom if his son ask bread, will
10 he give him a stone? Or if he ask a fish,
11 will he give him a serpent? If ye then, being evil, know how to give good gifts unto your children, how much more shall your Father which is in heaven give good things to them that ask him?
12 Therefore all things whatsoever ye would that men should do to you, do ye even so to them: for this is the law and the prophets.
13 *Enter ye in at the strait gate: for wide is the gate, and broad is the way, that leadeth to destruction, and many there*
14 *be which go in thereat: because strait is the gate, and narrow is the way, which leadeth unto life, and few there be that find it.*
15 *Beware of false prophets, which come to you in sheep's clothing, but inwardly*
16 *they are ravening wolves. Ye shall know them by their fruits. Do men gather*
17 *grapes of thorns, or figs of thistles? Even so every good tree bringeth forth good fruit; but a corrupt tree bringeth forth*
18 *evil fruit. A good tree cannot bring forth evil fruit, neither can a corrupt tree bring*
19 *forth good fruit. Every tree that bringeth not forth good fruit is hewn down, and*
20 *cast into the fire. Wherefore by their*
21 *fruits ye shall know them. Not every one that saith unto me, Lord, Lord, shall enter into the kingdom of heaven; but he that doeth the will of my Father which*
22 *is in heaven. Many will say to me in that day, Lord, Lord, have we not prophesied in thy name? and in thy name have cast out devils? and in thy name done many*
23 *wonderful works? And then will I profess unto them, I never knew you: depart*
24 *from me, ye that work iniquity. Therefore whosoever heareth these sayings of mine, and doeth them, I will liken him unto a wise man, which built his house*
25 *upon a rock: and the rain descended, and the floods came, and the winds blew, and beat upon that house; and it fell not: for*
26 *it was founded upon a rock. And every one that heareth these sayings of mine, and doeth them not, shall be likened unto a foolish man, which built his house upon*
27 *the sand: and the rain descended and*

Luke xii. 34.
Luke xi. 34.
Luke xvi. 13.
Luke xii. 22-31.
Luke vi. 37, 38, 41, 42.
Luke xi. 9-13.
Luke vi. 31.

S. MATTHEW.

the floods came, and the winds blew, and beat upon that house; and it fell: and great was the fall of it.

Cf. Mark i. 22.

23 [And it came to pass, when Jesus had ended these sayings,] the people were
29 astonished at his doctrine: for he taught them as one having authority, and not as the scribes.

8 *When he was come down from the mountain, great multitudes followed*
2 *him.* And, behold, there came a leper and worshipped him, saying, Lord, if thou wilt, thou canst make me clean.
3 And Jesus put forth his hand, and touched him, saying, I will; be thou clean. And immediately his leprosy was
4 cleansed. And Jesus saith unto him, See thou tell no man; but go thy way, shew thyself to the priest, and offer the gift that Moses commanded, for a testimony unto them.

5 *And when Jesus was entered into Capernaum, there came unto him a cen-*
6 *turion, beseeching him, and saying, Lord,*
7 *my servant lieth at home sick of the palsy, grievously tormented.* [And Jesus saith
8 unto him, I will come and heal him. The centurion answered and said], Lord, I am not worthy that thou shouldest come under my roof: but speak the word only,

Luke vii. 6-9.

9 and my servant shall be healed. For I am a man under authority, having soldiers under me: and I say to this man, Go, and he goeth; and to another, Come, and he cometh; and to my servant,
10 Do this, and he doeth it. When Jesus heard it, he marvelled, and said to them that followed, Verily I say unto you, I have not found so great faith, no, not in
11 Israel. *And I say unto you, That many shall come from the east and west, and shall sit down with Abraham, and Isaac, and Jacob, in the kingdom of heaven.*
12 *But the children of the kingdom shall be cast out into outer darkness: there shall*
13 *be weeping and gnashing of teeth.* And Jesus said unto the centurion, Go thy way; and as thou hast believed, so be it done unto thee. And his servant was healed in the self-same hour.

14 And when Jesus was come into Peter's house, he saw his wife's mother laid, and
15 sick of a fever. And he touched her hand, and the fever left her: and she
16 arose, and ministered unto them. When the even was come, they brought unto him many that were possessed with devils: and he cast out the spirits with his word, and healed all that were sick:
17 that it might be fulfilled which was spoken by Esaias the prophet, saying, Himself took our infirmities, and bare our sicknesses.

18 Now when Jesus saw great multitudes about him, he gave commandment to
19 depart unto the other side. And a certain scribe came, and said unto him, Master, I will follow thee whitherso-
20 ever thou goest. And Jesus saith unto him, The foxes have holes, and the birds of the air have nests; but the Son of man hath not where to lay his head.
21 And another of his disciples said unto him, Lord, suffer me first to go and
22 bury my father. But Jesus said unto him, Follow me; and let the dead bury their dead.

Luke ix. 57-60.

23 And when he was entered into a ship,
24 [his disciples followed him.] And, behold, there arose a great tempest in the sea, insomuch that the ship was covered with the waves: but he was asleep.
25 And his disciples came to him, and awoke him, saying, Lord, save us: we
26 perish. And he saith unto them, Why are ye fearful, O ye of little faith? Then he arose, and rebuked the winds and the
27 sea; and there was a great calm. But the men marvelled, saying, What manner of man is this, that even the winds and the sea obey him!

Cf. Mark i. 36.

28 And when he was come to the other side into the country of the Gergesenes, there met him two possessed with devils, coming out of the tombs, exceeding fierce, so that no man might pass by that
29 way. And, behold, they cried out, saying, What have we to do with thee, Jesus, thou Son of God? art thou come hither
30 to torment us before the time? And there was a good way off from them an
31 herd of many swine feeding. So the devils besought him, saying, If thou cast us out, suffer us to go away into the herd
32 of swine. And he said unto them, Go. And when they were come out, they went into the herd of swine: and, behold, the whole herd of swine ran violently down a steep place into the sea, and
33 perished in the waters. And they that kept them fled, and went their ways into the city, and told every thing, and what was befallen to the possessed of the
34 devils. And, behold, the whole city came out to meet Jesus: and when they saw him, they besought him that he would depart out of their coasts.

9 And he entered into a ship, and passed
2 over, and came into his own city. And, behold, they brought to him a man sick of the palsy, lying on a bed: and Jesus, seeing their faith, said unto the sick of the palsy; Son, be of good cheer; thy
3 sins be forgiven thee. And, behold, certain of the scribes said within them-
4 selves, This man blasphemeth. And Jesus knowing their thoughts, said, Wherefore think ye evil in your hearts?
5 For whether is easier, to say, Thy sins be forgiven thee; or to say, Arise, and
6 walk? But that ye may know that the Son of man hath power on earth to for-

give sins, (then saith he to the sick of the palsy,) Arise, take up thy bed, and go
7 unto thine house. And he arose, and
8 departed to his house. But when the multitudes saw it, they marvelled, and glorified God, which had given such power unto men.
9 And as Jesus passed forth from thence, he saw a man, named Matthew, sitting at the receipt of custom: and he saith unto him, Follow me. And he arose, and followed him.
10 And it came to pass, as Jesus sat at meat in the house, behold, many publicans and sinners came and sat down with
11 him and his disciples. And when the Pharisees saw it, they said unto his disciples, Why eateth your Master with
12 publicans and sinners? But when Jesus heard that, he said unto them, They that be whole need not a physician, but they
13 that are sick. But go ye and learn what that meaneth, I will have mercy, and not sacrifice: for I am not come to call the righteous, but sinners to repentance.
14 Then came to him the disciples of John, saying, Why do we and the Pharisees fast oft, but thy disciples fast not?
15 And Jesus said unto them, Can the children of the bride-chamber mourn, as long as the bridegroom is with them? but the days will come, when the bridegroom shall be taken from them, and
16 then shall they fast. No man putteth a piece of new cloth unto an old garment, for that which is put in to fill it up taketh from the garment, and the rent is made
17 worse. Neither do men put new wine into old bottles: else the bottles break, and the wine runneth out, and the bottles perish: but they put new wine into new bottles, and both are preserved.
18 While he spake these things unto them, behold, there came a certain ruler, and worshipped him, saying, My daughter is even now dead: but come and lay thy
19 hand upon her, and she shall live. And Jesus arose, and followed him, and so
20 did his disciples. And, behold, a woman, which was diseased with an issue of blood twelve years, came behind him, and touched the hem of his garment:
21 for she said within herself, If I may but touch his garment, I shall be whole.
22 But Jesus turned him about, and when he saw her, he said, Daughter, be of good comfort; thy faith hath made thee whole. And the woman was made
23 whole from that hour. And when Jesus came into the ruler's house, and saw the minstrels and the people making a noise,
24 he said unto them, Give place; for the maid is not dead, but sleepeth. And
25 they laughed him to scorn. But when the people were put forth, he went in, and took her by the hand, and the maid
26 arose. And the fame hereof went abroad into all that land.
27 And when Jesus departed thence, two blind men followed him, crying, and saying, Thou son of David, have mercy
28 on us. And when he was come into the house, the blind men came to him: and Jesus saith unto them, Believe ye that I am able to do this? They said unto him,
29 Yea, Lord. Then touched he their eyes, saying, According to your faith be it unto
30 you. And their eyes were opened; and Jesus straitly charged them, saying, See
31 that no man know it. But they, when they were departed, spread abroad his fame in all that country.
32 As they went out, behold, they brought to him a dumb man possessed with a
33 devil. And when the devil was cast out, the dumb spake: and the multitudes marvelled, saying, It was never so seen
34 in Israel. But the Pharisees said, He casteth out devils through the prince of the devils.
35 And Jesus went about all the cities and villages, teaching in their synagogues, and preaching the gospel of the kingdom, and healing every sickness and every
36 disease among the people. But when he saw the multitudes, he was moved with compassion on them, because they fainted, and were scattered abroad, as
37 sheep having no shepherd. Then saith Luke he unto his disciples, The harvest truly x. 2. is plenteous, but the labourers are few;
38 pray ye therefore the Lord of the harvest, that he will send forth labourers
10 into his harvest. And when he had called unto him his twelve disciples, he gave them power against unclean spirits, to cast them out, and to heal all manner of sickness and all manner of disease.
2 Now the names of the twelve apostles are these; The first, Simon, who is called Peter, and Andrew his brother; James the son of Zebedee, and John his brother;
3 Philip, and Bartholomew; Thomas, and Matthew the publican; James the son of Alpheus, and Lebbeus, whose surname
4 was Thaddeus; Simon the Cannanite, and Judas Iscariot, who also betrayed
5 him. These twelve Jesus sent forth, and commanded them, saying,
Go not into the way of the Gentiles, and into any city of the Samaritans enter
6 ye not: but go rather to the lost sheep
7 of the house of Israel. And as ye go, preach, saying, The kingdom of heaven
8 is at hand. Heal the sick, cleanse the lepers, raise the dead, cast out devils: freely ye have received, freely give.
9 Provide neither gold, nor silver, nor
10 brass in your purses, nor scrip for your journey, neither two coats, neither shoes, nor yet staves: for the workman is

11 worthy of his meat. And into whatsoever city or town ye shall enter, enquire who in it is worthy; and there abide till
12 ye go thence. And when ye come into
13 an house, salute it. And if the house be worthy, let your peace come upon it: but if it be not worthy, let your peace
14 return to you. And whosoever shall not receive you, nor hear your words, when ye depart out of that house or city, shake
15 off the dust of your feet. Verily I say unto you, It shall be more tolerable for the land of Sodom and Gomorrha in the day of judgment, than for that city.
16 Behold, I send you forth as sheep in the midst of wolves: be ye therefore wise
17 as serpents, and harmless as doves. But beware of men: for they will deliver you up to the councils, and they will scourge
18 you in their synagogues; and ye shall be brought before governors and kings for my sake, for a testimony against
19 them and the Gentiles. But when they deliver you up, take no thought how or what ye shall speak: for it shall be given you in that same hour what ye shall
20 speak. For it is not ye that speak, but the Spirit of your Father which speaketh
21 in you. And the brother shall deliver up the brother to death, and the father the child: and the children shall rise up against their parents, and cause them to
22 be put to death. And ye shall be hated of all men for my name's sake: but he that endureth to the end shall be saved.
23 But when they persecute you in this city, flee ye into another: for verily I say unto you, Ye shall not have gone over the cities of Israel, till the Son of man be come.
24 The disciple is not above his master,
25 nor the servant above his lord. It is enough for the disciple that he be as his master, and the servant as his lord. If they have called the master of the house Beelzebub, how much more shall they call
26 them of his household? Fear them not therefore: for there is nothing covered, that shall not be revealed; and hid, that
27 shall not be known. What I tell you in darkness, that speak ye in light: and what ye hear in the ear, that preach ye
28 upon the house-tops. And fear not them which kill the body, but are not able to kill the soul: but rather fear him which is able to destroy both soul and body in hell.
29 Are not two sparrows sold for a farthing? and one of them shall not fall on the
30 ground without your Father. But the very hairs of your head are all numbered.
31 Fear ye not therefore, ye are of more
32 value than many sparrows. Whosoever therefore shall confess me before men, him will I confess also before my Father
33 which is in heaven. But whosoever shall deny me before men, him will I also deny before my Father which is in heaven.

34 Think not that I am come to send peace on earth: I came not to send
35 peace, but a sword. For I am come to set a man at variance against his father, and the daughter against her mother, and the daughter-in-law against her
36 mother-in-law. And a man's foes shall
37 be they of his own household. He that loveth father or mother more than me is not worthy of me: and he that loveth son or daughter more than me is not
38 worthy of me. And he that taketh not his cross, and followeth after me, is not
39 worthy of me. He that findeth his life shall lose it: and he that loseth his life for my sake shall find it.
40 He that receiveth you receiveth me, and he that receiveth me receiveth him
41 that sent me. He that receiveth a prophet in the name of a prophet shall receive a prophet's reward; and he that receiveth a righteous man in the name of a righteous man shall receive a righteous
42 man's reward. And whosoever shall give to drink unto one of these little ones a cup of cold water only in the name of a disciple, verily I say unto you, he shall in no wise lose his reward.

11 And it came to pass, when Jesus had made an end of commanding his twelve disciples, he departed thence to teach and to preach in their cities.
2 Now when John had heard in the prison the works of Christ, he sent two
3 of his disciples, and said unto him, Art thou he that should come, or do we look
4 for another? Jesus answered and said unto them, Go and shew John again those things which ye do hear and see:
5 the blind receive their sight, and the lame walk, the lepers are cleansed, and the deaf hear, the dead are raised up, and the poor have the gospel preached
6 to them. And blessed is he, whosoever
7 shall not be offended in me. And as they departed, Jesus began to say unto the multitudes concerning John, What went ye out into the wilderness to see?
8 A reed shaken with the wind? But what went ye out for to see? A man clothed in soft raiment? behold, they that wear
9 soft clothing are in kings' houses. But what went ye out for to see? A prophet? yea, I say unto you, and more than a
10 prophet. For this is he, of whom it is written,
Behold, I send my messenger before thy face,
Which shall prepare thy way before thee.
11 Verily I say unto you, Among them that are born of women there hath not risen a greater than John the Baptist: notwithstanding he that is least in the kingdom of heaven is greater than
12 he. And from the days of John the

Baptist until now the kingdom of heaven suffereth violence, and the violent take
13 it by force. For all the prophets and
14 the law prophesied until John. And if ye will receive it, this is Elias, which was
15 for to come. He that hath ears to hear,
16 let him hear. But whereunto shall I liken this generation? It is like unto children sitting in the markets, and call-
17 ing unto their fellows, and saying, We have piped unto you, and ye have not danced; we have mourned unto you, and
18 ye have not lamented. For John came neither eating nor drinking, and they
19 say, He hath a devil. The Son of man came eating and drinking, and they say, Behold a man gluttonous, and a winebibber, a friend of publicans and sinners. But wisdom is justified of her children.
20 Then began he to upbraid the cities wherein most of his mighty works were
21 done, because they repented not: Woe unto thee, Chorazin! woe unto thee, Bethsaida! for if the mighty works, which were done in you, had been done in Tyre and Sidon, they would have repented long ago in sackcloth and ashes.
22 But I say unto you, It shall be more tolerable for Tyre and Sidon at the day
23 of judgment, than for you. And thou, Capernaum, which art exalted unto heaven, shalt be brought down to hell: for if the mighty works, which have been done in thee, had been done in Sodom, it would have remained until this day.
24 But I say unto you, That it shall be more tolerable for the land of Sodom in the day of judgment, than for thee.
25 At that time Jesus answered and said, I thank thee, O Father, Lord of heaven and earth, because thou hast hid these things from the wise and prudent, and
26 hast revealed them unto babes. Even so, Father: for so it seemed good in thy
27 sight. All things are delivered unto me of my Father: and no man knoweth the Son, but the Father; neither knoweth any man the Father, save the Son, and he to whomsoever the Son will reveal
28 him. Come unto me, all ye that labour and are heavy laden, and I will give you
29 rest. Take my yoke upon you, and learn of me; for I am meek and lowly in heart: and ye shall find rest unto your
30 souls. For my yoke is easy, and my burden is light.

12 At that time Jesus went on the sabbath-day through the corn; and his disciples were an hungered, and began to pluck
2 the ears of corn, and to eat. But when the Pharisees saw it, they said unto him, Behold, thy disciples do that which is not
3 lawful to do upon the sabbath-day. But he said unto them, Have ye not read what David did, when he was an hungered, and
4 they that were with him; how he entered into the house of God, and did eat the shew-bread, which was not lawful for him to eat, neither for them which were with
5 him, but only for the priests? Or have ye not read in the law, how that on the sabbath-days the priests in the temple profane the sabbath, and are blameless?
6 But I say unto you, That in this place is
7 one greater than the temple. But if ye had known what this meaneth, I will have mercy, and not sacrifice, ye would
8 not have condemned the guiltless. For the Son of man is Lord even of the sabbath-day.
9 And when he was departed thence, he
10 went into their synagogue: and, behold, there was a man which had his hand withered. And they asked him, saying, Is it lawful to heal on the sabbath-days?
11 that they might accuse him. And he said unto them, What man shall there be among you, that shall have one sheep, and if it fall into a pit on the sabbath-day, will he not lay hold on it, and lift it out?
12 How much then is a man better than a sheep? Wherefore it is lawful to do well
13 on the sabbath-days. Then saith he to the man, Stretch forth thine hand. And he stretched it forth; and it was restored
14 whole, like as the other. Then the Pharisees went out, and held a council against
15 him, how they might destroy him. But when Jesus knew it, he withdrew himself from thence: and great multitudes fol-
16 lowed him, and he healed them all; and
17 charged them that they should not make him known: that it might be fulfilled which was spoken by Esaias the prophet, saying,
18 Behold my servant, whom I have chosen;
My beloved, in whom my soul is well pleased:
I will put my Spirit upon him,
And he shall shew judgment to the Gentiles.
19 He shall not strive, nor cry;
Neither shall any man hear his voice in the streets.
20 A bruised reed shall he not break,
And smoking flax shall he not quench,
Till he send forth judgment unto victory.
21 And in his name shall the Gentiles trust.
22 Then was brought unto him one possessed with a devil, blind, and dumb: and he healed him, insomuch that the blind and dumb both spake and saw.
23 And all the people were amazed, and said,
24 Is not this the son of David? But when the Pharisees heard it, they said, This fellow doth not cast out devils, but by
25 Beelzebub the prince of the devils. And Jesus knew their thoughts, and said unto them, Every kingdom divided against itself is brought to desolation; and every city

S. MATTHEW.

or house divided against itself shall not
26 stand: and if Satan cast out Satan, he
is divided against himself; how shall
27 then his kingdom stand? And if I by *Luke xi. 9, 20*
Beelzebub cast out devils, by whom do
your children cast them out? therefore
28 they shall be your judges. But if I cast
out devils by the Spirit of God, then the
29 kingdom of God is come unto you. Or
else how can one enter into a strong man's
house, and spoil his goods, except he first
bind the strong man? and then he will
30 spoil his house. He that is not with me *Luke xi. 23.*
is against me; and he that gathereth not
31 with me scattereth abroad. Wherefore
I say unto you, All manner of sin and
blasphemy shall be forgiven unto men:
but the blasphemy against the Holy Ghost
32 shall not be forgiven unto men. And *Luke xii. 10.*
whosoever speaketh a word against the
Son of man, it shall be forgiven him:
but whosoever speaketh against the
Holy Ghost, it shall not be forgiven
him, neither in this world, neither in the
33 world to come. Either make the tree *Luke vi. 43-45.*
good, and his fruit good; or else make
the tree corrupt, and his fruit corrupt:
34 for the tree is known by his fruit. O
generation of vipers, how can ye, being
evil, speak good things? for out of the
abundance of the heart the mouth
35 speaketh. A good man out of the good
treasure of the heart bringeth forth good
things: and an evil man out of the evil
36 treasure bringeth forth evil things. But
I say unto you, That every idle word
that men shall speak, they shall give
account thereof in the day of judgment.
37 For by thy words thou shalt be justified, and by thy words thou shalt be
condemned.
38 Then certain of the scribes and of the
Pharisees answered, saying, Master, we
39 would see a sign from thee. But he answered and said unto them, An evil and
adulterous generation seeketh after a
sign; and there shall no sign be given to
it, but the sign of the prophet Jonas:
40 for as Jonas was three days and three
nights in the whale's belly; so shall the
Son of man be three days and three
41 nights in the heart of the earth. The *Luke xi. 29-32.*
men of Nineveh shall rise in judg-
ment with this generation, and shall
condemn it: because they repented at
the preaching of Jonas; and, behold, a
42 greater than Jonas is here. The queen
of the south shall rise up in the judgment
with this generation, and shall condemn
it: for she came from the uttermost
parts of the earth to hear the wisdom of
Solomon; and, behold, a greater than
43 Solomon is here. When the unclean
spirit is gone out of a man, he walketh
through dry places, seeking rest, and
44 findeth none. Then he saith, I will
return into my house from whence I
came out; and when he is come, he
findeth it empty, swept, and garnished.
45 Then goeth he, and taketh with himself
seven other spirits more wicked than
himself, and they enter in and dwell
there: and the last state of that man is
worse than the first. Even so shall it be
also unto this wicked generation.
46 While he yet talked to the people, behold,
his mother and his brethren stood without,
47 desiring to speak with him. Then one
said unto him, Behold, thy mother and
thy brethren stand without, desiring to
48 speak with thee. But he answered and
said unto him that told him, Who is my
49 mother? and who are my brethren? And
he stretched forth his hand toward his
disciples, and said, Behold my mother
50 and my brethren! For whosoever shall
do the will of my Father which is in
heaven, the same is my brother, and
sister, and mother.

13 The same day went Jesus out of
the house, and sat by the sea-side.
2 And great multitudes were gathered
together unto him, so that he went into
a ship, and sat; and the whole multitude
3 stood on the shore. And he spake many
things unto them in parables, saying,
4 Behold, a sower went forth to sow; and
when he sowed, some seeds fell by the
way-side, and the fowls came and de-
5 voured them up: some fell upon stony
places, where they had not much earth:
and forthwith they sprung up, because
6 they had no deepness of earth: and
when the sun was up, they were scorched;
and because they had no root, they
7 withered away. And some fell among
thorns; and the thorns sprung up, and
8 choked them: but other fell into good
ground, and brought forth fruit, some
an hundred-fold, some sixty-fold, some
9 thirty-fold. Who hath ears to hear, let
him hear.
10 And the disciples came, and said unto
him, Why speakest thou unto them in
11 parables? He answered and said unto
them, Because it is given unto you to
know the mysteries of the kingdom of
heaven, but to them it is not given.
12 [For whosoever hath, to him shall be Cf. Mark iv. 25.
given, and he shall have more abund-
ance: but whosoever hath not, from him
shall be taken away even that he hath.]
13 Therefore speak I to them in parables:
because they seeing see not; and hearing
they hear not, neither do they under-
14 stand. And in them is fulfilled the prophecy of Esaias, which saith,
By hearing ye shall hear, and shall not
understand;
And seeing ye shall see, and shall not
perceive:
15 For this people's heart is waxed gross,

And their ears are dull of hearing,
And their eyes they have closed;
Lest at any time they should see with their eyes,
And hear with their ears,
And should understand with their heart,
And should be converted,
And I should heal them.

Luke x. 23, 24.
16 But blessed are your eyes, for they see: and your ears, for they hear. 17 For verily I say unto you, That many prophets and righteous men have desired to see those things which ye see, and have not seen them; and to hear those things which ye hear, and have not heard them.

18 Hear ye therefore the parable of the sower. 19 When any one heareth the word of the kingdom, and understandeth it not, then cometh the wicked one, and catcheth away that which was sown in his heart. This is he which received 20 seed by the way-side. But he that received the seed into stony places, the same is he that heareth the word, and 21 anon with joy receiveth it; yet hath he not root in himself, but dureth for a while: for when tribulation or persecution ariseth because of the word, by and 22 by he is offended. He also that received seed among the thorns is he that heareth the word; and the care of this world, and the deceitfulness of riches, choke the 23 word, and he becometh unfruitful. But he that received seed into the good ground, is he that heareth the word, and understandeth it; which also beareth fruit, and bringeth forth, some an hundred-fold, some sixty, some thirty.

24 *Another parable put he forth unto them, saying, The kingdom of heaven is likened unto a man which sowed good* 25 *seed in his field: but while men slept, his enemy came and sowed tares among the* 26 *wheat, and went his way. But when the blade was sprung up, and brought forth* 27 *fruit, then appeared the tares also. So the servants of the householder came and said unto him, Sir, didst not thou sow good seed in thy field? from whence then* 28 *hath it tares? He said unto them, An enemy hath done this. The servants said unto him, Wilt thou then that we go and* 29 *gather them up? But he said, Nay; lest while ye gather up the tares, ye root up* 30 *also the wheat with them. Let both grow together until the harvest: and in the time of harvest I will say to the reapers, Gather ye together first the tares, and bind them in bundles to burn them: but gather the wheat into my barn.*

31 Another parable put he forth unto them, saying, The kingdom of heaven is
Luke xiii. 18-21.
like to a grain of mustard seed, which a 32 man took, and sowed in his field. Which indeed is the least of all seeds: but when it is grown, it is the greatest among herbs, and becometh a tree, so that the birds of the air come and lodge in the branches thereof.

33 Another parable spake he unto them; The kingdom of heaven is like unto leaven, which a woman took, and hid in three measures of meal, till the whole was leavened.

34 All these things spake Jesus unto the multitude in parables; and without a 35 parable spake he not unto them: that it might be fulfilled which was spoken by the prophet, saying,
I will open my mouth in parables;
I will utter things which have been kept secret from the foundation of the world.

36 *Then Jesus sent the multitude away, and went into the house: and his disciples came unto him, saying, Declare unto us the parable of the tares of the* 37 *field. He answered and said unto them, He that soweth the good seed is the Son of* 38 *man; the field is the world; the good seed are the children of the kingdom; but the tares are the children of the wicked one;* 39 *the enemy that sowed them is the devil; the harvest is the end of the world; and* 40 *the reapers are the angels. As therefore the tares are gathered and burned in the fire; so shall it be in the end of this* 41 *world. The Son of man shall send forth his angels, and they shall gather out of his kingdom all things that offend, and* 42 *them which do iniquity; and shall cast them into a furnace of fire: there shall* 43 *be wailing and gnashing of teeth. Then shall the righteous shine forth as the sun in the kingdom of their Father. Who hath ears to hear, let him hear.*

44 *Again, the kingdom of heaven is like unto treasure hid in a field; the which when a man hath found, he hideth, and for joy thereof goeth and selleth all that he hath, and buyeth that field.*

45 *Again, the kingdom of heaven is like unto a merchant-man, seeking goodly* 46 *pearls: who, when he had found one pearl of great price, went and sold all that he had, and bought it.*

47 *Again, the kingdom of heaven is like unto a net, that was cast into the sea,* 48 *and gathered of every kind: which, when it was full, they drew to shore, and sat down, and gathered the good into vessels,* 49 *but cast the bad away. So shall it be at the end of the world: the angels shall come forth, and sever the wicked from* 50 *among the just, and shall cast them into the furnace of fire: there shall be wailing and gnashing of teeth.*

51 *Jesus saith unto them, Have ye understood all these things? They say unto* 52 *him, Yea, Lord. Then said he unto them, Therefore every scribe which is*

K

instructed unto the kingdom of heaven is like unto a man that is an householder, which bringeth forth out of his treasure things new and old.

53 [And it came to pass, that when Jesus had finished these parables,] he departed
54 thence. And when he was come into his own country, he taught them in their synagogue, insomuch that they were astonished, and said, Whence hath this man this wisdom, and these mighty
55 works? Is not this the carpenter's son? is not his mother called Mary? and his brethren, James, and Joses, and Simon,
56 and Judas? And his sisters, are they not all with us? Whence then hath this
57 man all these things? And they were offended in him. But Jesus said unto them, A prophet is not without honour, save in his own country, and in his own
58 house. And he did not many mighty works there because of their unbelief.

14 At that time Herod the tetrarch heard
2 of the fame of Jesus, and said unto his servants, This is John the Baptist; he is risen from the dead; and therefore mighty works do shew forth themselves in
3 him. For Herod had laid hold on John, and bound him, and put him in prison for Herodias' sake, his brother Philip's
4 wife. For John said unto him, It is not
5 lawful for thee to have her. And when he would have put him to death, he feared the multitude, because they counted him
6 as a prophet. But when Herod's birthday was kept, the daughter of Herodias danced before them, and pleased Herod.
7 Whereupon he promised with an oath to
8 give her whatsoever she would ask. And she, being before instructed of her mother, said, Give me here John Baptist's head
9 in a charger. And the king was sorry: nevertheless for the oath's sake, and them which sat with him at meat, he com-
10 manded it to be given her. And he sent,
11 and beheaded John in the prison. And his head was brought in a charger, and given to the damsel: and she brought it
12 to her mother. And his disciples came, and took up the body, and buried it, and went and told Jesus.
13 When Jesus heard of it, he departed thence by ship into a desert place apart: and when the people had heard thereof, they followed him on foot out of the cities.
14 And Jesus went forth, and saw a great multitude, and was moved with compassion toward them, and he healed their
15 sick. And when it was evening, his disciples came to him, saying, This is a desert place, and the time is now past; send the multitude away, that they may go into the villages, and buy themselves
16 victuals. But Jesus said unto them, They need not depart; give ye them to eat.
17 And they say unto him, We have here
18 but five loaves, and two fishes. He said,
19 Bring them hither to me. And he commanded the multitude to sit down on the grass, and took the five loaves, and the two fishes, and looking up to heaven, he blessed, and brake, and gave the loaves to his disciples, and the disciples to the
20 multitude. And they did all eat, and were filled: and they took up of the fragments that remained twelve baskets full.
21 And they that had eaten were about five thousand men, beside women and children.
22 And straightway Jesus constrained his disciples to get into a ship, and to go before him unto the other side, while he
23 sent the multitudes away. And when he had sent the multitudes away, he went up into a mountain apart to pray: and when the evening was come, he was there
24 alone. But the ship was now in the midst of the sea, tossed with waves: for the wind
25 was contrary. And in the fourth watch of the night Jesus went unto them, walk-
26 ing on the sea. And when the disciples saw him walking on the sea, they were troubled, saying, It is a spirit; and they
27 cried out for fear. But straightway Jesus spake unto them, saying, Be of
28 good cheer; it is I; be not afraid. And Peter answered him and said, Lord, if it be thou, bid me come unto thee on the
29 water. And he said, Come. And when Peter was come down out of the ship, he
30 walked on the water, to go to Jesus. But when he saw the wind boisterous, he was afraid; and beginning to sink, he cried,
31 saying, Lord, save me. And immediately Jesus stretched forth his hand, and caught him, and said unto him, O thou of little faith, wherefore didst thou doubt?
32 And when they were come into the ship,
33 the wind ceased. Then they that were in the ship came and worshipped him, saying, Of a truth thou art the Son of God.
34 And when they were gone over, they
35 came into the land of Gennesaret. And when the men of that place had knowledge of him, they sent out into all that country round about, and brought unto
36 him all that were diseased: and besought him that they might only touch the hem of his garment: and as many as touched were made perfectly whole.

15 Then came to Jesus scribes and Pharisees, which were of Jerusalem, saying,
2 Why do thy disciples transgress the tradition of the elders? for they wash not their hands when they eat bread.
3 But he answered and said unto them, Why do ye also transgress the commandment of God by your tradition?
4 For God commanded, saying, Honour thy father and mother: and, He that curseth father or mother, let him die
5 the death. But ye say, Whosoever

shall say to his father or his mother, It is a gift, by whatsoever thou mightest
6 be profited by me; and honour not his father or his mother, he shall be free. Thus have ye made the commandment of God of none effect by your tradition.
7 *Ye hypocrites, well did Esaias prophesy of you, saying,*
8 *This people draweth nigh unto me with their mouth, and honoureth me with their lips;*
But their heart is far from me.
9 *But in vain they do worship me, Teaching for doctrines the commandments of men.*
10 And he called the multitude, and said
11 unto them, Hear, and understand: Not that which goeth into the mouth defileth a man; but that which cometh out of the
12 mouth, this defileth a man. Then came his disciples, and said unto him, Knowest thou that the Pharisees were offended,
13 after they heard this saying? But he answered and said, Every plant, which my heavenly Father hath not planted,
14 shall be rooted up. Let them alone: they be blind leaders of the blind. And if the blind lead the blind, both
15 shall fall into the ditch. Then answered Peter, and said unto him, De-
16 clare unto us this parable. And Jesus said, Are ye also yet without under-
17 standing? Do not ye yet understand, that whatsoever entereth in at the mouth goeth into the belly, and is cast out into
18 the draught? But those things which proceed out of the mouth come forth from
19 the heart; and they defile the man. For out of the heart proceed evil thoughts, murders, adulteries, fornications, thefts,
20 false witness, blasphemies: these are the things which defile a man: but to eat with unwashen hands defileth not a man.
21 Then Jesus went thence, and departed into the coasts of Tyre [and Sidon].
22 And, behold, a woman of Canaan came out of the same coasts, and cried unto him, saying, Have mercy on me, O Lord, thou son of David; my daughter is
23 grievously vexed with a devil. But he answered her not a word. And his disciples came and besought him, saying, Send her away; for she crieth after us.
24 But he answered and said, I am not sent but unto the lost sheep of the house of
25 Israel. Then came she and worshipped
26 him, saying, Lord, help me. But he answered and said, It is not meet to take the children's bread, and to cast it to
27 dogs. And she said, Truth, Lord: yet the dogs eat of the crumbs which fall
28 from their master's table. Then Jesus answered and said unto her, O woman, great is thy faith: be it unto thee even as thou wilt. And her daughter was made whole from that very hour.

29 And Jesus departed from thence, and came nigh unto the sea of Galilee; and went up into a mountain, and sat down
30 there. And great multitudes came unto him, having with them those that were lame, blind, dumb, maimed, and many others, and cast them down at Jesus'
31 feet; and he healed them: insomuch that the multitude wondered, when they saw the dumb to speak, the maimed to be whole, the lame to walk, and the blind to see: and they glorified the God of Israel.
32 Then Jesus called his disciples unto him, and said, I have compassion on the multitude, because they continue with me now three days, and have nothing to eat: and I will not send them away fast-
33 ing, lest they faint in the way. And his disciples say unto him, Whence should we have so much bread in the wilderness,
34 as to fill so great a multitude? And Jesus saith unto them, How many loaves have ye? And they said, Seven, and a
35 few little fishes. And he commanded the multitude to sit down on the ground.
36 And he took the seven loaves and the fishes, and gave thanks, and brake them, and gave to his disciples, and the dis-
37 ciples to the multitude. And they did all eat, and were filled: and they took up of the broken meat that was left
38 seven baskets full. And they that did eat were four thousand men, besides
39 women and children. And he sent away the multitude, and took ship, and came into the coasts of Magdala.

16 The Pharisees also with the Sadducees came, and tempting, desired him that he would shew them a sign
2 from heaven. He answered and said unto them, When it is evening, ye say, It will be fair weather: for the sky is
3 red. And in the morning, It will be foul weather to-day: for the sky is red and lowring. O ye hypocrites, ye can discern the face of the sky; but can ye not dis-
4 cern the signs of the times? A wicked and adulterous generation seeketh after a sign; and there shall no sign be given unto it, but the sign of the prophet Jonas. And he left them, and departed.
5 And when his disciples were come to the other side, they had forgotten to
6 take bread. Then Jesus said unto them, Take heed and beware of the leaven of the
7 Pharisees and of the Sadducees. And they reasoned among themselves, saying, It is because we have taken no bread.
8 Which when Jesus perceived, he said unto them, O ye of little faith, why reason ye among yourselves, because ye
9 have brought no bread? Do ye not yet understand, neither remember [the five loaves of the five thousand, and how many
10 baskets ye took up? Neither] the seven

S. MATTHEW.

loaves of the four thousand, and how
11 many baskets ye took up? How is it
that ye do not understand that I spake
it not to you concerning bread, that ye
should beware of the leaven of the Phari-
12 sees and of the Sadducees? Then understood they how that he bade them not
beware of the leaven of bread, but of the
doctrine of the Pharisees and of the
Sadducees.
13 When Jesus came into the coasts of
Cesarea Philippi, he asked his disciples,
saying, Whom do men say that I the Son
14 of man am? And they said, Some say
that thou art John the Baptist: some,
Elias; and others, Jeremias, or one of
15 the prophets. He saith unto them, But
16 whom say ye that I am? And Simon
Peter answered and said, Thou art the
17 Christ, the Son of the living God. And
Jesus answered and said unto him,
Blessed art thou, Simon Bar-jona: for
flesh and blood hath not revealed it unto
thee, but my Father which is in heaven.
18 And I say also unto thee, That thou art
Peter, and upon this rock I will build my
church; and the gates of hell shall not
19 prevail against it. And I will give unto
thee the keys of the kingdom of heaven:
and whatsoever thou shalt bind on earth
shall be bound in heaven: and whatsoever thou shalt loose on earth shall be
20 loosed in heaven. Then charged he his
disciples that they should tell no man that
he was Jesus the Christ.
21 From that time forth began Jesus to
shew unto his disciples, how that he must
go unto Jerusalem, and suffer many
things of the elders and chief priests and
scribes, and be killed, and be raised again
22 the third day. Then Peter took him, and
began to rebuke him, saying, Be it far
from thee, Lord: this shall not be unto
23 thee. But he turned, and said unto
Peter, Get thee behind me, Satan: thou
art an offence unto me: for thou savourest not the things that be of God, but
24 those that be of men. Then said Jesus
unto his disciples, If any man will come
after me, let him deny himself, and take
25 up his cross, and follow me. For whosoever will save his life shall lose it: and
whosoever will lose his life for my sake
26 shall find it. For what is a man profited, if he shall gain the whole world, and
lose his own soul? or what shall a man
27 give in exchange for his soul? For the
Son of man shall come in the glory of his
Father with his angels; and then he shall
reward every man according to his works.
28 Verily I say unto you, There be some
standing here, which shall not taste of
death, till they see the Son of man coming
in his kingdom.
17 And after six days Jesus taketh Peter,
James, and John his brother, and bringeth

them up into an high mountain apart,
2 and was transfigured before them: and
his face did shine as the sun, and his
3 raiment was white as the light. And,
behold, there appeared unto them Moses
4 and Elias talking with him. Then answered Peter, and said unto Jesus, Lord,
it is good for us to be here: if thou wilt,
let us make here three tabernacles; one
for thee, and one for Moses, and one for
5 Elias. While he yet spake, behold, a
bright cloud overshadowed them: and behold a voice out of the cloud, which said,
This is my beloved Son, in whom I am
6 well pleased; hear ye him. And when
the disciples heard it, they fell on their
7 face, and were sore afraid. And Jesus
came and touched them, and said, Arise,
8 and be not afraid. And when they had
lifted up their eyes, they saw no man,
save Jesus only.
9 And as they came down from the
mountain, Jesus charged them, saying,
Tell the vision to no man, until the Son
of man be risen again from the dead.
10 And his disciples asked him, saying, Why
then say the scribes that Elias must first
11 come? And Jesus answered and said
unto them, Elias truly shall first come,
12 and restore all things. But I say unto
you, That Elias is come already, and
they knew him not, but have done unto
him whatsoever they listed. Likewise
shall also the Son of man suffer of them.
13 Then the disciples understood that he
spake unto them of John the Baptist.
14 And when they were come to the multitude, there came to him a certain man,
15 kneeling down to him, and saying, Lord,
have mercy on my son; for he is lunatick,
and sore vexed: for oft-times he falleth
16 into the fire, and oft into the water. And
I brought him to thy disciples, and they
17 could not cure him. Then Jesus answered
and said, O faithless and perverse generation, how long shall I be with you? how
long shall I suffer you? bring him hither
18 to me. And Jesus rebuked the devil; and
he departed out of him: and the child
19 was cured from that very hour. Then
came the disciples to Jesus apart, and
said, Why could not we cast him out?
20 And Jesus said unto them, Because of
your unbelief: for verily I say unto you,
If ye have faith as a grain of mustard-
seed, ye shall say unto this mountain,
Remove hence to yonder place; and it
shall remove; and nothing shall be im-
21 possible unto you. Howbeit this kind
goeth not out but by prayer and fasting.
22 And while they abode in Galilee, Jesus
said unto them, The Son of man shall be
23 betrayed into the hands of men: and
they shall kill him, and the third day he
shall be raised again. And they were
exceeding sorry.

S. MATTHEW.

24 And when they were come to Capernaum, they that received tribute-money came to Peter, and said, Doth not your
25 master pay tribute? He saith, Yes. And when he was come into the house, Jesus prevented him, saying, What thinkest thou, Simon? of whom do the kings of the earth take custom or tribute? of their
26 own children, or of strangers? Peter saith unto him, Of strangers. Jesus saith unto him, Then are the children free.
27 Notwithstanding, lest we should offend them, go thou to the sea, and cast an hook, and take up the fish that first cometh up; and when thou hast opened his mouth, thou shalt find a piece of money: that take, and give unto them for me and thee.

18 At the same time came the disciples unto Jesus, saying, Who is the greatest
2 in the kingdom of heaven? And Jesus called a little child unto him, and set
3 him in the midst of them, and said, Verily I say unto you, Except ye be converted, and become as little children, ye shall not enter into the kingdom
4 of heaven. Whosoever therefore shall humble himself as this little child, the same is greatest in the kingdom of
5 heaven. And whoso shall receive one such little child in my name receiveth me.
6 But whoso shall offend one of these little ones which believe in me, it were better for him that a millstone were hanged about his neck, and that he were drowned
7 in the depth of the sea. Woe unto the world because of offences! for it must needs be that offences come; but woe to that man by whom the offence cometh!
8 Wherefore if thy hand or thy foot offend thee, cut them off, and cast them from thee: it is better for thee to enter into life halt or maimed, rather than having two hands or two feet to be cast
9 into everlasting fire. And if thine eye offend thee, pluck it out, and cast it from thee: it is better for thee to enter into life with one eye, rather than having
10 two eyes to be cast into hell fire. Take heed that ye despise not one of these little ones; for I say unto you, That in heaven their angels do always behold the face of my Father which is in heaven.
11 For the Son of man is come to save
12 that which was lost. How think ye? if a man have an hundred sheep, and one of them be gone astray, doth he not leave the ninety and nine, and goeth into the mountains, and seeketh that
13 which is gone astray? And if so be that he find it, verily I say unto you, he rejoiceth more of that sheep, than of the ninety and nine which went not astray.
14 Even so it is not the will of your Father which is in heaven, that one of these little ones should perish.

15 Moreover if thy brother shall trespass against thee, go and tell him his fault between thee and him alone: if he shall hear thee, thou hast gained thy brother.
16 But if he will not hear thee, then take with thee one or two more, that in the mouth of two or three witnesses every
17 word may be established. And if he shall neglect to hear them, tell it unto the church: but if he neglect to hear the church, let him be unto thee as an
18 heathen man and a publican. Verily I say unto you, Whatsoever ye shall bind on earth shall be bound in heaven: and whatsoever ye shall loose on earth shall
19 be loosed in heaven. Again I say unto you, That if two of you shall agree on earth as touching any thing that they shall ask, it shall be done for them of
20 my Father which is in heaven. For where two or three are gathered together in my name, there am I in the midst of them.

21 Then came Peter to him, and said, Lord, how oft shall my brother sin against me, and I forgive him? till seven times?
22 Jesus saith unto him, I say not unto thee, Until seven times: but, Until
23 seventy times seven. Therefore is the kingdom of heaven likened unto a certain king, which would take account of his
24 servants. And when he had begun to reckon, one was brought unto him, which
25 owed him ten thousand talents. But forasmuch as he had not to pay, his lord commanded him to be sold, and his wife, and children, and all that he had, and
26 payment to be made. The servant therefore fell down, and worshipped him, saying, Lord, have patience with me, and I
27 will pay thee all. Then the lord of that servant was moved with compassion, and loosed him, and forgave him the debt.
28 But the same servant went out, and found one of his fellowservants, which owed him an hundred pence: and he laid hands on him, and took him by the throat, saying, Pay me that thou owest.
29 And his fellowservant fell down at his feet, and besought him, saying, Have patience with me, and I will pay thee all.
30 And he would not: but went and cast him into prison, till he should pay the
31 debt. So when his fellowservants saw what was done, they were very sorry, and came and told unto their lord all that
32 was done. Then his lord, after that he had called him, said unto him, O thou wicked servant, I forgave thee all that
33 debt, because thou desiredst me: shouldest not thou also have had compassion on thy fellowservant, even as I had pity on
34 thee? And his lord was wroth, and delivered him to the tormentors, till he should pay all that was due unto him.
35 So likewise shall my heavenly Father do

also unto you, if ye from your hearts forgive not every one his brother their trespasses.

19 And it came to pass, that when Jesus had finished these sayings, he departed from Galilee, and came into the coasts of
2 Judæa beyond Jordan; and great multitudes followed him; and he healed them there.
3 The Pharisees also came unto him, tempting him, and saying unto him, Is it lawful for a man to put away his wife
4 for every cause? And he answered and said unto them, Have ye not read, that he which made them at the beginning
5 made them male and female, and said, For this cause shall a man leave father and mother, and shall cleave to his wife: and they twain shall be one flesh?
6 Wherefore they are no more twain, but one flesh. What therefore God hath joined together, let not man put asunder.
7 They say unto him, Why did Moses then command to give a writing of divorce-
8 ment, and to put her away? He saith unto them, Moses because of the hardness of your hearts suffered you to put away your wives: but from the begin-
9 ning it was not so. And I say unto you, Whosoever shall put away his wife, except it be for fornication, and shall marry another, committeth adultery; and whoso marrieth her which is put
10 away doth commit adultery. His disciples say unto him, If the case of the man be so with his wife, it is not good
11 to marry. But he said unto them, All men cannot receive this saying, save
12 they to whom it is given. For there are some eunuchs, which were so born from their mother's womb: and there are some eunuchs, which were made eunuchs of men: and there be eunuchs, which have made themselves eunuchs for the kingdom of heaven's sake. He that is able to receive it, let him receive it.
13 Then were there brought unto him little children, that he should put his hands on them, and pray: and the disciples re-
14 buked them. But Jesus said, Suffer little children, and forbid them not, to come unto me: for of such is the kingdom of
15 heaven. And he laid his hands on them, and departed thence.
16 And, behold, one came and said unto him, Good Master, what good thing shall
17 I do, that I may have eternal life? And he said unto him, Why callest thou me good? there is none good but one, that is God: but if thou wilt enter into life, keep
18 the commandments. He saith unto him, Which? Jesus said, Thou shalt do no murder, Thou shalt not commit adultery, Thou shalt not steal, Thou shalt not bear
19 false witness, Honour thy father and thy mother: and, Thou shalt love thy neigh-
20 bour as thyself. The young man saith unto him, All these things have I kept from my youth up: what lack I yet?
21 Jesus said unto him, If thou wilt be perfect, go and sell that thou hast, and give to the poor, and thou shalt have treasure in heaven: and come and follow me.
22 But when the young man heard that saying, he went away sorrowful: for he had great possessions.
23 Then said Jesus unto his disciples, Verily I say unto you, That a rich man shall hardly enter into the kingdom of
24 heaven. And again I say unto you, It is easier for a camel to go through the eye of a needle, than for a rich man to enter
25 into the kingdom of God. When his disciples heard it, they were exceedingly amazed, saying, Who then can be saved?
26 But Jesus beheld them, and said unto them, With men this is impossible; but
27 with God all things are possible. Then answered Peter and said unto him, Behold, we have forsaken all, and followed
28 thee; what shall we have therefore? And Jesus said unto them, Verily I say unto you, That ye which have followed me, in the regeneration when the Son of man shall sit in the throne of his glory, ye also shall sit upon twelve thrones, judging the
29 twelve tribes of Israel. And every one that hath forsaken houses, or brethren, or sisters, or father, or mother, or wife, or children, or lands, for my name's sake, shall receive an hundred-fold, and shall
30 inherit everlasting life. But many that are first shall be last: and the last shall be first.

20 For the kingdom of heaven is like unto a man that is an householder, which went out early in the morning to hire labourers
2 into his vineyard. And when he had agreed with the labourers for a penny a
3 day, he sent them into his vineyard. And he went out about the third hour, and saw others standing idle in the market-
4 place, and said unto them; Go ye also into the vineyard, and whatsoever is right I will give you. And they went their
5 way. Again he went out about the sixth
6 and ninth hour, and did likewise. And about the eleventh hour he went out, and found others standing idle, and saith unto them, Why stand ye here all the day
7 idle? They say unto him, Because no man hath hired us. He saith unto them, Go ye also into the vineyard; and what-
8 soever is right, that shall ye receive. So when even was come, the lord of the vineyard saith unto his steward, Call the labourers, and give them their hire, be-
9 ginning from the last unto the first. And when they came that were hired about the eleventh hour, they received every man a
10 penny. But when the first came, they supposed that they should have received

more; and they likewise received every
11 man a penny. And when they had received it, they murmured against the
12 good man of the house, saying, These last have wrought but one hour, and thou hast made them equal unto us, which have borne the burden and heat of the day.
13 But he answered one of them, and said, Friend, I do thee no wrong: didst not
14 thou agree with me for a penny? Take that thine is, and go thy way: I will give
15 unto this last, even as unto thee. Is it not lawful for me to do what I will with mine own? Is thine eye evil, because I am
16 good? So the last shall be first, and the first last: for many be called, but few chosen.
17 And Jesus going up to Jerusalem took the twelve disciples apart in the way,
18 and said unto them, Behold, we go up to Jerusalem; and the Son of man shall be betrayed unto the chief priests and unto the scribes, and they shall condemn
19 him to death, and shall deliver him to the Gentiles to mock, and to scourge, and to crucify him: and the third day he shall rise again.
20 Then came to him the mother of Zebedee's children with her sons, worshipping him, and desiring a certain thing of
21 him. And he said unto her, What wilt thou? She saith unto him, Grant that these my two sons may sit, the one on thy right hand, and the other on the left, in
22 thy kingdom. But Jesus answered and said, Ye know not what ye ask. Are ye able to drink of the cup that I shall drink of, and to be baptized with the baptism that I am baptized with. They say unto
23 him, We are able. And he saith unto them, Ye shall drink indeed of my cup, and be baptized with the baptism that I am baptized with: but to sit on my right hand, and on my left, is not mine to give, but it shall be given to them for whom it is prepared of my Father.
24 And when the ten heard it, they were moved with indignation against the two
25 brethren. But Jesus called them unto him, and said, Ye know that the princes of the Gentiles exercise dominion over them, and they that are great exercise
26 authority upon them. But it shall not be so among you: but whosoever will be great among you, let him be your
27 minister; and whosoever will be chief among you, let him be your servant:
28 even as the Son of man came not to be ministered unto, but to minister, and to give his life a ransom for many.
29 And as they departed from Jericho, a
30 great multitude followed him. And, behold, two blind men sitting by the wayside, when they heard that Jesus passed by, cried out, saying, Have mercy on us,
31 O Lord, thou son of David. And the multitude rebuked them, because they should hold their peace: but they cried the more, saying, Have mercy on us, O
32 Lord, thou son of David. And Jesus stood still, and called them, and said, What will ye that I shall do unto you?
33 They say unto him, Lord, that our eyes
34 may be opened. So Jesus had compassion on them, and touched their eyes: and immediately their eyes received sight, and they followed him.

21 And when they drew nigh unto Jerusalem, and were come to Bethphage, unto the mount of Olives, then sent
2 Jesus two disciples, saying unto them, Go into the village over against you, and straightway ye shall find an ass tied, and a colt with her: loose them, and
3 bring them unto me. And if any man say ought unto you, ye shall say, The Lord hath need of them; and straight-
4 way he will send them. All this was done, that it might be fulfilled which was spoken by the prophet, saying,
5 Tell ye the daughter of Zion,
   Behold, thy King cometh unto thee,
   Meek, and sitting upon an ass,
   And a colt the foal of an ass.
6 And the disciples went, and did as Jesus
7 commanded them, and brought the ass, and the colt, and put on them their
8 clothes, and they set him thereon. And a very great multitude spread their garments in the way; others cut down branches from the trees, and strawed
9 them in the way. And the multitudes that went before, and that followed, cried, saying, Hosanna to the son of David: Blessed is he that cometh in the name of the Lord; Hosanna in the
10 highest. And when he was come into Jerusalem, all the city was moved, say-
11 ing, Who is this? And the multitude said, This is Jesus the prophet of Nazareth of Galilee.
12 And Jesus went into the temple of God, and cast out all them that sold and bought in the temple, and overthrew the tables of the money-changers, and the
13 seats of them that sold doves, and said unto them, It is written, My house shall be called the house of prayer; but ye
14 have made it a den of thieves. And the blind and the lame came to him in the
15 temple; and he healed them. And when the chief priests and scribes saw the wonderful things that he did, and the children crying in the temple, and saying, Hosanna to the son of David; they were sore dis-
16 pleased, and said unto him, Hearest thou what these say? And Jesus saith unto them, Yea; have ye never read, Out of the mouth of babes and sucklings thou
17 hast perfected praise? And he left them, and went out of the city into Bethany; and he lodged there.

18 Now in the morning as he returned in-
19 to the city, he hungered. And when he saw a fig tree in the way, he came to it, and found nothing thereon, but leaves only, and said unto it, Let no fruit grow on thee henceforward for ever. And presently the fig tree withered away.
20 And when the disciples saw it, they marvelled, saying, How soon is the fig
21 tree withered away! Jesus answered and said unto them, Verily I say unto you, If ye have faith, and doubt not, ye shall not only do this which is done to the fig tree, but also if ye shall say unto this mountain, Be thou removed, and be thou cast into the sea; it shall be done.
22 And all things, whatsoever ye shall ask in prayer, believing, ye shall receive.
23 And when he was come into the temple, the chief priests and the elders of the people came unto him as he was teaching, and said, By what authority doest thou these things? and who gave
24 thee this authority? And Jesus answered and said unto them, I also will ask you one thing, which if ye tell me, I in likewise will tell you by what authority I do these
25 things. The baptism of John, whence was it? from heaven, or of men? And they reasoned with themselves, saying, If we shall say, From heaven; he will say unto us, Why did ye not then believe
26 him? But if we shall say, Of men; we fear the people; for all hold John
27 as a prophet. And they answered Jesus, and said, We cannot tell. And he said unto them, Neither tell I you by what
28 authority I do these things. *But what think ye? A certain man had two sons; and he came to the first, and said, Son,*
29 *go work to-day in my vineyard. He answered and said, I will not: but after-*
30 *ward he repented, and went. And he came to the second, and said likewise. And he answered and said, I go, sir:*
31 *and went not. Whether of them twain did the will of his father? They say unto him, The first. Jesus saith unto them, Verily I say unto you, That the publicans and the harlots go into the king-*
32 *dom of God before you. For John came unto you in the way of righteousness, and ye believed him not: but the publicans and the harlots believed him: and ye, when ye had seen it, repented not afterward, that ye might believe him.*
33 *Hear another parable: There was a certain householder, which planted a vineyard, and hedged it round about, and digged a winepress in it, and built a tower, and let it out to husbandmen, and*
34 *went into a far country: and when the time of the fruit drew near, he sent his servants to the husbandmen, that they*
35 *might receive the fruits of it. And the husbandmen took his servants, and beat*
one, *and killed another, and stoned an-*
30 *other. Again, he sent other servants more than the first: and they did unto*
37 *them likewise. But last of all he sent unto them his son, saying, They will rever-*
38 *ence my son. But when the husbandmen saw the son, they said among themselves, This is the heir; come, let us kill him, and let us seize on his inheritance.*
39 *And they caught him, and cast him out*
40 *of the vineyard, and slew him. When the lord therefore of the vineyard cometh, what will he do unto those husbandmen?*
41 *They say unto him, He will miserably destroy those wicked men, and will let out his vineyard unto other husbandmen, which shall render him the fruits in their*
42 *seasons. Jesus saith unto them, Did ye never read in the scriptures,*
The stone which the builders rejected,
The same is become the head of the corner:
This is the Lord's doing,
And it is marvellous in our eyes?
43 *Therefore say I unto you, The kingdom of God shall be taken from you, and given to a nation bringing forth the fruits there-*
44 *of. And whosoever shall fall on this stone shall be broken: but on whomsoever it shall fall, it will grind him to powder.*
45 *And when the chief priests and Pharisees had heard his parables, they per-*
46 *ceived that he spake of them. But when they sought to lay hands on him, they feared the multitude, because they took him for a prophet.*

22 *And Jesus answered and spake unto*
2 *them again by parables, and said, The kingdom of heaven is like unto a certain king, which made a marriage for his son,*
3 *and sent forth his servants to call them that were bidden to the wedding: and*
4 *they would not come. Again, he sent forth other servants, saying, Tell them which are bidden, Behold, I have prepared my dinner: my oxen and my fatlings are killed, and all things are ready: come*
5 *unto the marriage. But they made light of it, and went their ways, one to his*
6 *farm, another to his merchandise: and the remnant took his servants, and entreated them spitefully, and slew them.*
7 *But when the king heard thereof, he was wroth: and he sent forth his armies, and destroyed those murderers, and burned*
8 *up their city. Then saith he to his servants, The wedding is ready, but they*
9 *which were bidden were not worthy. Go ye therefore into the highways, and as many as ye shall find, bid to the marriage.*
10 *So those servants went out into the highways, and gathered together all as many as they found, both bad and good: and the wedding was furnished with guests.*
11 *And when the king came in to see the guests, he saw there a man which had*

S. MATTHEW.

12 *not on a wedding garment: and he saith unto him, Friend, how camest thou in hither not having a wedding garment?*
13 *And he was speechless. Then said the king to the servants, Bind him hand and foot, and take him away, and cast him into outer darkness; there shall be weep-*
14 *ing and gnashing of teeth. For many are called, but few are chosen.*
15 Then went the Pharisees, and took counsel how they might entangle him in
16 his talk. And they sent out unto him their disciples with the Herodians, saying, Master, we know that thou art true, and teachest the way of God in truth, neither carest thou for any man: for thou regardest not the person of men.
17 Tell us therefore, What thinkest thou? Is it lawful to give tribute unto Cæsar,
18 or not? But Jesus perceived their wickedness, and said, Why tempt ye me,
19 ye hypocrites? Shew me the tribute money. And they brought unto him a
20 penny. And he saith unto them, Whose
21 is this image and superscription? They say unto him, Cæsar's. Then saith he unto them, Render therefore unto Cæsar the things which are Cæsar's; and unto
22 God the things that are God's. When they had heard these words, they marvelled, and left him, and went their way.
23 The same day came to him the Sadducees, which say that there is no resur-
24 rection, and asked him, saying, Master, Moses said, If a man die, having no children, his brother shall marry his wife,
25 and raise up seed unto his brother. Now there were with us seven brethren: and the first, when he had married a wife, deceased, and, having no issue, left his
26 wife unto his brother: likewise the second also, and the third, unto the
27 seventh. And last of all the woman
28 died also. Therefore in the resurrection whose wife shall she be of the seven?
29 for they all had her. Jesus answered and said unto them, Ye do err, not knowing the scriptures, nor the power
30 of God. For in the resurrection they neither marry, nor are given in marriage, but are as the angels of God in heaven.
31 But as touching the resurrection of the dead, have ye not read that which was
32 spoken unto you by God, saying, I am the God of Abraham, and the God of Isaac, and the God of Jacob? God is not the God of the dead, but of the living.
33 And when the multitude heard this, they were astonished at his doctrine.
34 But when the Pharisees had heard that he had put the Sadducees to silence,
35 they were gathered together. Then one of them, which was a lawyer, asked him a question, tempting him, and saying,
36 Master, which is the great command-
37 ment in the law? Jesus said unto him, Thou shalt love the Lord thy God with all thy heart, and with all thy soul, and
38 with all thy mind. This is the first and
39 great commandment. And the second is like unto it, Thou shalt love thy neigh-
40 bour as thyself. On these two commandments hang all the law and the prophets.
41 While the Pharisees were gathered to-
42 gether, Jesus asked them, saying, What think ye of Christ? whose son is he? They say unto him, The son of David.
43 He saith unto them, How then doth David in spirit call him Lord, saying,
44 The Lord said unto my Lord, Sit thou on my right hand, Till I make thine enemies thy footstool?
45 If David then call him Lord, how is he
46 his son? And no man was able to answer him a word, neither durst any man from that day forth ask him any more questions.

23 Then spake Jesus to the multitude,
2 and to his disciples, saying, The scribes and the Pharisees sit in Moses' seat:
3 all therefore whatsoever they bid you observe, that observe and do; but do not ye after their works: for they say, and
4 do not. For they bind heavy burdens and grievous to be borne, and lay them on men's shoulders: but they themselves will not move them with one of their
5 fingers. But all their works they do for to be seen of men: they make broad their phylacteries, and enlarge the bor-
6 ders of their garments, and love the uppermost rooms at feasts, and the chief
7 seats in the synagogues, and greetings in the markets, and to be called of men,
8 Rabbi, Rabbi. But be not ye called Rabbi: for one is your Master, even
9 Christ; and all ye are brethren. And call no man your father upon the earth: for one is your Father, which is in heaven.
10 Neither be ye called masters: for one is
11 your master, even Christ. But he that Luke is greatest among you shall be your xxii. 26
12 servant. And whosoever shall exalt himself shall be abased; and he that shall 11; xvii humble himself shall be exalted. 14
13 But woe unto you, scribes and Pharisees, hypocrites! for ye shut up the kingdom of heaven against men: for ye neither go in yourselves, neither suffer ye them that are entering to go in.
14 Woe unto you, scribes and Pharisees, hypocrites! for ye devour widows' houses, and for a pretence make long prayer: therefore ye shall receive the greater damnation.
15 Woe unto you, scribes and Pharisees, hypocrites! for ye compass sea and land to make one proselyte, and when he is made, ye make him twofold more the child of hell than yourselves.

L

16 Woe unto you, ye blind guides, which say, Whosoever shall swear by the temple, it is nothing; but whosoever shall swear by the gold of the temple, he is a debtor! 17 Ye fools and blind: for whether is greater, the gold, or the temple that 18 sanctifieth the gold? And, Whosoever shall swear by the altar, it is nothing; but whosoever sweareth by the gift that 19 is upon it, he is guilty. Ye fools and blind: for whether is greater, the gift, or the altar that sanctifieth the gift? 20 Whoso therefore shall swear by the altar, sweareth by it, and by all things thereon. 21 And whoso shall swear by the temple, sweareth by it, and by him that dwelleth 22 therein. And he that shall swear by heaven, sweareth by the throne of God, and by him that sitteth thereon. 23 Woe unto you, scribes and Pharisees, hypocrites! for ye pay tithe of mint and anise and cummin, and have omitted the weightier matters of the law, judgment, mercy, and faith: these ought ye to have done, and not to leave the other undone. 24 Ye blind guides, which strain at a gnat, and swallow a camel. 25 Woe unto you, scribes and Pharisees, hypocrites! for ye make clean the outside of the cup and of the platter, but within they are full of extortion and 26 excess. Thou blind Pharisee, cleanse first that which is within the cup and platter, that the outside of them may be clean also. 27 Woe unto you, scribes and Pharisees, hypocrites! for ye are like unto whited sepulchres, which indeed appear beautiful outward, but are within full of dead men's bones, and of all uncleanness. 28 Even so ye also outwardly appear righteous unto men, but within ye are full of hypocrisy and iniquity. 29 Woe unto you, scribes and Pharisees, hypocrites! because ye build the tombs of the prophets, and garnish the sepul- 30 chres of the righteous, and say, If we had been in the days of our fathers, we would not have been partakers with them 31 in the blood of the prophets. Wherefore ye be witnesses unto yourselves, that ye are the children of them that killed the 32 prophets. Fill ye up then the measure 33 of your fathers. Ye serpents, ye generation of vipers, how can ye escape the 34 damnation of hell? Wherefore, behold, I send unto you prophets, and wise men, and scribes: and some of them ye shall kill and crucify; and some of them shall ye scourge in your synagogues, and persecute them from city to city: 35 that upon you may come all the righteous blood shed upon the earth, from the blood of righteous Abel unto the blood of Zacharias son of Barachias, whom ye slew between the temple and the altar.

Luke xi. 49.

36 Verily I say unto you All these things shall come upon this generation. 37 O Jerusalem, Jerusalem, thou that killest the prophets, and stonest them which are sent unto thee, how often would I have gathered thy children together, even as a hen gathereth her chickens under her wings, and ye would 38 not! Behold, your house is left unto 39 you desolate. For I say unto you, Ye shall not see me henceforth, till ye shall say, Blessed is he that cometh in the name of the Lord.

Luke xiii. 34, 35.

24 And Jesus went out, and departed from the temple: and his disciples came to him for to shew him the buildings of 2 the temple. And Jesus said unto them, See ye not all these things? verily I say unto you, There shall not be left here one stone upon another, that shall not be thrown down. 3 And as he sat upon the mount of Olives, the disciples came unto him privately, saying, Tell us, when shall these things be? and what shall be the sign of thy coming, and of the end of the world? 4 And Jesus answered and said unto them, 5 Take heed that no man deceive you. For many shall come in my name, saying, I 6 am Christ; and shall deceive many. And ye shall hear of wars and rumours of wars: see that ye be not troubled: for all these things must come to pass, but the 7 end is not yet. [For nation shall rise against nation, and kingdom against kingdom: and there shall be famines, and pestilences, and earthquakes, in 8 divers places. All these are the begin 9 ning of sorrows.] Then shall they deliver you up to be afflicted, and shall kill you: and ye shall be hated of all nations for 10 my name's sake. And then shall many be offended, and shall betray one another, 11 and shall hate one another. And many false prophets shall rise, and shall de- 12 ceive many. And because iniquity shall abound, the love of many shall wax cold. 13 But he that shall endure unto the end, the 14 same shall be saved. And this gospel of the kingdom shall be preached in all the world for a witness unto all nations; and then shall the end come. 15 When ye therefore shall see the abomination of desolation, spoken of by Daniel the prophet, stand in the holy place, (whoso 16 readeth, let him understand:) then let them which be in Judæa flee into the 17 mountains: let him which is on the housetop not come down to take any thing 18 out of his house: neither let him which is in the field return back to take his clothes. 19 And woe unto them that are with child, and to them that give suck in those days! 20 But pray ye that your flight be not in the 21 winter, neither on the sabbath day: for then shall be great tribulation, such as

Luke xvii. 20.

Belongs after ver. 25

was not since the beginning of the world
22 to this time, no, nor ever shall be. And except those days should be shortened, there should no flesh be saved: but for the elect's sake those days shall be shortened.
23 Then if any man shall say unto you, Lo, here is Christ, or there; believe it not.
24 For there shall arise false Christs, and false prophets, and shall shew great signs and wonders; insomuch that, if it were possible, they shall deceive the very elect. Behold, I have told you before.
26 Wherefore if they shall say unto you, Behold, he is in the desert; go not forth: behold, he is in the secret chambers;
27 believe it not. For as the lightning cometh out of the east, and shineth even unto the west; so shall also the coming
28 of the Son of man be. For wheresoever the carcase is, there will the eagles be gathered together.
29 Immediately after the tribulation of those days shall the sun be darkened, and the moon shall not give her light, and the stars shall fall from heaven, and the powers of the heavens shall be shaken:
30 and then shall appear the sign of the Son of man in heaven: and then shall all the tribes of the earth mourn, and they shall see the Son of man coming in the clouds of heaven with power and great glory.
31 And he shall send his angels with a great sound of a trumpet, and they shall gather together his elect from the four winds, from one end of heaven to the other.
32 Now learn a parable of the fig tree; When his branch is yet tender, and putteth forth leaves, ye know that summer
33 is nigh: so likewise ye, when ye shall see all these things, know that it is near,
34 even at the doors. Verily I say unto you, This generation shall not pass, till
35 all these things be fulfilled. Heaven and earth shall pass away, but my
36 words shall not pass away. But of that day and hour knoweth no man, no, not the angels of heaven, but my Father
37 only. But as the days of Noe were, so shall also the coming of the Son of
38 man be. For as in the days that were before the flood they were eating and drinking, marrying and giving in marriage, until the day that Noe entered into
39 the ark, and knew not until the flood came, and took them all away; so shall also the coming of the Son of man be.
40 Then shall two be in the field; the one
41 shall be taken, and the other left. Two women shall be grinding at the mill; the one shall be taken, and the other left.
42 Watch therefore: for ye know not what
43 hour your Lord doth come. But know this, that if the goodman of the house had known in what watch the thief would come, he would have watched,
44 and would not have suffered his house to be broken up. Therefore be ye also ready: for in such an hour as ye think
45 not the Son of man cometh. Who then is a faithful and wise servant, whom his lord hath made ruler over his household, to give them meat in due season?
46 Blessed is that servant, whom his lord when he cometh shall find so doing.
47 Verily I say unto you, That he shall
48 make him ruler over all his goods. But and if that evil servant shall say in his heart, My lord delayeth his coming;
49 and shall begin to smite his fellowservants, and to eat and drink with the
50 drunken; the lord of that servant shall come in a day when he looketh not for him, and in an hour that he is not aware
51 of, and shall cut him asunder, and appoint him his portion with the hypocrites: there shall be weeping and gnashing of teeth

25 Then shall the kingdom of heaven be likened unto ten virgins, which took their lamps, and went forth to meet
2 the bridegroom. And five of them were
3 wise, and five were foolish. They that were foolish took their lamps, and took no oil
4 with them: but the wise took oil in their
5 vessels with their lamps. While the bridegroom tarried, they all slumbered
6 and slept. And at midnight there was a cry made, Behold, the bridegroom cometh;
7 go ye out to meet him. Then all those virgins arose, and trimmed their lamps.
8 And the foolish said unto the wise, Give us of your oil; for our lamps are gone
9 out. But the wise answered, saying, Not so; lest there be not enough for us and you: but go ye rather to them that sell,
10 and buy for yourselves. And while they went to buy, the bridegroom came; and they that were ready went in with him to the marriage: and the door was shut.
11 Afterward came also the other virgins,
12 saying, Lord, Lord, open to us. But he answered and said, Verily I say unto
13 you, I know you not. Watch therefore, for ye know neither the day nor the hour wherein the Son of man cometh.
14 For the kingdom of heaven is as a man travelling into a far country, who called his own servants, and delivered unto
15 them his goods. And unto one he gave five talents, to another two, and to another one; to every man according to his several ability; and straightway took his journey.
16 Then he that had received the five talents went and traded with the same, and
17 made them other five talents. And likewise he that had received two, he also
18 gained other two. But he that had received one went and digged in the earth,
19 and hid his lord's money. After a long time the lord of those servants cometh,
20 and reckoneth with them. And so he

that had received *five talents* came and brought other *five talents*, saying, Lord, thou deliveredst unto me *five talents*: behold, I have gained beside them *five*
21 *talents* more. His lord said unto him, Well done, thou good and faithful servant: thou hast been faithful over a few things, I will make thee ruler over many things: enter thou into the joy of thy
22 lord. He also that had received *two talents* came and said, Lord, thou deliveredst unto me *two talents*: behold, I have gained *two* other *talents* beside
23 them. His lord said unto him, Well done, good and faithful servant: thou hast been faithful over a few things, I will make thee ruler over many things: enter thou into the joy of thy lord.
24 Then he which had received the *one talent* came and said, Lord, I knew thee that thou art an hard man, reaping where thou hast not sown, and gathering where
25 thou hast not strawed: and I was afraid, and went and hid thy talent in the earth:
26 lo, there thou hast that is thine. His lord answered and said unto him, Thou wicked and slothful servant, thou knewest that I reap where I sowed not, and gather
27 where I have not strawed: thou oughtest therefore to have put my money to the exchangers, and then at my coming I should have received mine own with
28 usury. Take therefore the talent from him, and give it unto him which hath ten
29 talents. For unto every one that hath shall be given, and he shall have abundance; but from him that hath not shall be taken away even that which he hath.
30 And cast ye the unprofitable servant into outer darkness: there shall be weeping and gnashing of teeth.
31 When the Son of man shall come in his glory, and all the holy angels with him, then shall he sit upon the throne of his
32 glory: and before him shall be gathered all nations: and he shall separate them one from another, as a shepherd divideth
33 his sheep from the goats: and he shall set the sheep on his right hand, but the goats
34 on the left. Then shall the King say unto them on his right hand, Come, ye blessed of my Father, inherit the kingdom prepared for you from the foundation of
35 the world: for I was an hungred, and ye gave me meat: I was thirsty, and ye gave me drink: I was a stranger, and ye
36 took me in: naked, and ye clothed me: I was sick, and ye visited me: I was in
37 prison, and ye came unto me. Then shall the righteous answer him, saying, Lord, when saw we thee an hungred, and fed thee? or thirsty, and gave thee drink?
38 When saw we thee a stranger, and took
39 thee in? or naked, and clothed thee? or when saw we thee sick, or in prison, and
40 came unto thee? And the King shall answer and say unto them, Verily I say unto you, Inasmuch as ye have done it unto one of the least of these my brethren,
41 ye have done it unto me. Then shall he say also unto them on the left hand, Depart from me, ye cursed, into everlasting fire, prepared for the devil and
42 his angels: for I was an hungred, and ye gave me no meat: I was thirsty, and
43 ye gave me no drink: I was a stranger, and ye took me not in: naked, and ye clothed me not: sick, and in prison, and
44 ye visited me not. Then shall they also answer him, saying, Lord, when saw we thee an hungred, or athirst, or a stranger, or naked, or sick, or in prison, and did
45 not minister unto thee? Then shall he answer them, saying, Verily I say unto you, Inasmuch as ye did it not to one of the least of these, ye did it not to me.
46 And these shall go away into everlasting punishment: but the righteous into life eternal.

26 And it came to pass, when Jesus had finished all these sayings, he said unto
2 his disciples, Ye know that after two days is the feast of the passover, and the Son
3 of man is betrayed to be crucified. Then assembled together the chief priests, and the scribes, and the elders of the people, unto the palace of the high priest, who
4 was called Caiaphas, and consulted that they might take Jesus by subtilty, and
5 kill him. But they said, Not on the feast day, lest there be an uproar among the people.
6 Now when Jesus was in Bethany, in
7 the house of Simon the leper, there came unto him a woman having an alabaster box of very precious ointment, and poured
8 it on his head, as he sat at meat. But when his disciples saw it, they had indignation, saying, To what purpose is this
9 waste? For this ointment might have been sold for much, and given to the poor.
10 When Jesus understood it, he said unto them, Why trouble ye the woman? for she
11 hath wrought a good work upon me. For ye have the poor always with you; but
12 me ye have not always. For in that she hath poured this ointment on my body,
13 she did it for my burial. Verily I say unto you, Wheresoever this gospel shall be preached in the whole world, there shall also this, that this woman hath done, be told for a memorial of her.
14 Then one of the twelve, called Judas Iscariot, went unto the chief priests,
15 and said unto them, What will ye give me, and I will deliver him unto you? And they covenanted with him for thirty
16 pieces of silver. And from that time he sought opportunity to betray him.
17 Now the first day of the feast of unleavened bread the disciples came to Jesus, saying unto him, Where wilt thou

31 the head. And after that they had mocked him, they took the robe off from him, and put his own raiment on him, and led him away to crucify him.

32 And as they came out, they found a man of Cyrene, Simon by name: him
33 they compelled to bear his cross. And when they were come unto a place called Golgotha, that is to say, a place of a
34 skull, they gave him vinegar to drink mingled with gall: and when he had tasted thereof, he would not drink.
35 And they crucified him, and parted his garments, casting lots: that it might be fulfilled which was spoken by the prophet, They parted my garments among them, and upon my vesture did they cast lots.
36 And sitting down they watched him
37 there; and set up over his head his accusation written, This is Jesus the
38 King of the Jews. Then were there two thieves crucified with him, one on the right hand, and another on the left.
39 And they that passed by reviled him,
40 wagging their heads, and saying, Thou that destroyest the temple, and buildest it in three days, save thyself. If thou be the Son of God, come down from the
41 cross. Likewise also the chief priests mocking him, with the scribes and
42 elders, said, He saved others; himself he cannot save. If he be the King of Israel, let him now come down from
43 the cross, and we will believe him. He trusted in God; let him deliver him now, if he will have him: for he said, I
44 am the Son of God. The thieves also, which were crucified with him, cast the same in his teeth.
45 Now from the sixth hour there was darkness over all the land unto the ninth
46 hour. And about the ninth hour Jesus cried with a loud voice, saying, Eli, Eli, lama sabachthani? that is to say, My God, my God, why hast thou forsaken
47 me? Some of them that stood there, when they heard that, said, This man
48 calleth for Elias. And straightway one of them ran, and took a spunge, and filled it with vinegar, and put it on a
49 reed, and gave him to drink.ᵃ The rest said, Let be, let us see whether Elias
50 will come to save him. Jesus, when he had cried again with a loud voice, yielded
51 up the ghost. And, behold, the veil of the temple was rent in twain from the top to the bottom; and the earth did quake,
52 and the rocks rent; and the graves were opened; and many bodies of the saints
53 which slept arose, and came out of the graves after his resurrection, and went into the holy city, and appeared unto
54 many. Now when the centurion, and they that were with him, watching Jesus, saw the earthquake, and those things

ᵃ Some authorities add "And another took a spear and pierced his side, and there came out water and blood."

that we prepare for thee to eat the pass-
18 over? And he said, Go into the city to such a man, and say unto him, The Master saith, My time is at hand; I will keep the passover at thy house with my
19 disciples. And the disciples did as Jesus had appointed them; and they made
20 ready the passover. Now when the even was come, he sat down with the twelve.
21 And as they did eat, he said, Verily I say unto you, that one of you shall be-
22 tray me. And they were exceeding sorrowful, and began every one of them to
23 say unto him, Lord, is it I? And he answered and said, He that dippeth his hand with me in the dish, the same shall
24 betray me. The Son of man goeth as it is written of him: but woe unto that man by whom the Son of man is betrayed! it had been good for that man if he had
25 not been born. Then Judas, which betrayed him, answered and said, Master, is it I? He said unto him, Thou hast
26 said. And as they were eating, Jesus took bread, and blessed it, and brake it, and gave it to the disciples, and said,
27 Take, eat; this is my body. And he took the cup, and gave thanks, and gave
28 it to them, saying, Drink ye all of it; for this is my blood of the new testament, which is shed for many for the remission
29 of sins. But I say unto you, I will not drink henceforth of this fruit of the vine, until that day when I drink it new with you in my Father's kingdom.
30 And when they had sung an hymn, they went out into the mount of Olives.
31 Then saith Jesus unto them, All ye shall be offended because of me this night: for it is written, I will smite the shepherd, and the sheep of the flock
32 shall be scattered abroad. But after I am risen again, I will go before you into
33 Galilee. Peter answered and said unto him, Though all men shall be offended because of thee, yet will I never be
34 offended. Jesus said unto him, Verily I say unto thee, That this night, before the cock crow, thou shalt deny me thrice.
35 Peter said unto him, Though I should die with thee, yet will I not deny thee. Likewise also said all the disciples.
36 Then cometh Jesus with them unto a place called Gethsemane, and saith unto the disciples, Sit ye here, while I go and
37 pray yonder. And he took with him Peter and the two sons of Zebedee, and began to be sorrowful and very heavy.
38 Then saith he unto them, My soul is exceeding sorrowful, even unto death: tarry
39 ye here, and watch with me. And he went a little farther, and fell on his face, and prayed, saying, O my Father, if it be possible, let this cup pass from me: nevertheless not as I will, but as thou
40 wilt. And he cometh unto the disciples,

and findeth them asleep, and saith unto Peter, What, could ye not watch with me
41 one hour? Watch and pray, that ye enter not into temptation: the spirit indeed is
42 willing, but the flesh is weak. He went away again the second time, and prayed, saying, O my Father, if this cup may not pass away from me, except I drink it,
43 thy will be done. And he came and found them asleep again: for their eyes were
44 heavy. And he left them, and went away again, and prayed the third time, saying
45 the same words. Then cometh he to his disciples, and saith unto them, Sleep on now, and take your rest: behold, the hour is at hand, and the Son of man is be-
46 trayed into the hands of sinners. Rise, let us be going: behold, he is at hand that doth betray me.
47 And while he yet spake, lo, Judas, one of the twelve, came, and with him a great multitude with swords and staves, from the chief priests and elders of the
48 people. Now he that betrayed him gave them a sign, saying, Whomsoever I shall kiss, that same is he: hold him fast.
49 Forthwith he came to Jesus, and said,
50 Hail, master; and kissed him. And Jesus said unto him, Friend, wherefore art thou come? Then came they, and
51 laid hands on Jesus, and took him. And behold, one of them which were with Jesus stretched out his hand, and drew his sword, and struck a servant of the high priest's, and smote off his ear.
52 Then said Jesus unto him, Put up again thy sword into his place; for all they that take the sword shall perish with
53 the sword. Thinkest thou that I cannot now pray to my Father, and he shall presently give me more than twelve
54 legions of angels? But how then shall the scriptures be fulfilled, that thus it
55 must be? In that same hour said Jesus to the multitudes, Are ye come out as against a thief with swords and staves for to take me? I sat daily with you teaching in the temple, and ye laid no
56 hold on me. But all this was done, that the scriptures of the prophets might be fulfilled. Then all the disciples forsook him, and fled.
57 And they that had laid hold on Jesus led him away to Caiaphas the high priest, where the scribes and the elders were
58 assembled. But Peter followed him afar off unto the high priest's palace, and went in, and sat with the servants, to
59 see the end. Now the chief priests, and elders, and all the council, sought false witness against Jesus, to put him to
60 death; but found none: yea, though many false witnesses came, yet found they none. At the last came two false
61 witnesses, and said, This fellow said, I am able to destroy the temple of God,

62 and to build it in three days.
  high priest arose, and said u[nto]
  Answerest thou nothing? what is
63 these witness against thee? B[ut]
  held his peace. And the high p[riest]
  swered and said unto him, I adj[ure]
  by the living God, that thou tell
  ther thou be the Christ, the Son
64 Jesus saith unto him, Thou ha[st]
  nevertheless I say unto you, H[ereafter]
  shall ye see the Son of man si[tting]
  the right hand of power, and co[ming]
65 the clouds of heaven. Then t[he]
  priest rent his clothes, saying,
  spoken blasphemy; what furth[er]
  have we of witnesses? behold,
66 have heard his blasphemy. Wh[at think]
  ye? They answered and said
67 guilty of death. Then did they
  his face, and buffeted him; an[d others]
  smote him with the palms of thei[r hands]
68 saying, Prophesy unto us, thou
  Who is he that smote thee?
69 Now Peter sat without in the
  and a damsel came unto him,
  Thou also wast with Jesus of
70 But he denied before them all,
  I know not what thou sayest. A[nd]
71 he was gone out into the porch,
  maid saw him, and said unto th[em]
  were there, This fellow was a[lso with]
72 Jesus of Nazareth. And again h[e denied]
  with an oath, I do not know t[he man]
73 And after a while came unto h[im they]
  that stood by, and said to Peter
  thou also art one of them; for th[y speech]
74 bewrayeth thee. Then began he
  and to swear, saying, I know
  man. And immediately the co[ck crew]
75 And Peter remembered the word
  which said unto him, Before t[he cock]
  crow, thou shalt deny me thri[ce. And]
  he went out, and wept bitterly.
27 *When the morning was come*
  chief priests and elders of th[e people]
  took counsel against Jesus to pu[t him to]
2 *death: and when they had bou[nd him]*
  they led him away, and delivere[d him to]
  Pontius Pilate the governor.
3 Then Judas, which had betray[ed him]
  when he saw that he was con[demned,]
  repented himself, and brought a[gain the]
  thirty pieces of silver to the chie[f priests]
4 and elders, saying, I have sinned
  I have betrayed the innocent
  And they said, What is that to
5 thou to that. And he cast do[wn the]
  pieces of silver in the temple,
  parted, and went and hanged
6 And the chief priests took the
  pieces, and said, It is not lawfu[l for to]
  put them into the treasury, bec[ause]
7 is the price of blood. And th[ey took]
  counsel, and bought with th[em the]
  potter's field, to bury strang[ers.]
8 Wherefore that field was called,

---

10 shipped him. Then said Jesus unto them,
  Be not afraid: go tell my brethren that
  they go into Galilee, and there shall they
  see me.
11 Now when they were going, behold,
  some of the watch came into the city,
  and shewed unto the chief priests all the
12 things that were done. And when they
  were assembled with the elders, and had
  taken counsel, they gave large money
13 unto the soldiers, saying, Say ye, His
  disciples came by night, and stole him
14 away while we slept. And if this come
  to the governor's ears, we will persuade
15 him, and secure you. So they took the
  money, and did as they were taught: and

this saying is commonly reported among
  the Jews until this day.
16 Then the eleven disciples went away
  into Galilee, into a mountain where Jesus
17 *had appointed them. And when they saw*
  him, they worshipped him: but some
18 *doubted. And Jesus came and spake*
  unto them, saying, All power is given
19 *unto me in heaven and in earth. Go ye*
  therefore, and teach all nations, baptizing
  them in the name of the Father, and of
20 *the Son, and of the Holy Ghost: teaching*
  them to observe all things whatsoever I
  have commanded you: and, lo, I am
  with you alway, even unto the end of the
  world. Amen

THE GOSPEL ACCORDING TO
S. MARK.

1 *The beginning of the gospel of Jesus*
  Christ, the Son of God;
2 As it is written in the prophets,[a]

<small>a R. V. in Isaiah.</small>

  Behold, I send my messenger before
    thy face,
  Which shall prepare thy way before
    thee.
3 The voice of one crying in the
    wilderness,
  Prepare ye the way of the Lord,
  Make his paths straight.
4 *John did baptize in the wilderness, and*
  preach the baptism of repentance for the
5 *remission of sins. And there went out*
  unto him all the land of Judæa, and
  they of Jerusalem, and were all baptized
  of him in the river of Jordan, confessing
6 *their sins.* And John was clothed with
  camel's hair, and with a girdle of skin
  about his loins; and he did eat locusts
7 and wild honey; and preached, saying,
  There cometh one mightier than I after
  me, the latchet of whose shoes I am not
8 worthy to stoop down and unloose. I
  indeed have baptized you with water:
  but he shall baptize you with the Holy
  Ghost.
9 And it came to pass in those days,
  that Jesus came from Nazareth of Galilee, and was baptized of John in Jordan.
10 And straightway coming up out of the
  water, he saw the heavens opened, and
  the Spirit like a dove descending upon
11 him: and there came a voice from
  heaven, saying, Thou art my beloved
  Son, in whom I am well pleased.
12 And immediately the Spirit driveth
13 him into the wilderness. And he was
  there in the wilderness forty days, tempted of Satan; and was with the wild
  beasts; and the angels ministered unto
  him.
14 Now after that John was put in
  prison, Jesus came into Galilee, preaching the gospel of the kingdom of God,
15 and saying, The time is fulfilled, and the
  kingdom of God is at hand: repent ye,
  and believe the gospel.
16 Now as he walked by the sea of Galilee, he saw Simon and Andrew his
  brother casting a net into the sea: for
17 they were fishers. And Jesus said unto
  them, Come ye after me, and I will make
18 you to become fishers of men. And
  straightway they forsook their nets, and
19 followed him. And when he had gone a
  little farther thence, he saw James the
  son of Zebedee, and John his brother,
  who also were in the ship mending their
20 nets. And straightway he called them:
  and they left their father Zebedee in the
  ship with the hired servants, and went
  after him.
21 And they went into Capernaum; and
  straightway on the sabbath day he entered into the synagogue, and taught.
22 And they were astonished at his doctrine: for he taught them as one
  that had authority, and not as the
23 scribes. And there was in their synagogue a man with an unclean spirit; and
24 he cried out, saying, Let us alone; what
  have we to do with thee, thou Jesus of
  Nazareth? art thou come to destroy us?

I know thee who thou art, the Holy One 25 of God. And Jesus rebuked him, saying, Hold thy peace, and come out of him. 26 And when the unclean spirit had torn him, and cried with a loud voice, he 27 came out of him. And they were all amazed, insomuch that they questioned among themselves, saying, What thing is this? what new doctrine is this? for with authority commandeth he even the unclean spirits, and they do obey him. 28 And immediately his fame spread abroad throughout all the region round about Galilee. 29 And forthwith, when they were come out of the synagogue, they entered into the house of Simon and Andrew, with 30 James and John. But Simon's wife's mother lay sick of a fever, and anon 31 they tell him of her. And he came and took her by the hand, and lifted her up; and immediately the fever left her, and she ministered unto them. 32 And at even, when the sun did set, they brought unto him all that were diseased, and them that were possessed 33 with devils. And all the city was 34 gathered together at the door. And he healed many that were sick of divers diseases, and cast out many devils; and suffered not the devils to speak, because they knew him. 35 And in the morning, rising up a great while before day, he went out, and departed into a solitary place, and there 36 prayed. And Simon and they that were 37 with him followed after him. And when they had found him, they said unto him, 38 All men seek for thee. And he said unto them, Let us go into the next towns, that I may preach there also: for there-

·Matt. 39 fore came I forth. *And he preached in*
·23. *their synagogues throughout all Galilee, and cast out devils.*
40 And there came a leper to him, beseeching him, and kneeling down to him, and saying unto him, If thou wilt, thou 41 canst make me clean. And Jesus, moved with compassion, put forth his hand, and touched him, and saith unto him, 42 I will; be thou clean. And as soon as he had spoken, immediately the leprosy departed from him, and he was 43 cleansed. And he straitly charged him, 44 and forthwith sent him away; and saith unto him, See thou say nothing to any man: but go thy way, shew thyself to the priest, and offer for thy cleansing those things which Moses commanded, 45 for a testimony unto them. But he went out, and began to publish it much, and to blaze abroad the matter, insomuch that Jesus could no more openly enter into the city, but was without in desert places: and they came to him from every quarter.

2 And again he entered into Capernaum, after some days; and it was noised that 2 he was in the house. And straightway many were gathered together, insomuch that there was no room to receive them, no, not so much as about the door: and 3 he preached the word unto them. And they come unto him, bringing one sick of the palsy, which was borne of four. 4 And when they could not come nigh unto him for the press, they uncovered the roof where he was: and when they had broken it up, they let down the bed 5 wherein the sick of the palsy lay. When Jesus saw their faith, he said unto the sick of the palsy, Son, thy sins be for- 6 given thee. But there were certain of the scribes sitting there, and reasoning 7 in their hearts, Why doth this man thus speak blasphemies? who can forgive sins 8 but God only? And immediately when Jesus perceived in his spirit that they so reasoned within themselves, he said unto them, Why reason ye these things in your 9 hearts? Whether is it easier to say to the sick of the palsy, Thy sins be forgiven thee; or to say, Arise, and take up 10 thy bed, and walk? But that ye may know that the Son of man hath power on earth to forgive sins, (he saith to the 11 sick of the palsy,) I say unto thee, Arise, and take up thy bed, and go thy way 12 into thine house. And immediately he arose, took up the bed, and went forth before them all; insomuch that they were all amazed, and glorified God, saying, We never saw it on this fashion. 13 And he went forth again by the sea side; and all the multitude resorted unto 14 him, and he taught them. And as he passed by, he saw Levi the son of Alphæus sitting at the receipt of custom, and said unto him, Follow me. And he 15 arose and followed him. And it came to pass that, as Jesus sat at meat in his house, many publicans and sinners sat also together with Jesus and his disciples: for there were many, and they 16 followed him. And when the scribes and Pharisees saw him eat with publicans and sinners, they said unto his disciples. How is it that he eateth and drinketh 17 with publicans and sinners? When Jesus heard it, he saith unto them, They that are whole have no need of the physician, but they that are sick: I came not to call the righteous, but sinners to repentance. 18 And the disciples of John and of the Pharisees used to fast: and they come and say unto him, Why do the disciples of John and of the Pharisees fast, but 19 thy disciples fast not? And Jesus said unto them, Can the children of the bridechamber fast, while the bridegroom is with them? as long as they have the bridegroom with them, they cannot fast.

M

20 But the days will come, when the bridegroom shall be taken away from them, and then shall they fast in those days.
21 No man also seweth a piece of new cloth on an old garment: else the new piece that filled it up taketh away from the old, and the rent is made worse. And no man putteth new wine into old bottles: else the new wine doth burst the bottles, and the wine is spilled, and the bottles will be marred: but new wine must be put into new bottles.
23 And it came to pass, that he went through the corn fields on the sabbath day; and his disciples began, as they
24 went, to pluck the ears of corn. And the Pharisees said unto him, Behold, why do they on the sabbath day that which is not
25 lawful? And he said unto them, Have ye never read what David did, when he had need, and was an hungred, he, and
26 they that were with him? How he went into the house of God in the days of Abiathar the high priest, and did eat the shewbread, which is not lawful to eat but for the priests, and gave also to
27 them which were with him? And he said unto them, The sabbath was made for man, and not man for the sabbath:
28 therefore the Son of man is Lord also of the sabbath.

3 And he entered again into the synagogue; and there was a man there which
2 had a withered hand. And they watched him, whether he would heal him on the sabbath day; that they might accuse him.
3 And he saith unto the man which had
4 the withered hand, Stand forth. And he saith unto them, Is it lawful to do good on the sabbath days, or to do evil? to save life, or to kill? But they held their peace.
5 And when he had looked round about on them with anger, being grieved for the hardness of their hearts, he saith unto the man, Stretch forth thine hand. And he stretched it out: and his hand was
6 restored whole as the other. And the Pharisees went forth, and straightway took counsel with the Herodians against him, how they might destroy him.
7 But Jesus withdrew himself with his disciples to the sea: and a great multitude from Galilee followed him, [and from
8 Judea, and from Jerusalem, and from Idumæa, and from beyond Jordan; and they about Tyre and Sidon, a great multitude, when they had heard what great
9 things he did, came unto him.] And he spake to his disciples, that a small ship should wait on him because of the multitude, lest they should throng him. For
10 he had healed many; insomuch that they pressed upon him for to touch him, as many
11 as had plagues. And unclean spirits, when they saw him, fell down before him, and cried, saying, Thou art the Son of

12 God. And he straitly charged them that they should not make him known.
13 [And he goeth up into a mountain, and calleth unto him whom he would: and
14 they came unto him.] And he ordained twelve, that they should be with him, and that he might send them forth to preach,
15 and to have power to heal sicknesses, and
16 to cast out devils: and Simon he surnamed Peter; and James the son of
17 Zebedee, and John the brother of James; and he surnamed them Boanerges, which
18 is, The sons of thunder: and Andrew, and Philip, and Bartholomew, and Matthew, and Thomas, and James the son of Alphæus, and Thaddæus, and Simon the
19 Canaanite, and Judas Iscariot, which also betrayed him:
20 And they went into an house. And the multitude cometh together again, so that they could not so much as eat
21 bread. And when his friends heard of it, they went out to lay hold on him: for they said, He is beside himself.
22 And the scribes which came down from Jerusalem said, He hath Beelzebub, and by the prince of the devils casteth he out
23 devils. And he called them unto him, and said unto them in parables, How can
24 Satan cast out Satan? And if a kingdom be divided against itself, that king-
25 dom cannot stand. And if a house be divided against itself, that house cannot
26 stand. And if Satan rise up against himself, and be divided, he cannot stand,
27 but hath an end. No man can enter into a strong man's house, and spoil his goods, except he will first bind the strong man; and then he will spoil his house.
28 Verily I say unto you, All sins shall be forgiven unto the sons of men, and blasphemies wherewith soever they shall
29 blaspheme: but he that shall blaspheme against the Holy Ghost hath never forgiveness, but is in danger of eternal
30 damnation: because they said, He hath an unclean spirit.
31 There came then his brethren and his mother, and, standing without, sent unto
32 him, calling him. And the multitude sat about him, and they said unto him, Behold, thy mother and thy brethren
33 without seek for thee. And he answered them, saying, Who is my mother, or my
34 brethren? And he looked round about on them which sat about him, and said, Behold my mother and my brethren!
35 For whosoever shall do the will of God, the same is my brother, and my sister, and mother.

4 And he began again to teach by the seaside: and there was gathered unto him a great multitude, so that he entered into a ship, and sat in the sea; and the whole multitude was by the sea on the land.
2 And he taught them many things by par-

ables, and said unto them in his doctrine,
3 Hearken; Behold, there went out a
4 sower to sow: and it came to pass, as
he sowed, some fell by the wayside, and
the fowls of the air came and devoured
5 it up. And some fell on stony ground,
where it had not much earth; and immediately it sprang up, because it had
6 no depth of earth: but when the sun
was up, it was scorched; and because it
7 had no root, it withered away. And
some fell among thorns, and the thorns
grew up, and choked it, and it yielded
8 no fruit. And other fell on good ground,
and did yield fruit that sprang up and
increased; and brought forth, some
thirty, and some sixty, and some an
9 hundred. And he said unto them, He
that hath ears to hear, let him hear.
10 And when he was alone, they that
were about him with the twelve asked
11 of him the parable. And he said unto
them, Unto you it is given to know the
mystery of the kingdom of God: but
unto them that are without, all these
12 things are done in parables: that seeing
they may see, and not perceive; and
hearing they may hear, and not understand; lest at any time they should be
converted, and their sins should be for-
13 given them. And he said unto them,
Know ye not this parable? and how then
14 will ye know all parables? The sower
15 soweth the word. And these are they
by the way side, where the word is sown;
but when they have heard, Satan cometh
immediately, and taketh away the word
16 that was sown in their hearts. And
these are they likewise which are sown
on stony ground; who, when they have
heard the word, immediately receive it
17 with gladness; and have no root in
themselves, and so endure but for a
time: afterward, when affliction or persecution ariseth for the word's sake,
18 immediately they are offended. And
these are they which are sown among
19 thorns; such as hear the word, and the
cares of this world, and the deceitfulness
of riches, and the lusts of other things
entering in, choke the word, and it be-
20 cometh unfruitful. And these are they
which are sown on good ground; such
as hear the word, and receive it, and
bring forth fruit, some thirty-fold, some
sixty, and some an hundred.
21 And he said unto them, Is a candle
brought to be put under a bushel, or
under a bed? and not to be set on a
22 candlestick? For there is nothing hid,
which shall not be manifested; neither
was any thing kept secret, but that it
23 should come abroad. If any man have
24 ears to hear, let him hear. And he said
unto them, Take heed what ye hear:
with what measure ye mete, it shall be
measured to you: and unto you that
25 hear shall more be given. For he that
hath, to him shall be given: and he that
hath not, from him shall be taken even
that which he hath.
26 And he said, So is the kingdom of God,
as if a man should cast seed into the
27 ground; and should sleep, and rise night
and day, and the seed should spring and
28 grow up, he knoweth not how. For the
earth bringeth forth fruit of herself; first
the blade, then the ear, after that the
29 full corn in the ear. But when the fruit
is brought forth, immediately he putteth
in the sickle, because the harvest is
come.
30 And he said, Whereunto shall we
liken the kingdom of God? or with what
31 comparison shall we compare it? It is
like a grain of mustard seed, which,
when it is sown in the earth, is less than
32 all the seeds that be in the earth: but
when it is sown, it groweth up, and becometh greater than all herbs, and
shooteth out great branches; so that the
fowls of the air may lodge under the
shadow of it.
33 And with many such parables spake
he the word unto them, as they were
34 able to hear it. But without a parable
spake he not unto them: and when they
were alone, he expounded all things to
his disciples.
35 And the same day, when the even was
come, he saith unto them, Let us pass
36 over unto the other side. And when
they had sent away the multitude, they
took him even as he was in the ship.
And there were also with him other
37 little ships. And there arose a great
storm of wind, and the waves beat into
38 the ship, so that it was now full. And
he was in the hinder part of the ship,
asleep on a pillow: and they awake
him, and say unto him, Master, carest
39 thou not that we perish? And he arose,
and rebuked the wind, and said unto
the sea, Peace, be still. And the wind
ceased, and there was a great calm.
40 And he said unto them, Why are ye so
fearful? how is it that ye have no faith?
41 And they feared exceedingly, and said
one to another, What manner of man is
this, that even the wind and the sea
obey him?

5 And they came over unto the other
side of the sea, into the country of the
2 Gadarenes. And when he was come out
of the ship, immediately there met him
out of the tombs a man with an unclean
3 spirit, who had his dwelling among the
tombs; and no man could bind him,
4 no, not with chains: because that he
had been often bound with fetters and
chains, and the chains had been plucked
asunder by him, and the fetters broken

S. MARK.

in pieces: neither could any man tame
5 him. And always, night and day, he
was in the mountains, and in the tombs,
crying, and cutting himself with stones.
6 But when he saw Jesus afar off, he ran
7 and worshipped him, and cried with a
loud voice, and said, What have I to do
with thee, Jesus, thou Son of the most
high God? I adjure thee by God, that
8 thou torment me not. ' For he said unto
him, Come out of the man, thou unclean
9 spirit. And he asked him, What is thy
name? And he answered, saying, My
10 name is Legion: for we are many. And
he besought him much that he would
not send them away out of the country.
11 Now there was there nigh unto the
mountains a great herd of swine feeding.
12 And all the devils besought him, saying,
Send us into the swine, that we may
13 enter into them. And forthwith Jesus
gave them leave. And the unclean
spirits went out, and entered into the
swine: and the herd ran violently down
a steep place into the sea, (they were
about two thousand;) and were choked
14 in the sea. And they that fed the swine
fled, and told it in the city, and in the
country. And they went out to see
15 what it was that was done. And they
come to Jesus, and see him that was
possessed with the devil, and had the
legion, sitting, and clothed, and in his
16 right mind: and they were afraid. And
they that saw it told them how it befell
to him that was possessed with the
devil, and also concerning the swine.
17 And they began to pray him to depart
18 out of their coasts. And when he was
come into the ship, he that had been
possessed with the devil prayed him that
19 he might be with him. Howbeit Jesus
suffered him not, but saith unto him,
Go home to thy friends, and tell them
how great things the Lord hath done for
thee, and hath had compassion on thee.
20 And he departed, and began to publish
in Decapolis how great things Jesus had
done for him: and all men did marvel.
21 And when Jesus was passed over
again by ship unto the other side, much
people gathered unto him: and he was
22 nigh unto the sea. And, behold, there
cometh one of the rulers of the synagogue,
Jairus by name; and when he
23 saw him, he fell at his feet, and besought
him greatly, saying, My little daughter
lieth at the point of death: I pray thee,
come and lay thy hands on her, that she
24 may be healed; and she shall live. And
Jesus went with him; and much people
followed him, and thronged him.
25 And a certain woman, which had an
26 issue of blood twelve years, and had
suffered many things of many physicians,
and had spent all that she had, and was
nothing bettered, but rather grew worse,
27 when she had heard of Jesus, came in
the press behind, and touched his gar-
28 ment. For she said, If I may touch but
29 his clothes, I shall be whole. And
straightway the fountain of her blood
was dried up; and she felt in her body
that she was healed of that plague.
30 And Jesus, immediately knowing in
himself that virtue had gone out of him,
turned him about in the press, and said,
31 Who touched my clothes? And his
disciples said unto him, Thou seest the
multitude thronging thee, and sayest
32 thou, Who touched me? And he looked
round about to see her that had done
33 this thing. But the woman fearing and
trembling, knowing what was done in
her, came and fell down before him, and
34 told him all the truth. And he said
unto her, Daughter, thy faith hath made
thee whole; go in peace, and be whole
of thy plague.
35 While he yet spake, there came from
the ruler of the synagogue's house certain
which said, Thy daughter is dead: why
troublest thou the Master any further?
36 As soon as Jesus heard the word that
was spoken, he saith unto the ruler of
the synagogue, Be not afraid, only be-
37 lieve. And he suffered no man to follow
him, save Peter, and James, and John
38 the brother of James. And he cometh
to the house of the ruler of the synagogue,
and seeth the tumult, and them
39 that wept and wailed greatly. And
when he was come in, he saith unto
them, Why make ye this ado, and weep?
the damsel is not dead, but sleepeth.
40 And they laughed him to scorn. But
when he had put them all out, he taketh
the father and the mother of the damsel,
and them that were with him, and
entereth in where the damsel was lying.
41 And he took the damsel by the hand,
and said unto her, Talitha cumi; which
is, being interpreted, Damsel, I say unto
42 thee, arise. And straightway the damsel
arose, and walked: for she was of the
age of twelve years. And they were
astonished with a great astonishment.
43 And he charged them straitly that no
man should know it; and commanded
that something should be given her to
eat.

6 And he went out from thence, and
came into his own country; and his dis-
2 ciples follow him. And when the sabbath
day was come, he began to teach in
the synagogue; and many hearing him
were astonished, saying, From whence
hath this man these things? and what
wisdom is this which is given unto him,
that even such mighty works are wrought
3 by his hands? Is not this the carpenter,
the son of Mary, the brother of James,

and Joses, and of Juda, and Simon? and are not his sisters here with us? And
4 they were offended at him. But Jesus said unto them, A prophet is not without honour, but in his own country, and among his own kin, and in his own house.
5 And he could there do no mighty work, save that he laid his hands upon a few
6 sick folk, and healed them. And he marvelled because of their unbelief.

And he went round about the villages, teaching.
7 And he called unto him the twelve, and began to send them forth by two and two; and gave them power over
8 unclean spirits; and commanded them that they should take nothing for their journey, save a staff only; no scrip, no
9 bread, no money in their purse: but be shod with sandals; and not put on two
10 coats. And he said unto them, In what place soever ye enter into an house, there abide till ye depart from that place.
11 And whosoever shall not receive you, nor hear you, when ye depart thence, shake off the dust under your feet for a testimony against them. Verily I say unto you, It shall be more tolerable for Sodom and Gomorrha in the day of judg-
12 ment, than for that city. And they went out, and preached that men should re-
13 pent. And they cast out many devils, and anointed with oil many that were sick, and healed them.
14 And king Herod heard of him; (for his name was spread abroad;) and he said, That John the Baptist was risen from the dead, and therefore mighty works do shew forth themselves in him.
15 Others said, That it is Elias. And others said, That it is a prophet, or as one of
16 the prophets. But when Herod heard thereof, he said, It is John, whom I be-
17 headed: he is risen from the dead. For Herod himself had sent forth and laid hold upon John, and bound him in prison for Herodias' sake, his brother Philip's
18 wife: for he had married her. For John had said unto Herod, It is not lawful for
19 thee to have thy brother's wife. Therefore Herodias had a quarrel against him, and would have killed him; but she could not:
20 for Herod feared John, knowing that he was a just man and an holy, and observed him; and when he heard him, he did many things, and heard him
21 gladly. And when a convenient day was come, that Herod on his birthday made a supper to his lords, high captains, and
22 chief estates of Galilee; and when the daughter of the said Herodias came in, and danced, and pleased Herod and them that sat with him, the king said unto the damsel, Ask of me whatsoever thou wilt,
23 and I will give it thee. And he sware unto her, Whatsoever thou shalt ask of me, I will give it thee, unto the half of
24 my kingdom. And she went forth, and said unto her mother, What shall I ask? And she said, The head of John the Bap-
25 tist. And she came in straightway with haste unto the king, and asked, saying, I will that thou give me by and by in a charger the head of John the Baptist.
26 And the king was exceeding sorry; yet for his oath's sake, and for their sakes which sat with him, he would not reject
27 her. And immediately the king sent an executioner, and commanded his head to be brought: and he went and beheaded
28 him in the prison, and brought his head in a charger, and gave it to the damsel: and the damsel gave it to the mother.
29 And when his disciples heard of it, they came and took up his corpse, and laid it in a tomb.
30 [And the apostles gathered themselves together unto Jesus, and told him all things, both what they had done, and
31 what they had taught. And he said unto them, Come ye yourselves apart into a desert place, and rest a while: for there were many coming and going, and they
32 had no leisure so much as to eat.] And they departed into a desert place by ship
33 privately. And the people saw them departing, and many knew him, and ran afoot thither out of all cities, and outwent them, and came together unto him.
34 And Jesus, when he came out, saw much people, and was moved with compassion toward them, [because they were as sheep not having a shepherd:] and he began to Cf. Matt. ix. 36.
35 teach them many things. And when the day was now far spent, his disciples came unto him, and said, This is a desert place,
36 and now the time is far passed; send them away, that they may go into the country round about, and into the villages, and buy themselves bread: for they
37 have nothing to eat. He answered and said unto them, Give ye them to eat. And they say unto him, Shall we go and buy two hundred pennyworth of bread,
38 and give them to eat? He saith unto them, How many loaves have ye? go and see. And when they knew, they say, Five,
39 and two fishes. And he commanded them to make all sit down by companies
40 upon the green grass. And they sat down in ranks, by hundreds, and by fifties.
41 And when he had taken the five loaves and the two fishes, he looked up to heaven, and blessed, and brake the loaves, and gave them to his disciples to set before them; and the two fishes divided he
42 among them all. And they did all eat,
43 and were filled. And they took up twelve baskets full of the fragments, and of the
44 fishes. And they that did eat of the loaves were about five thousand men.
45 And straightway he constrained his

disciples to get into the ship, and to go to the other side before unto Bethsaida, while
46 he sent away the people. And when he had sent them away, he departed into a
47 mountain to pray. And when even was come, the ship was in the midst of the
48 sea, and he alone on the land. And he saw them toiling in rowing; for the wind was contrary unto them: and about the fourth watch of the night he cometh unto them, walking upon the sea, and would
49 have passed by them. But when they saw him walking upon the sea, they supposed
50 it had been a spirit, and cried out: for they all saw him, and were troubled. And immediately he talked with them, and saith unto them, Be of good cheer:
51 it is I; be not afraid. And he went up unto them into the ship; and the wind ceased: and they were sore amazed in themselves beyond measure, and won-
52 dered. For they considered not the miracle of the loaves: for their heart was hardened.
53 And when they had passed over, they came into the land of Gennesaret, and
54 drew to the shore. And when they were come out of the ship, straightway they
55 knew him, and ran through that whole region round about, and began to carry about in beds those that were sick, where
56 they heard he was. And whithersoever he entered, into villages, or cities, or country, they laid the sick in the streets, and besought him that they might touch if it were but the border of his garment: and as many as touched him were made whole.

7 Then came together unto him the Pharisees, and certain of the scribes, which
2 came from Jerusalem. And when they saw some of his disciples eat bread with defiled, that is to say, with unwashen,
3 hands, they found fault. For the Pharisees, and all the Jews, except they wash their hands oft, eat not, holding the
4 tradition of the elders. And when they come from the market, except they wash, they eat not. And many other things there be, which they have received to hold, as the washing of cups, and pots,
5 brasen vessels, and of tables. Then the Pharisees and scribes asked him, Why walk not thy disciples according to the tradition of the elders, but eat bread with
6 unwashen hands? He answered and said unto them, Well hath Esaias prophesied of you hypocrites, as it is written,
This people honoureth me with their lips,
But their heart is far from me.
7 Howbeit in vain do they worship me, Teaching for doctrines the commandments of men.
8 For laying aside the commandment of God, ye hold the tradition of men, as the

washing of pots and cups: and many
9 other such like things ye do. And he said unto them, Full well ye reject the commandment of God, that ye may keep
10 your own tradition. For Moses said, Honour thy father and thy mother; and Whoso curseth father or mother, let him
11 die the death: but ye say, If a man shall say to his father or mother, It is Corban, that is to say, a gift, by whatsoever thou mightest be profited by me; he shall be
12 free. And ye suffer him no more to do ought for his father or his mother;
13 making the word of God of none effect through your tradition, which ye have delivered: and many such like things do
14 ye. And when he had called all the people unto him, he said unto them, Hearken unto me every one of you, and
15 understand: there is nothing from without a man, that entering into him can defile him: but the things which come out of him, those are they that defile the man.
16 If any man have ears to hear, let him
17 hear. And when he was entered into the house from the people, his disciples asked
18 him concerning the parable. And he saith unto them, Are ye so without understanding also? Do ye not perceive, that whatsoever thing from without entereth
19 into the man, it cannot defile him; because it entereth not into his heart, but into the belly, and goeth out into the
20 draught, purging all meats? And he said, That which cometh out of the man,
21 that defileth the man. For from within, out of the heart of men, proceed evil thoughts, adulteries, fornications, mur-
22 ders, thefts, covetousness, wickedness, deceit, lasciviousness, an evil eye, blasphemy,
23 pride, foolishness: all these evil things come from within, and defile the man.
24 And from thence he arose, and went into the borders of Tyre [and Sidon], and *Some ancient authori-* entered into an house, and would have *ties omit* no man know it: but he could not be *and*
25 hid. For a certain woman, whose young *Sidon.* daughter had an unclean spirit, heard of
26 him, and came and fell at his feet: the woman was a Greek, a Syrophenician by nation; and she besought him that he would cast forth the devil out of her
27 daughter. But Jesus said unto her, Let the children first be filled: for it is not meet to take the children's bread, and
28 to cast it unto the dogs. And she answered and said unto him, Yes, Lord: yet the dogs under the table eat of the
29 children's crumbs. And he said unto her, For this saying go thy way; the
30 devil is gone out of thy daughter. And when she was come to her house, she found the devil gone out, and her daughter laid upon the bed.
31 And again, departing from the coasts of Tyre [and Sidon], he came unto the

sea of Galilee, through the midst of the
32 coasts of Decapolis. [And they bring
unto him one that was deaf, and had
an impediment in his speech; and they
beseech him to put his hand upon him.
33 And he took him aside from the multitude, and put his fingers into his ears,
and he spit, and touched his tongue;
34 and looking up to heaven, he sighed,
and saith unto him, Ephphatha, that is,
35 Be opened. And straightway his ears
were opened, and the string of his tongue
36 was loosed, and he spake plain. And he
charged them that they should tell no
man: but the more he charged them, so
much the more a great deal they pub-
37 lished it;) and were beyond measure
astonished, saying, He hath done all
things well: he maketh both the deaf to
hear, and the dumb to speak.

8 In those days the multitude being
very great, and having nothing to eat,
Jesus called his disciples unto him, and
2 saith unto them, I have compassion on
the multitude, because they have now
been with me three days, and have
3 nothing to eat: and if I send them away
fasting to their own houses, they will
faint by the way: for divers of them
4 came from far. And his disciples answered him, From whence can a man
satisfy these men with bread here in the
5 wilderness? And he asked them, How
many loaves have ye? And they said,
6 Seven. And he commanded the people
to sit down on the ground: and he took
the seven loaves, and gave thanks, and
brake, and gave to his disciples to set
before them; and they did set them
7 before the people. And they had a few
small fishes: and he blessed, and commanded to set them also before them.
8 So they did eat, and were filled; and
they took up of the broken meat that
9 was left seven baskets. And they that
had eaten were about four thousand:
10 and he sent them away. And straightway he entered into a ship with his
disciples, and came into the parts of
Dalmanutha.
11 And the Pharisees came forth, and
began to question with him, seeking of
him a sign from heaven, tempting him.
12 And he sighed deeply in his spirit, and
saith, Why doth this generation seek
after a sign? verily I say unto you,
There shall no sign be given unto this
13 generation. And he left them, and
entering into the ship again departed to
the other side.
14 Now the disciples had forgotten to
take bread, neither had they in the ship
15 with them more than one loaf. And he
charged them, saying, Take heed, beware
of the leaven of the Pharisees, and of the
16 leaven of Herod. And they reasoned
among themselves," saying, It is because *a* Or,
17 we have no bread. And when Jesus Because
knew it, he saith unto them, Why reason no bread.
ye, because ye have no bread? perceive
ye not yet, neither understand? have ye
18 your heart yet hardened? Having eyes,
see ye not? and having ears, hear ye not?
19 and do ye not remember? When I brake
[the five loaves among five thousand,
how many baskets full of fragments took
ye up? They say unto him, Twelve.
20 And when] the seven among four thousand, how many baskets full of fragments took ye up? And they said,
21 Seven. And he said unto them, How is
it that ye do not understand?
22 [And he cometh to Bethsaida; and Cf. Matt.
they bring a blind man unto him, and ix. 27-31.
23 besought him to touch him. And he
took the blind man by the hand, and led
him out of the town; and when he had
spit on his eyes, and put his hands upon
24 him, he asked him if he saw ought. And
he looked up, and said, I see men as
25 trees, walking. After that he put his
hands again upon his eyes, and made
him look up: and he was restored, and
26 saw every man clearly. And he sent
him away to his house, saying, Neither
go into the town, nor tell it to any in the
town.]
27 *And Jesus went out, and his disciples,
into the towns of Cæsarea Philippi: and
by the way he asked his disciples, saying
unto them, Whom do men say that I am?*
28 *And they answered, John the Baptist:
but some say, Elias; and others, One of*
29 *the prophets. And he saith unto them,
But whom say ye that I am? And Peter
answereth and saith unto him, Thou art*
30 *the Christ. And he charged them that*
31 *they should tell no man of him. And he
began to teach them, that the Son of man
must suffer many things, and be rejected
of the elders, and of the chief priests, and
scribes, and be killed, and after three days*
32 *rise again. And he spake that saying
openly. And Peter took him, and began*
33 *to rebuke him. But when he had turned
about and looked on his disciples, he rebuked Peter, saying, Get thee behind me,
Satan: for thou savourest not the things
that be of God, but the things that be of*
34 *men. And when he had called the people
unto him with his disciples also, he said
unto them, Whosoever will come after
me, let him deny himself, and take up*
35 *his cross, and follow me. For whosoever
will save his life shall lose it; but whosoever shall lose his life for my sake and the*
36 *gospel's, the same shall save it. For what
shall it profit a man, if he shall gain the*
37 *whole world, and lose his own soul? Or
what shall a man give in exchange for*
38 *his soul? Whosoever therefore shall be
ashamed of me and of my words in this*

adulterous and sinful generation; of him also shall the Son of man be ashamed, when he cometh in the glory of his Father
9 with the holy angels. And he said unto them, Verily I say unto you, That there be some of them that stand here, which shall not taste of death, till they have seen the kingdom of God come with power.
2 And after six days Jesus taketh with him Peter, and James, and John, and leadeth them up into an high mountain apart by themselves: and he was trans-
3 figured before them. And his raiment became shining, exceeding white as snow; so as no fuller on earth can white them.
4 And there appeared unto them Elias with Moses: and they were talking with Jesus.
5 And Peter answered and said to Jesus, Master, it is good for us to be here: and let us make three tabernacles; one for thee, and one for Moses, and one for
6 Elias. For he wist not what to say; for
7 they were sore afraid. And there was a cloud that overshadowed them: and a voice came out of the cloud, saying, This
8 is my beloved Son: hear him. And suddenly, when they had looked round about, they saw no man any more, save Jesus only with themselves.
9 And as they came down from the mountain, he charged them that they should tell no man what things they had seen, till the Son of man were risen from
10 the dead. And they kept that saying with themselves, questioning one with another what the rising from the dead
11 should mean. And they asked him, saying, Why say the scribes that Elias must
12 first come? And he answered and told them, Elias verily cometh first, and restoreth all things; and how it is written of the Son of man, that he must suffer
13 many things, and be set at nought. But I say unto you, That Elias is indeed come, and they have done unto him whatsoever they listed, as it is written of him.
14 And when he came to his disciples, he saw a great multitude about them, and
15 the scribes questioning with them. And straightway all the people, when they beheld him, were greatly amazed, and
16 running to him saluted him. And he asked the scribes, What question ye with
17 them? And one of the multitude answered and said, Master, I have brought unto thee my son, which hath a dumb
18 spirit; and wheresoever he taketh him, he teareth him: and he foameth, and gnasheth with his teeth, and pineth away: and I spake to thy disciples that they should cast him out; and they could not.
19 He answereth him, and saith, O faithless generation, how long shall I be with you? how long shall I suffer you? bring
20 him unto me. And they brought him unto him: and when he saw him, straightway the spirit tare him; and he fell on
21 the ground, and wallowed foaming. And he asked his father, How long is it ago since this came unto him? And he said,
22 Of a child. And ofttimes it hath cast him into the fire, and into the waters, to destroy him: but if thou canst do any thing, have compassion on us, and help
23 us. Jesus said unto him, If thou canst believe, all things are possible to him that
24 believeth. And straightway the father of the child cried out, and said with tears, Lord, I believe; help thou mine unbelief.
25 When Jesus saw that the people came running together, he rebuked the foul spirit, saying unto him, Thou dumb and deaf spirit, I charge thee, come out of
26 him, and enter no more into him. And the spirit cried, and rent him sore, and came out of him: and he was as one dead; insomuch that many said, He is
27 dead. But Jesus took him by the hand,
28 and lifted him up; and he arose. And when he was come into the house, his disciples asked him privately, Why could
29 not we cast him out? And he said unto them, This kind can come forth by nothing, but by prayer and fasting.
30 And they departed thence, and passed through Galilee; and he would not that
31 any man should know it. For he taught his disciples, and said unto them, The Son of man is delivered into the hands of men, and they shall kill him; and after that he is killed, he shall rise the
32 third day. But they understood not that saying, and were afraid to ask him.
33 And he came to Capernaum: and being in the house he asked them, What was it that ye disputed among yourselves by
34 the way? But they held their peace: for by the way they had disputed among themselves, who should be the greatest.
35 And he sat down, and called the twelve, and saith unto them, If any man desire to be first, the same shall be last of all,
36 and servant of all. And he took a child, and set him in the midst of them: and when he had taken him in his arms, he
37 said unto them, Whosoever shall receive one of such children in my name, receiveth me: and whosoever shall receive me, receiveth not me, but him that sent me.
38 And John answered him, saying, Master, we saw one casting out devils in thy name, and he followeth not us: and we forbade him, because he followeth not
39 us. But Jesus said, Forbid him not: for there is no man which shall do a miracle in my name, that can lightly speak evil
40 of me. For he that is not against us is
41 on our part. [For whosoever shall give you a cup of water to drink in my name, because ye belong to Christ, verily I say

Cf. Matt. x. 42.

unto you, he shall not lose his reward.]
42 *And whosoever shall offend one of these little ones that believe in me, it is better for him that a millstone were hanged about his neck, and he were cast into the*
43 *sea.* And if thy hand offend thee, cut it off: it is better for thee to enter into life maimed, than having two hands to go into hell, into the fire that never shall
44 be quenched : where their worm dieth
45 not, and the fire is not quenched. And if thy foot offend thee, cut it off: it is better for thee to enter halt into life, than having two feet to be cast into hell, into the fire that never shall be quenched:
46 where their worm dieth not, and the fire
47 is not quenched. And if thine eye offend thee, pluck it out: it is better for thee to enter into the kingdom of God with one eye, than having two eyes to be cast
48 into hell fire: where their worm dieth
49 not, and the fire is not quenched. For every one shall be salted with fire, and every sacrifice shall be salted with salt.
50 Salt is good : but if the salt have lost his saltness, wherewith will ye season it? Have salt in yourselves, and have peace one with another.

10 *And he arose from thence, and cometh into the coasts of Judea by the farther side of Jordan: and the people resort unto him again; and, as he was wont,*
2 *he taught them again.* And the Pharisees came to him, and asked him, Is it lawful for a man to put away his wife?
3 tempting him. And he answered and said unto them, What did Moses com-
4 mand you? And they said, Moses suffered to write a bill of divorcement, and
5 to put her away. And Jesus answered and said unto them, For the hardness of your heart he wrote you this precept.
6 But from the beginning of the creation
7 God made them male and female. For this cause shall a man leave his father
8 and mother, and cleave to his wife ; and they twain shall be one flesh: so then they are no more twain, but one flesh.
9 What therefore God hath joined together,
10 let not man put asunder. And in the house his disciples asked him again of
11 the same matter. And he saith unto them, Whosoever shall put away his wife, and marry another, committeth
12 adultery against her. And if a woman shall put away her husband, and be married to another, she committeth adultery.
13 *And they brought young children to him, that he should touch them: and his disciples rebuked those that brought them.*
14 *But when Jesus saw it, he was much displeased, and said unto them, Suffer the little children to come unto me, and forbid them not: for of such is the king-*
15 *dom of God. Verily I say unto you, Whosoever shall not receive the kingdom*

of God as a little child, he shall not enter
16 *therein. And he took them up in his arms, put his hands upon them, and blessed them.*
17 *And when he was gone forth into the way, there came one running, and kneeled to him, and asked him, Good Master, what shall I do that I may inherit eternal life?*
18 *And Jesus said unto him, Why callest thou me good? there is none good but one,*
19 *that is, God. Thou knowest the commandments, Do not commit adultery, Do not kill, Do not steal, Do not bear false witness, Defraud not, Honour thy father*
20 *and mother. And he answered and said unto him, Master, all these have I ob-*
21 *served from my youth. Then Jesus beholding him loved him, and said unto him, One thing thou lackest: go thy way, sell whatsoever thou hast, and give to the poor, and thou shalt have treasure in heaven: and come, take up the cross, and*
22 *follow me. And he was sad at that saying, and went away grieved: for he had great possessions.*
23 *And Jesus looked round about, and saith unto his disciples, How hardly shall they that have riches enter into the king-*
24 *dom of God! And the disciples were astonished at his words. But Jesus answereth again, and saith unto them, Children, how hard is it for them that trust in riches to enter into the kingdom*
25 *of God! It is easier for a camel to go through the eye of a needle, than for a rich man to enter into the kingdom of God.*
26 *And they were astonished out of measure, saying among themselves, Who then can*
27 *be saved? And Jesus looking upon them saith, With men it is impossible, but not with God: for with God all things are*
28 *possible.* Then Peter began to say unto him, Lo, we have left all, and have fol-
29 lowed thee. And Jesus answered and said, Verily I say unto you, There is no man that hath left house, or brethren, or sisters, or father, or mother, or wife, or children, or lands, for my sake, and the
30 gospel's, but he shall receive an hundredfold now in this time, houses, and brethren, and sisters, and mothers, and children, and lands, with persecutions ; and
31 in the world to come eternal life. But many that are first shall be last ; and the last first.
32 *And they were in the way going up to Jerusalem ; and Jesus went before them : and they were amazed ; and as they followed, they were afraid.* And he took again the twelve, and began to tell them what things should happen unto him,
33 saying, Behold, we go up to Jerusalem ; and the Son of man shall be delivered unto the chief priests, and unto the scribes ; and they shall condemn him to death, and shall deliver him to the

N

34 Gentiles: and they shall mock him, and shall scourge him, and shall spit upon him, and shall kill him: and the third day he shall rise again.

35 *And James and John, the sons of Zebedee, come unto him, saying, Master, we would that thou shouldest do for us whatsoever we shall desire. And he said unto them, What would ye that I should do for you? They said unto him, Grant unto us that we may sit, one on thy right hand, and the other on thy left hand, in thy glory. But Jesus said unto them, Ye know not what ye ask: can ye drink of the cup that I drink of? and be baptized with the baptism that I am baptized with? And they said unto him, We can. And Jesus said unto them, Ye shall indeed drink of the cup that I drink of; and with the baptism that I am baptized withal shall ye be baptized: but to sit on my right hand and on my left hand is not mine to give; but it shall be given to them for whom it is prepared. And when the ten heard it, they began to be much displeased with James and John. But Jesus called them to him, and saith unto them, Ye know that they which are accounted to rule over the Gentiles exercise lordship over them; and their great ones exercise authority upon them. But so shall it not be among you: but whosoever will be great among you, shall be your minister: and whosoever of you will be the chiefest, shall be servant of all. For even the Son of man came not to be ministered unto, but to minister, and to give his life a ransom for many.*

46 And they came to Jericho: and as he went out of Jericho with his disciples and a great number of people, blind Bartimæus, the son of Timæus, sat by the highway side begging. And when he heard that it was Jesus of Nazareth, he began to cry out, and say, Jesus, thou son of David, have mercy on me. And many charged him that he should hold his peace: but he cried the more a great deal, Thou son of David, have mercy on me. And Jesus stood still, and commanded him to be called. And they call the blind man, saying unto him, Be of good comfort, rise; he calleth thee. And he, casting away his garment, rose, and came to Jesus. And Jesus answered and said unto him, What wilt thou that I should do unto thee? The blind man said unto him, Lord, that I might receive my sight. And Jesus said unto him, Go thy way; thy faith hath made thee whole. And immediately he received his sight, and followed Jesus in the way.

11 And when they came nigh to Jerusalem, unto Bethphage and Bethany, at the mount of Olives, he sendeth forth two of his disciples, and saith unto them, Go your way into the village over against you: and as soon as ye be entered into it, ye shall find a colt tied, whereon never man sat; loose him, and bring him. And if any man say unto you, Why do ye this? say ye that the Lord hath need of him; and straightway he will send him hither. And they went their way, and found the colt tied by the door without in a place where two ways met; and they loose him. And certain of them that stood there said unto them, What do ye, loosing the colt? And they said unto them even as Jesus had commanded: and they let them go. And they brought the colt to Jesus, and cast their garments on him; and he sat upon him. And many spread their garments in the way: and others cut down branches off the trees, and strawed them in the way. And they that went before, and they that followed, cried, saying, Hosanna; Blessed is he that cometh in the name of the Lord: Blessed be the kingdom of our father David, that cometh in the name of the Lord: Hosanna in the highest.

11 *And Jesus entered into Jerusalem, and into the temple: and when he had looked round about upon all things, and now the even-tide was come, he went out unto Bethany with the twelve.*

12 And on the morrow, when they were come from Bethany, he was hungry: and seeing a fig-tree afar off having leaves, he came, if haply he might find any thing thereon: and when he came to it, he found nothing but leaves; for the time of figs was not yet. And Jesus answered and said unto it, No man eat fruit of thee hereafter for ever. And his disciples heard it.

15 And they come to Jerusalem: and Jesus went into the temple, and began to cast out them that sold and bought in the temple, and overthrew the tables of the money-changers, and the seats of them that sold doves; and would not suffer that any man should carry any vessel through the temple. And he taught, saying unto them, Is it not written, My house shall be called of all nations the house of prayer? but ye have made it a den of thieves. And the scribes and chief priests heard it, and sought how they might destroy him: for they feared him, because all the people was astonished at his doctrine. And when even was come, he went out of the city.

20 And in the morning, as they passed by, they saw the fig-tree dried up from the roots. And Peter, calling to remembrance, saith unto him, Master, behold, the fig-tree which thou cursedst is withered away. And Jesus answering,

S. MARK.

23 saith unto them, Have faith in God. For verily I say unto you, That whosoever shall say unto this mountain, Be thou removed, and be thou cast into the sea; and shall not doubt in his heart, but shall believe that those things which he saith shall come to pass; he shall have what-
24 soever he saith. Therefore I say unto you, What things soever ye desire, when ye pray, believe that ye receive them,
25 and ye shall have them. And when ye stand praying, forgive, if ye have ought against any: that your Father also which is in heaven may forgive you your tres-
26 passes. But if ye do not forgive, neither will your Father which is in heaven forgive your trespasses.

27 And they come again to Jerusalem: and as he was walking in the temple, there come to him the chief priests, and the
28 scribes, and the elders, and say unto him, By what authority doest thou these things? and who gave thee this authority
29 to do these things? And Jesus answered and said unto them, I will also ask of you one question, and answer me, and I will tell you by what authority I do these
30 things. The baptism of John, was it from heaven, or of men? answer me.
31 And they reasoned with themselves, saying, If we shall say, From heaven; he will say, Why then did ye not believe
32 him? But if we shall say, Of men; they feared the people: for all men counted John, that he was a prophet indeed.
33 And they answered and said unto Jesus, We cannot tell. And Jesus answering, saith unto them, Neither do I tell you by what authority I do these things.

12 And he began to speak unto them by parables. A certain man planted a vineyard, and set an hedge about it, and digged a place for the wine-fat, and built a tower, and let it out to husbandmen,
2 and went into a far country. And at the season he sent to the husbandmen a servant, that he might receive from the husbandmen of the fruit of the vineyard.
3 And they caught him, and beat him, and
4 sent him away empty. And again he sent unto them another servant; and at him they cast stones, and wounded him in the head, and sent him away shame-
5 fully handled. And again he sent another; and him they killed, and many others: beating some, and killing some.
6 Having yet therefore one son, his wellbeloved, he sent him also last unto them,
7 saying, They will reverence my son. But those husbandmen said among themselves, This is the heir; come, let us kill him,
8 and the inheritance shall be ours. And they took him, and killed him, and cast
9 him out of the vineyard. What shall therefore the lord of the vineyard do? he will come and destroy the husbandmen, and will give the vineyard unto others.
10 And have ye not read this scripture;
 The stone which the builders rejected
 Is become the head of the corner:
11 This was the Lord's doing,
 And it is marvellous in our eyes?
12 And they sought to lay hold on him, but feared the people: for they knew that he had spoken the parable against them: and they left him, and went their way.

13 And they send unto him certain of the Pharisees and of the Herodians, to catch
14 him in his words. And when they were come, they say unto him, Master, we know that thou art true, and carest for no man: for thou regardest not the person of men, but teachest the way of God in truth: Is it lawful to give
15 tribute to Cæsar, or not? Shall we give, or shall we not give? But he, knowing their hypocrisy, said unto them, Why tempt ye me? Bring me a penny, that
16 I may see it. And they brought it. And he saith unto them, Whose is this image and superscription? And they said unto
17 him, Cæsar's. And Jesus answering, said unto them, Render to Cæsar the things that are Cæsar's, and to God the things that are God's. And they marvelled at him.

18 Then come unto him the Sadducees, which say there is no resurrection; and
19 they asked him, saying, Master, Moses wrote unto us, If a man's brother die, and leave his wife behind him, and leave no children, that his brother should take his wife, and raise up seed unto his brother.
20 Now there were seven brethren: and the first took a wife, and dying left no seed.
21 And the second took her, and died, neither left he any seed: and the third likewise.
22 And the seven had her, and left no seed:
23 last of all the woman died also. In the resurrection, therefore, when they shall rise, whose wife shall she be of them? for
24 the seven had her to wife. And Jesus answering, said unto them, Do ye not therefore err, because ye know not the scriptures, neither the power of God?
25 For when they shall rise from the dead, they neither marry, nor are given in marriage; but are as the angels which
26 are in heaven. And as touching the dead, that they rise: have ye not read in the book of Moses, how in the bush God spake unto him, saying, I am the God of Abraham, and the God of Isaac,
27 and the God of Jacob? He is not the God of the dead, but the God of the living: ye therefore do greatly err.

28 And one of the scribes came, and having heard them reasoning together, and perceiving that he had answered them well, asked him, Which is the
29 first commandment of all? And Jesus answered him, The first of all the com-

mandments is, Hear, O Israel; The Lord
30 our God is one Lord; and thou shalt love the Lord thy God with all thy heart, and with all thy soul, and with all thy mind, and with all thy strength: this is the first
31 commandment. And the second is like, namely this, Thou shalt love thy neighbour as thyself. There is none other com-
32 mandment greater than these. And the scribe said unto him, Well, Master, thou hast said the truth: for there is one God;
33 and there is none other but he: and to love him with all the heart, and with all the understanding, and with all the soul, and with all the strength, and to love his neighbour as himself, is more than all whole burnt-offerings and sacrifices.
34 And when Jesus saw that he answered discreetly, he said unto him, Thou art not far from the kingdom of God. And no man after that durst ask him any question.
35 And Jesus answered and said, while he taught in the temple, How say the scribes
36 that Christ is the son of David? For David himself said by the Holy Ghost,
The LORD said to my Lord,
Sit thou on my right hand,
Till I make thine enemies thy footstool.
37 David therefore himself calleth him Lord; and whence is he then his son? And the common people heard him gladly.
38 And he said unto them in his doctrine, Beware of the scribes, which love to go in long clothing, and love salutations in the
39 market-places, and the chief seats in the synagogues, and the uppermost rooms at
40 feasts: which devour widows' houses, and for a pretence make long prayers: these shall receive greater damnation.
41 *And Jesus sat over against the treasury, and beheld how the people cast money into the treasury: and many*
42 *that were rich cast in much. And there came a certain poor widow, and she threw in two mites, which make a farth-*
43 *ing. And he called unto him his disciples, and saith unto them, Verily I say unto you, That this poor widow hath cast more in, than all they which have cast*
44 *into the treasury: for all they did cast in of their abundance; but she of her want did cast in all that she had, even all her living.*

13 *And as he went out of the temple, one of his disciples saith unto him, Master, see what manner of stones and what*
2 *buildings are here! And Jesus answering, said unto him, Seest thou these great buildings? there shall not be left one stone upon another, that shall not be thrown down.*
3 *And as he sat upon the mount of Olives over against the temple, Peter, and James, and John, and Andrew, asked*
4 *him privately, Tell us, when shall these*

things be? and what shall be the sign when all these things shall be fulfilled?
5 And Jesus answering them, began to say, Take heed lest any man deceive you:
6 for many shall come in my name, saying, I am Christ; and shall deceive many.
7 And when ye shall hear of wars and rumours of wars, be ye not troubled: for such things must needs be; but the
8 end shall not be yet. For nation shall rise against nation, and kingdom against kingdom: and there shall be earthquakes in divers places, and there shall be famines and troubles: these are the beginnings of sorrows.
9 [But take heed to yourselves: for they Cf. Matt. shall deliver you up to councils; and in x. 17-22 the synagogues ye shall be beaten: and ye shall be brought before rulers and kings for my sake, for a testimony against
10 them. And the gospel must first be pub-
11 lished among all nations. But when they shall lead you, and deliver you up, take no thought beforehand what ye shall speak, neither do ye premeditate: but whatsoever shall be given you in that hour, that speak ye: for it is not ye that
12 speak, but the Holy Ghost. Now the brother shall betray the brother to death, and the father the son; and children shall rise up against their parents, and shall cause them to be put to death.
13 And ye shall be hated of all men for my name's sake: but he that shall endure unto the end, the same shall be saved.]
14 *But when ye shall see the abomination of desolation, spoken of by Daniel the prophet, standing where it ought not, (let him that readeth understand,) then let them that be in Judea flee to the moun-*
15 *tains: and let him that is on the housetop not go down into the house, neither enter therein, to take any thing out of his house:*
16 *and let him that is in the field not turn back again for to take up his garment.*
17 *But woe to them that are with child, and to them that give suck in those days!*
18 *And pray ye that your flight be not in*
19 *the winter. For in those days shall be affliction, such as was not from the beginning of the creation which God created*
20 *unto this time, neither shall be. And except that the Lord had shortened those days, no flesh should be saved: but for the elect's sake, whom he hath chosen, he*
21 *hath shortened the days.* And then if any man shall say to you, Lo, here is Christ; or, lo, he is there; believe him
22 not: for false Christs and false prophets shall rise, and shall shew signs and wonders, to seduce, if it were possible, even
23 the elect. But take ye heed: behold, I have foretold you all things.
24 *But in those days, after that tribulation, the sun shall be darkened, and the*
25 *moon shall not give her light, and the*

stars *of heaven shall fall, and the powers* that *are in heaven shall be shaken. And then shall they see the Son of man coming in the clouds with great power and glory.*

27 *And then shall he send his angels, and shall gather together his elect from the four winds, from the uttermost part of the earth to the uttermost part of heaven.*

28 Now learn a parable of the fig-tree; When her branch is yet tender, and putteth forth leaves, ye know that sum-

29 mer is near: so ye in like manner, when ye shall see these things come to pass, know that it is nigh, even at the doors.

30 *Verily I say unto you, that this generation shall not pass, till all these things*

31 *be done. Heaven and earth shall pass away: but my words shall not pass away.*

32 *But of that day and that hour knoweth no man, no, not the angels which are in heaven, neither the Son, but the Father.*

33 Take ye heed, watch and pray: for ye

34 know not when the time is. For the Son of man is as a man taking a far journey, who left his house, and gave authority to his servants, and to every man his work, and commanded the

35 porter to watch. Watch ye therefore: for ye know not when the master of the house cometh, at even, or at midnight, or at the cock-crowing, or in the morn-

36 ing: lest coming suddenly he find you

37 sleeping. And what I say unto you I say unto all, Watch.

14 *After two days was the feast of the passover, and of unleavened bread:* and the chief priests and the scribes sought how they might take him by craft, and

2 put him to death. But they said, Not on the feast-day, lest there be an uproar of the people.

3 *And being in Bethany in the house of Simon the leper, as he sat at meat, there came a woman having an alabaster-box of ointment of spikenard very precious; and she brake the box, and poured it on*

4 *his head.* And there were some that had indignation within themselves, and said, Why was this waste of the ointment made?

5 *For it might have been sold for more than three hundred pence, and have been given to the poor.* And they murmured against

6 her. *And Jesus said, Let her alone; why trouble ye her? she hath wrought a good*

7 *work on me. For ye have the poor with you always, and whensoever ye will ye may do them good: but me ye have not*

8 *always. She hath done what she could: she is come aforehand to anoint my body*

9 *to the burying. Verily I say unto you, Wheresoever this gospel shall be preached throughout the whole world, this also that she hath done shall be spoken of for a memorial of her.*

10 And Judas Iscariot, one of the twelve, went unto the chief priests, to betray

11 him unto them. And when they heard it, they were glad, and promised to give him money. And he sought how he might conveniently betray him.

12 And the first day of unleavened bread, when they killed the passover, his disciples said unto him, Where wilt thou that we go and prepare that thou mayest

13 eat the passover? And he sendeth forth two of his disciples, and saith unto them, Go ye into the city, and there shall meet you a man bearing a pitcher of water:

14 follow him. And wheresoever he shall go in, say ye to the goodman of the house, The Master saith, Where is the guest-chamber, where I shall eat the passover

15 with my disciples? And he will shew you a large upper room furnished and

16 prepared: there make ready for us. And his disciples went forth, and came into the city, and found as he had said unto them: and they made ready the passover.

17 And in the evening he cometh with the

18 twelve. And as they sat and did eat, Jesus said, Verily I say unto you, One of you which eateth with me shall betray

19 me. And they began to be sorrowful, and to say unto him one by one, Is it I?

20 and another said, Is it I? And he answered and said unto them, It is one of the twelve, that dippeth with me in

21 the dish. The Son of man indeed goeth, as it is written of him: but woe to that man by whom the Son of man is betrayed! good were it for that man if he had never been born.

22 And as they did eat, Jesus took bread, and blessed, and brake it, and gave to them, and said, Take, eat: this is my

23 body. And he took the cup, and when he had given thanks, he gave it to them:

24 and they all drank of it. And he said unto them, This is my blood of the new testament, which is shed for many.

25 Verily I say unto you, I will drink no more of the fruit of the vine, until that day that I drink it new in the kingdom of God.

26 And when they had sung an hymn, they went out into the Mount of Olives.

27 And Jesus saith unto them, All ye shall be offended because of me this night: for it is written, I will smite the Shepherd,

28 and the sheep shall be scattered. But after that I am risen, I will go before

29 you into Galilee. But Peter said unto him, Although all shall be offended, yet

30 will not I. And Jesus saith unto him, Verily I say unto thee, that this day, even in this night, before the cock crow

31 twice, thou shalt deny me thrice. But he spake the more vehemently, If I should die with thee, I will not deny thee in any wise. Likewise also said they all.

32 *And they came to a place which was*

named Gethsemane; and he saith to his disciples, Sit ye here, while I shall pray.
33 *And he taketh with him Peter, and James, and John, and began to be sore*
34 *amazed, and to be very heavy; and saith unto them, My soul is exceeding sorrowful unto death: tarry ye here, and*
35 *watch. And he went forward a little, and fell on the ground, and prayed that, if it were possible, the hour might pass from*
36 *him. And he said, Abba, Father, all things are possible unto thee; take away this cup from me: nevertheless not what*
37 *I will, but what thou wilt. And he cometh, and findeth them sleeping, and saith unto Peter, Simon, sleepest thou?*
38 *couldst not thou watch one hour? Watch ye and pray, lest ye enter into temptation. The spirit truly is ready, but the*
39 *flesh is weak. And again he went away, and prayed, and spake the same words.*
40 *And when he returned, he found them asleep again, (for their eyes were heavy,) neither wist they what to answer him.*
41 *And he cometh the third time, and saith unto them, Sleep on now, and take your rest: it is enough, the hour is come; behold, the Son of man is betrayed into the*
42 *hands of sinners. Rise up, let us go; lo, he that betrayeth me is at hand.*

43 And immediately, while he yet spake, cometh Judas, one of the twelve, and with him a great multitude with swords and staves, from the chief priests, and
44 the scribes, and the elders. *And he that betrayed him had given them a token, saying, Whomsoever I shall kiss, that same is he; take him, and lead him away*
45 *safely.* And as soon as he was come, he goeth straightway to him, and saith, Mas-
46 ter, master; and kissed him. And they laid their hands on him, and took him.
47 *And one of them that stood by drew a sword, and smote a servant of the high*
48 *priest, and cut off his ear.* And Jesus answered and said unto them, Are ye come out, as against a thief, with swords
49 and with staves to take me? I was daily with you in the temple teaching, and ye took me not: but the scriptures must be
50 fulfilled. And they all forsook him, and fled.

51 And there followed him a certain young man, having a linen cloth cast about his naked body; and the young men laid hold
52 on him: and he left the linen cloth, and fled from them naked.

53 And they led Jesus away to the high priest: and with him were assembled all the chief priests, and the elders, and
54 the scribes. And Peter followed him afar off, even into the palace of the high priest: and he sat with the servants, and
55 warmed himself at the fire. And the chief priests and all the council sought for witness against Jesus to put him to
56 death; and found none. For many bare false witness against him, but their wit-
57 ness agreed not together. And there arose certain, and bare false witness
58 against him, saying, We heard him say, I will destroy this temple that is made with hands, and within three days I will
59 build another made without hands. But neither so did their witness agree to-
60 gether. And the high priest stood up in the midst, and asked Jesus, saying, Answerest thou nothing? what is it
61 which these witness against thee? But he held his peace, and answered nothing. Again the high priest asked him, and said unto him, Art thou the Christ, the Son
62 of the Blessed? And Jesus said, I am: and ye shall see the Son of man sitting on the right hand of power, and coming
63 in the clouds of heaven. Then the high priest rent his clothes, and saith, What
64 need we any further witnesses? Ye have heard the blasphemy: what think ye? And they all condemned him to be guilty
65 of death. And some began to spit on him, and to cover his face, and to buffet him, and to say unto him, Prophesy: and the servants did strike him with the palms of their hands.

66 And as Peter was beneath in the palace,
67 there cometh one of the maids of the high priest: and when she saw Peter warming himself, she looked upon him, and said, And thou also wast with Jesus
68 of Nazareth. But he denied, saying, I know not, neither understand I what thou sayest. And he went out into the
69 porch; and the cock crew. And a maid saw him again, and began to say to them
70 that stood by, This is one of them. And he denied it again. And a little after, they that stood by said again to Peter, Surely thou art one of them: for thou art a Galilean, and thy speech agreeth
71 thereto. But he began to curse and to swear, saying, I know not this man of
72 whom ye speak. And the second time the cock crew. And Peter called to mind the word that Jesus said unto him, Before the cock crow twice, thou shalt deny me thrice. And when he thought thereon, he wept.

15 *And straightway in the morning the chief priests held a consultation with the elders, and scribes, and the whole council, and bound Jesus, and carried him away, and delivered him to Pilate.*
2 *And Pilate asked him, Art thou the king of the Jews? And he answering, said*
3 *unto him, Thou sayest it.* And the chief priests accused him of many things: but
4 he answered nothing. And Pilate asked him again, saying, Answerest thou nothing? behold how many things they wit-
5 ness against thee. But Jesus yet answered nothing; so that Pilate marvelled.

S. MARK.

6 Now at that feast he released unto them one prisoner, whomsoever they
7 desired. And there was one named Barabbas, which lay bound with them that had made insurrection with him, who had committed murder in the in-
8 surrection. And the multitude crying aloud began to desire him to do as he
9 had ever done unto them. But Pilate answered them, saying, Will ye that I release unto you the King of the Jews?
10 For he knew that the chief priests had
11 delivered him for envy. But the chief priests moved the people, that he should
12 rather release Barabbas unto them. And Pilate answered and said again unto them, What will ye then that I shall do unto him whom ye call the King of the
13 Jews? And they cried out again, Crucify
14 him. Then Pilate said unto them, Why, what evil hath he done? And they cried out the more exceedingly, Crucify him.
15 And so Pilate, willing to content the people, released Barabbas unto them, and delivered Jesus, *when he had scourged him, to be crucified.*
16 *And the soldiers led him away into the hall, called Pretorium; and they call*
17 *together the whole band. And they clothed him with purple, and platted a crown of thorns, and put it about his*
18 *head, and began to salute him, Hail,*
19 *King of the Jews! And they smote him on the head with a reed, and did spit upon him, and bowing their knees wor-*
20 *shipped him. And when they had mocked him, they took off the purple from him, and put his own clothes on him, and led him out to crucify him.*
21 And they compel one Simon a Cyrenian, who passed by, coming out of the country, the father of Alexander and
22 Rufus, to bear his cross. And they bring him unto the place Golgotha, which is being interpreted, The place of a scull.
23 And they gave him to drink wine mingled with myrrh: but he received it not.
24 *And when they had crucified him, they parted his garments, casting lots upon*
25 *them, what every man should take.* And it was the third hour, and they crucified
26 him. *And the superscription of his accusation was written over, the King*
27 *of the Jews. And with him they crucify two thieves; the one on his right hand,*
28 *and the other on his left. And the scripture was fulfilled which saith, And he was numbered with the transgressors.*
29 And they that passed by railed on him, wagging their heads, and saying, Ah, thou that destroyest the temple, and
30 buildest it in three days, save thyself,
31 and come down from the cross. Likewise also the chief priests, mocking, said among themselves with the scribes, He saved others; himself he cannot save.
32 Let Christ the King of Israel descend now from the cross, that we may see and believe. *And they that were crucified with him reviled him.*
33 And when the sixth hour was come, there was darkness over the whole land
34 *until the ninth hour.* And at the ninth hour Jesus cried with a loud voice, saying, Eloi, Eloi, lama sabachthani? which is, being interpreted, My God, my God,
35 why hast thou forsaken me? And some of them that stood by, when they heard
36 it, said, Behold, he calleth Elias. *And one ran and filled a spunge full of vinegar, and put it on a reed, and gave him to drink,* saying, Let alone; let us see whether Elias will come to take him
37 down. *And Jesus cried with a loud*
38 *voice, and gave up the ghost. And the veil of the temple was rent in twain from*
39 *the top to the bottom.* And when the centurion, which stood over against him, saw that he so cried out, and gave up the ghost, he said, Truly this man was
40 the Son of God. There were also women looking on afar off: among whom was Mary Magdalene, and Mary the mother of James the less and of Joses, and Sa-
41 lome; (who also, when he was in Galilee, followed him, and ministered unto him;) and many other women which came up with him unto Jerusalem.
42 And now when the even was come, because it was the preparation, that is,
43 the day before the sabbath, Joseph of Arimathea, an honourable counsellor, which also waited for the kingdom of God, came, and went in boldly unto Pilate,
44 and craved the body of Jesus. And Pilate marvelled if he were already dead: and calling unto him the centurion, he asked him whether he had been any while dead.
45 And when he knew it of the centurion,
46 he gave the body to Joseph. And he bought *fine linen,* and took him down, and wrapped him in *the linen,* and laid him in a sepulchre which was hewn out of a rock, and rolled a stone unto the
47 door of the sepulchre. And Mary Magdalene and Mary the mother of Joses beheld where he was laid.

16 And when the sabbath was past, Mary Magdalene, and Mary the mother of James, and Salome, had bought sweet spices, that they might come and anoint
2 him. And very early in the morning the first day of the week, they came unto the sepulchre at the rising of the sun.
3 And they said among themselves, Who shall roll us away the stone from the door
4 of the sepulchre? And when they looked, they saw that the stone was rolled away:
5 for it was very great. And entering into the sepulchre, they saw a young man sitting on the right side, clothed in a long white garment; and they were

6 affrighted. And he saith unto them, Be not affrighted: Ye seek Jesus of Nazareth, which was crucified: he is risen; he is not here: behold the place where
7 they laid him. But go your way, tell his disciples and Peter that he goeth before you into Galilee: there shall ye
8 see him, as he said unto you. And they went out quickly, and fled from the sepulchre; for they trembled and were amazed: neither said they any thing to any man; for they were afraid.

*The two oldest manuscripts and some other authorities omit ties omit from ver. 9 to the end.

9 *Now when Jesus was risen early the first day of the week, he appeared first to Mary Magdalene, out of whom he had
10 cast seven devils. And she went and told them that had been with him, as
11 they mourned and wept. And they, when they had heard that he was alive, and had been seen of her, believed not.
12 After that he appeared in another form unto two of them, as they walked, and
13 went into the country. And they went and told it unto the residue: neither believed they them.
14 Afterward he appeared unto the eleven as they sat at meat, and upbraided them with their unbelief and hardness of heart, because they believed not them which
15 had seen him after he was risen. And he said unto them, Go ye into all the world, and preach the gospel to every
16 creature. He that believeth and is baptized shall be saved; but he that be-
17 lieveth not shall be damned. And these signs shall follow them that believe; In my name shall they cast out devils; they
18 shall speak with new tongues; they shall take up serpents; and if they drink any deadly thing, it shall not hurt them; they shall lay hands on the sick, and they shall recover.
19 So then after the Lord had spoken unto them, he was received up into heaven, and sat on the right hand of
20 God. And they went forth, and preached every where, the Lord working with them, and confirming the word with signs following. Amen.

THE GOSPEL ACCORDING TO

S. LUKE.

1 FORASMUCH as many have taken in hand to set forth in order a declaration of those things which are most surely
2 believed among us, even as they delivered them unto us, which from the beginning were eye-witnesses, and ministers of the
3 word; it seemed good to me also, having had perfect understanding of all things from the very first, to write unto thee in
4 order, most excellent Theophilus, that thou mightest know the certainty of those things, wherein thou hast been instructed.

5 THERE was in the days of Herod, the king of Judea, a certain priest named Zacharias, of the course of Abia: and his wife was of the daughters of Aaron,
6 and her name was Elisabeth. And they were both righteous before God, walking in all the commandments and ordi-
7 nances of the Lord blameless. And they had no child, because that Elisabeth was barren, and they both were now well stricken in years.
8 And it came to pass, that while he executed the priest's office before God
9 in the order of his course, according to the custom of the priest's office, his lot was to burn incense when he went
10 into the temple of the Lord. And the whole multitude of the people were praying without at the time of incense.
11 And there appeared unto him an angel of the Lord standing on the right side
12 of the altar of incense. And when Zacharias saw him, he was troubled,
13 and fear fell upon him. But the angel said unto him, Fear not, Zacharias: for thy prayer is heard; and thy wife Elisabeth shall bear thee a son, and thou
14 shalt call his name John. And thou shalt have joy and gladness; and many
15 shall rejoice at his birth. For he shall be great in the sight of the Lord, and shall drink neither wine nor strong drink; and he shall be filled with the Holy Ghost, even from his mother's
16 womb. And many of the children of Israel shall he turn to the Lord their
17 God. And he shall go before him in the spirit and power of Elias, to turn the hearts of the fathers to the children, and the disobedient to the wisdom of the

just; to make ready a people prepared for the Lord.
18 And Zacharias said unto the angel, Whereby shall I know this? for I am an old man, and my wife well
19 stricken in years. And the angel answering, said unto him, I am Gabriel, that stand in the presence of God ; and am sent to speak unto thee, and to shew
20 thee these glad tidings. And, behold, thou shalt be dumb, and not able to speak, until the day that these things shall be performed, because thou believest not my words, which shall be fulfilled in
21 their season. And the people waited for Zacharias, and marvelled that he tarried
22 so long in the temple. And when he came out, he could not speak unto them : and they perceived that he had seen a vision in the temple : for he beckoned unto them, and remained speechless.
23 And it came to pass, that, as soon as the days of his ministration were accomplished, he departed to his own house.
24 And after those days his wife Elisabeth conceived, and hid herself five months,
25 saying, Thus hath the Lord dealt with me in the days wherein he looked on me, to take away my reproach among men.
26 And in the sixth month the angel Gabriel was sent from God unto a city
27 of Galilee, named Nazareth, to a virgin espoused to a man whose name was Joseph, of the house of David ; and the
28 virgin's name was Mary. And the angel came in unto her, and said, Hail, thou that art highly favoured, the Lord is with thee: blessed art thou among women.
29 And when she saw him, she was troubled at his saying, and cast in her mind what manner of salutation this should be.
30 And the angel said unto her, Fear not, Mary: for thou hast found favour with
31 God. And, behold, thou shalt conceive in thy womb, and bring forth a son, and
32 shalt call his name JESUS. He shall be great, and shall be called the Son of the Highest: and the Lord God shall give unto him the throne of his father David:
33 and he shall reign over the house of Jacob for ever; and of his kingdom
34 there shall be no end. Then said Mary unto the angel, How shall this be, see-
35 ing I know not a man? And the angel answered and said unto her, The Holy Ghost shall come upon thee, and the power of the Highest shall overshadow thee: therefore also that holy thing which shall be born of thee shall be
36 called The Son of God. And, behold, thy cousin Elisabeth, she hath also conceived a son in her old age : and this is the sixth month with her, who was called
37 barren. For with God nothing shall be
38 impossible. And Mary said, Behold the handmaid of the Lord ; be it unto me according to thy word. And the angel departed from her.
39 And Mary arose in those days, and went into the hill country with haste,
40 into a city of Juda ; and entered into the house of Zacharias, and saluted
41 Elisabeth. And it came to pass, that, when Elisabeth heard the salutation of Mary, the babe leaped in her womb ; and Elisabeth was filled with the Holy
42 Ghost : and she spake out with a loud voice, and said, Blessed art thou among women, and blessed is the fruit of thy
43 womb. And whence is this to me, that the mother of my Lord should come to
44 me? For, lo, as soon as the voice of thy salutation sounded in mine ears, the
45 babe leaped in my womb for joy. And blessed is she that believed : for there shall be a performance of those things which were told her from the Lord.
46 And Mary said,
My soul doth magnify the Lord,
47 And my spirit hath rejoiced in God my Saviour.
48 For he hath regarded the low estate of his handmaiden :
For, behold, from henceforth all generations shall call me blessed.
49 For he that is mighty hath done to me great things ;
And holy is his name.
50 And his mercy is on them that fear him from generation to generation.
51 He hath shewed strength with his arm ;
He hath scattered the proud in the imagination of their hearts.
52 He hath put down the mighty from their seats,
And exalted them of low degree.
53 He hath filled the hungry with good things ;
And the rich he hath sent empty away.
54 He hath holpen his servant Israel,
In remembrance of his mercy ;
55 As he spake to our fathers,
To Abraham, and to his seed for ever.
56 And Mary abode with her about three months, and returned to her own house.
57 Now Elisabeth's full time came that she should be delivered; and she brought
58 forth a son. And her neighbours and her cousins heard how the Lord had shewed great mercy upon her; and they
59 rejoiced with her. And it came to pass, that on the eighth day they came to circumcise the child ; and they called him Zacharias, after the name of his father.
60 And his mother answered and said, Not
61 so ; but he shall be called John. And they said unto her, There is none of thy kindred that is called by this name.
62 And they made signs to his father, how
63 he would have him called. And he

O

S. LUKE.

asked for a writing-table, and wrote, saying, His name is John. And they
64 marvelled all. And his mouth was opened immediately, and his tongue loosed, and he spake, and praised God.
65 And fear came on all that dwelt round about them: and all these sayings were noised abroad throughout all the hill
66 country of Judea. And all they that heard them laid them up in their hearts, saying, What manner of child shall this be! And the hand of the Lord was with him.
67 And his father Zacharias was filled with the Holy Ghost, and prophesied, saying,
68 Blessed be the Lord God of Israel;
For he hath visited and redeemed his people,
69 And hath raised up an horn of salvation for us
In the house of his servant David;
70 As he spake by the mouth of his holy prophets, which have been since the world began:
71 That we should be saved from our enemies, and from the hand of all that hate us;
72 To perform the mercy promised to our fathers,
And to remember his holy covenant;
73 The oath which he sware to our father Abraham,
74 That he would grant unto us, that we being delivered out of the hand of our enemies
Might serve him without fear,
75 In holiness and righteousness before him, all the days of our life.
76 And thou, child, shalt be called the Prophet of the Highest:
For thou shalt go before the face of the Lord to prepare his ways;
77 To give knowledge of salvation unto his people
By the remission of their sins,
78 Through the tender mercy of our God;
Whereby the day-spring from on high hath visited us,
79 To give light to them that sit in darkness and in the shadow of death,
To guide our feet into the way of peace.
80 And the child grew, and waxed strong in spirit, and was in the deserts till the day of his shewing unto Israel.

2 And it came to pass in those days, that there went out a decree from Cæsar Augustus, that all the world should be
2 taxed. (And this taxing was first made when Cyrenius was governor of Syria.)
3 And all went to be taxed, every one into
4 his own city. And Joseph also went up from Galilee, out of the city of Nazareth, into Judea, unto the city of David, which is called Bethlehem; (because he was
5 of the house and lineage of David:) to be taxed with Mary his espoused wife,
6 being great with child. And so it was, that, while they were there, the days were accomplished that she should be
7 delivered. And she brought forth her first-born son, and wrapped him in swaddling-clothes, and laid him in a manger; because there was no room for them in the inn.
8 And there were in the same country shepherds abiding in the field, keeping
9 watch over their flock by night. And, lo, the angel of the Lord came upon them, and the glory of the Lord shone round about them: and they were sore
10 afraid. And the angel said unto them, Fear not: for, behold, I bring you good tidings of great joy, which shall be to all
11 people. For unto you is born this day in the city of David, a Saviour, which is
12 Christ the Lord. And this shall be a sign unto you; Ye shall find the babe wrapped in swaddling clothes, lying in a
13 manger. And suddenly there was with the angel a multitude of the heavenly host praising God, and saying,
14 Glory to God in the highest,
And on earth peace, good will toward men.
15 And it came to pass, as the angels were gone away from them into heaven, the shepherds said one to another, Let us now go even unto Bethlehem, and see this thing which is come to pass, which the Lord hath made known unto us.
16 And they came with haste, and found Mary, and Joseph, and the babe lying in
17 a manger. And when they had seen it, they made known abroad the saying which was told them concerning this
18 child. And all they that heard it wondered at those things which were told
19 them by the shepherds. But Mary kept all these things, and pondered them in
20 her heart. And the shepherds returned, glorifying and praising God for all the things that they had heard and seen, as it was told unto them.
21 And when eight days were accomplished for the circumcising of the child, his name was called JESUS, which was so named of the angel before he was conceived in the womb.
22 And when the days of her purification according to the law of Moses were accomplished, they brought him to Jeru-
23 salem, to present him to the Lord: (as it is written in the law of the Lord, Every male that openeth the womb shall
24 be called holy to the Lord;) and to offer a sacrifice according to that which is said in the law of the Lord, A pair of turtle-
25 doves, or two young pigeons. And, behold, there was a man in Jerusalem, whose name was Simeon; and the same

S. LUKE.

man was just and devout, waiting for the consolation of Israel: and the Holy Ghost
26 was upon him. And it was revealed unto him by the Holy Ghost, that he should not see death, before he had seen the
27 Lord's Christ. And he came by the Spirit into the temple: and when the parents brought in the child Jesus, to do for him
28 after the custom of the law, then took he him up in his arms, and blessed God, and said,
29 Lord, now lettest thou thy servant depart in peace,
According to thy word:
30 For mine eyes have seen thy salvation,
31 Which thou hast prepared before the face of all people;
32 A light to lighten the Gentiles,
And the glory of thy people Israel.
33 And Joseph and his mother marvelled at those things which were spoken of him.
34 And Simeon blessed them, and said unto Mary his mother, Behold, this child is set for the fall and rising again of many in Israel; and for a sign which shall be
35 spoken against; (yea, a sword shall pierce through thy own soul also,) that the thoughts of many hearts may be revealed.
36 And there was one Anna, a prophetess, the daughter of Phanuel, of the tribe of Aser: she was of a great age, and had lived with an husband seven years from
37 her virginity; and she was a widow of about fourscore and four years, which departed not from the temple, but served God with fastings and prayers night and
38 day. And she coming in that instant gave thanks likewise unto the Lord, and spake of him to all them that looked for
39 redemption in Jerusalem. And when they had performed all things according to the law of the Lord, they returned into Galilee, to their own city Nazareth.
40 And the child grew, and waxed strong in spirit, filled with wisdom: and the grace of God was upon him.
41 Now his parents went to Jerusalem every year, at the feast of the passover.
42 And when he was twelve years old, they went up to Jerusalem after the custom
43 of the feast. And when they had fulfilled the days, as they returned, the child Jesus tarried behind in Jerusalem; and Joseph and his mother knew not of
44 it. But they, supposing him to have been in the company, went a day's journey; and they sought him among their
45 kinsfolk and acquaintance. And when they found him not, they turned back
46 again to Jerusalem, seeking him. And it came to pass, that after three days they found him in the temple, sitting in the midst of the doctors, both hearing
47 them, and asking them questions. And all that heard him were astonished at
48 his understanding and answers. And

when they saw him, they were amazed: and his mother said unto him, Son, why hast thou thus dealt with us? behold, thy father and I have sought thee sor-
49 rowing. And he said unto them, How is it that ye sought me? wist ye not that I must be about my Father's business?
50 And they understood not the saying
51 which he spake unto them. And he went down with them, and came to Nazareth, and was subject unto them: but his mother kept all these sayings in her heart.
52 And Jesus increased in wisdom and stature, and in favour with God and man.

3 Now in the fifteenth year of the reign of Tiberius Cæsar, Pontius Pilate being governor of Judea, and Herod being tetrarch of Galilee, and his brother Philip tetrarch of Iturea and of the region of Trachonitis, and Lysanias the
2 tetrarch of Abilene, Annas and Caiaphas being the high priests, the word of God came unto John the son of Zacharias in
3 the wilderness. And he came into all the country about Jordan, preaching the baptism of repentance for the remission
4 of sins; as it is written in the book of the words of Esaias the prophet, saying, The voice of one crying in the wilderness,
Prepare ye the way of the Lord,
Make his paths straight.
5 Every valley shall be filled,
And every mountain and hill shall be brought low;
And the crooked shall be made straight,
And the rough ways shall be made smooth;
6 And all flesh shall see the salvation of God.
7 Then said he to the multitude that came forth to be baptized of him, O generation of vipers, who hath warned you to flee
8 from the wrath to come? Bring forth therefore fruits worthy of repentance, and begin not to say within yourselves, We have Abraham to our father: for I say unto you, That God is able of these stones to raise up children unto Abra-
9 ham. And now also the axe is laid unto the root of the trees: every tree therefore which bringeth not forth good fruit is hewn down, and cast into the fire.
10 And the people asked him, saying, What
11 shall we do then? He answereth and saith unto them, He that hath two coats, let him impart to him that hath none; and he that hath meat, let him do like-
12 wise. Then came also publicans to be baptized, and said unto him, Master,
13 what shall we do? And he said unto them, Exact no more than that which is
14 appointed you. And the soldiers like-

S. LUKE.

wise demanded of him, saying, And what shall we do? And he said unto them, Do violence to no man, neither accuse any falsely; and be content with your wages.

15 And as the people were in expectation, and all men mused in their hearts of John, whether he were the Christ, or
16 not; John answered, saying unto them all, I indeed baptize you with water; but one mightier than I cometh, the latchet of whose shoes I am not worthy to unloose: he shall baptize you with the
17 Holy Ghost and with fire: whose fan is in his hand, and he will throughly purge his floor, and will gather the wheat into his garner; but the chaff he will burn with fire unquenchable.
18 And many other things in his exhorta-
19 tion preached he unto the people. But Herod the tetrarch, being reproved by him for Herodias his brother Philip's wife, and for all the evils which Herod
20 had done, added yet this above all, that he shut up John in prison.
21 Now when all the people were baptized, it came to pass, that Jesus also being baptized, and praying, the heaven
22 was opened, and the Holy Ghost descended in a bodily shape like a dove upon him, and a voice came from heaven, which said, Thou art my beloved Son; in thee I am well pleased.
23 And Jesus himself began to be about thirty years of age, being (as was supposed) the son of Joseph, which was
24 the son of Heli, which was the son of Matthat, which was the son of Levi, which was the son of Melchi, which was the son of Janna, which was the son of
25 Joseph, which was the son of Mattathias, which was the son of Amos, which was the son of Naum, which was the son of
26 Esli, which was the son of Nagge, which was the son of Maath, which was the son of Mattathias, which was the son of Semei, which was the son of Joseph,
27 which was the son of Juda, which was the son of Joanna, which was the son of Rhesa, which was the son of Zorobabel, which was the son of Salathiel, which
28 was the son of Neri, which was the son of Melchi, which was the son of Addi, which was the son of Cosam, which was the son of Elmodam, which was the son
29 of Er, which was the son of Jose, which was the son of Eliezer, which was the son of Jorim, which was the son of Matthat, which was the son of Levi,
30 which was the son of Simeon, which was the son of Juda, which was the son of Joseph, which was the son of Jonan, which was the son of Eliakim,
31 which was the son of Melea, which was the son of Menan, which was the son of Mattatha, which was the son of

Nathan, which was the son of David,
32 which was the son of Jesse, which was the son of Obed, which was the son of Booz, which was the son of Salmon,
33 which was the son of Naasson, which was the son of Aminadab, which was the son of Aram, which was the son of Esrom, which was the son of Phares,
34 which was the son of Juda, which was the son of Jacob, which was the son of Isaac, which was the son of Abraham, which was the son of Thara, which was
35 the son of Nachor, which was the son of Saruch, which was the son of Ragau, which was the son of Phalec, which was the son of Heber, which was the son of
36 Sala, which was the son of Cainan, which was the son of Arphaxad, which was the son of Sem, which was the son of Noe,
37 which was the son of Lamech, which was the son of Mathusala, which was the son of Enoch, which was the son of Jared, which was the son of Maleleel,
38 which was the son of Cainan, which was the son of Enos, which was the son of Seth, which was the son of Adam, which was the son of God.

4 And Jesus being full of the Holy Ghost returned from Jordan, and was led by
2 the Spirit into the wilderness, being forty days tempted of the devil. And in those days he did eat nothing: and when they were ended, he afterward hungered.
3 And the devil said unto him, If thou be the Son of God, command this stone that
4 it be made bread. And Jesus answered him, saying, It is written, That man shall not live by bread alone, but by
5 every word of God. And the devil, taking him up into an high mountain, shewed unto him all the kingdoms of
6 the world in a moment of time. And the devil said unto him, All this power will I give thee, and the glory of them: for that is delivered unto me; and to
7 whomsoever I will I give it. If thou therefore wilt worship me, all shall be
8 thine. And Jesus answered and said unto him, Get thee behind me, Satan: for it is written, Thou shalt worship the Lord thy God, and him only shalt thou
9 serve. And he brought him to Jerusalem, and set him on a pinnacle of the temple, and said unto him, If thou be the Son of God, cast thyself down from
10 hence: for it is written,
He shall give his angels charge over thee, to keep thee:
11 and
In their hands they shall bear thee up, Lest at any time thou dash thy foot against a stone.
12 And Jesus answering, said unto him, It is said, Thou shalt not tempt the Lord thy God.
13 [And when the devil had ended all the

temptation,] he departed from him for a season.

14 And Jesus returned in the power of the Spirit into Galilee: and there went out a fame of him through all the region
15 round about. And he taught in their synagogues, being glorified of all.
16 And he came to Nazareth, where he had been brought up: and, as his custom was, he went into the synagogue on the sabbath-day, and stood up for to read.
17 And there was delivered unto him the book of the prophet Esaias. And when he had opened the book, he found the place where it was written,
18 The Spirit of the Lord is upon me, Because he hath anointed me to preach the gospel to the poor;
He hath sent me to heal the brokenhearted,
To preach deliverance to the captives,
And recovering of sight to the blind,
To set at liberty them that are bruised,
19 To preach the acceptable year of the Lord.
20 And he closed the book, and he gave it again to the minister, and sat down. And the eyes of all them that were in the synagogue were fastened on him.
21 And he began to say unto them, This day is this scripture fulfilled in your
22 ears. And all bare him witness, and wondered at the gracious words which proceeded out of his mouth. And they
23 said, Is not this Joseph's son? And he said unto them, Ye will surely say unto me this proverb, Physician, heal thyself: whatsoever we have heard done in Caper-
24 naum, do also here in thy country. And he said, Verily I say unto you, No prophet
25 is accepted in his own country. But I tell you of a truth, many widows were in Israel in the days of Elias, when the heaven was shut up three years and six months, when great famine was through-
26 out all the land; but unto none of them was Elias sent, save unto Sarepta, a city of Sidon, unto a woman that was a
27 widow. And many lepers were in Israel in the time of Eliseus the prophet; and none of them was cleansed,
28 saving Naaman the Syrian. And all they in the synagogue, when they heard these
29 things, were filled with wrath, and rose up, and thrust him out of the city, and led him unto the brow of the hill whereon their city was built, that they might cast
30 him down headlong. But he passing through the midst of them went his way,
31 And came down to Capernaum, a city of Galilee, and taught them on the
32 sabbath-days. And they were astonished at his doctrine: for his word was
33 with power. And in the synagogue there was a man, which had a spirit of an unclean devil, and cried out with a loud
34 voice, saying, Let us alone; what have we to do with thee, thou Jesus of Nazareth? art thou come to destroy us? I know thee who thou art; the Holy
35 One of God. And Jesus rebuked him, saying, Hold thy peace, and come out of him. And when the devil had thrown him in the midst, he came out of him,
36 and hurt him not. And they were all amazed, and spake among themselves, saying, What a word is this! for with authority and power he commandeth the unclean spirits, and they come out.
37 And the fame of him went out into every place of the country round about.
38 And he arose out of the synagogue, and entered into Simon's house. And Simon's wife's mother was taken with a great fever; and they besought him for
39 her. And he stood over her, and rebuked the fever; and it left her: and immediately she arose and ministered unto them.
40 Now when the sun was setting, all they that had any sick with divers diseases brought them unto him; and he laid his hands on every one of them, and
41 healed them. And devils also came out of many, crying out, and saying, Thou art Christ the Son of God. And he rebuking them suffered them not to speak: for they knew that he was Christ.
42 And when it was day, he departed and went into a desert place: and the people sought him, and came unto him, and stayed him, that he should not depart
43 from them. And he said unto them, I must preach the kingdom of God to other cities also: for therefore am I sent.
44 And he preached in the synagogues of Galilee.

5 And it came to pass, that, as the people pressed upon him to hear the word of God, he stood by the lake of
2 Gennesaret, and saw two ships standing by the lake: but the fishermen were gone out of them, and were washing
3 their nets. And he entered into one of the ships, which was Simon's, and prayed him that he would thrust out a little from the land. And he sat down, and taught the people out of the ship.
4 Now when he had left speaking, he said unto Simon, Launch out into the deep, and let down your nets for a draught.
5 And Simon answering, said unto him, Master, we have toiled all the night, and have taken nothing: nevertheless at thy
6 word I will let down the net. And when they had this done, they inclosed a great multitude of fishes: and their net brake.
7 And they beckoned unto their partners, which were in the other ship, that they should come and help them. And they

came, and filled both the ships, so that
8 they began to sink. When Simon Peter
saw it, he fell down at Jesus' knees,
saying, Depart from me; for I am a
9 sinful man, O Lord. For he was astonished, and all that were with him, at the
draught of the fishes which they had
10 taken : and so was also James, and John,
the sons of Zebedee, which were partners with Simon. And Jesus said unto
Simon, Fear not; from henceforth thou
11 shalt catch men. [And when they had
brought their ships to land, they forsook
all, and followed him.]
12 And it came to pass, when he was in a
certain city, behold a man full of leprosy:
who seeing Jesus fell on his face, and
besought him, saying, Lord, if thou wilt,
13 thou canst make me clean. And he put
forth his hand, and touched him, saying,
I will : be thou clean. And immediately
14 the leprosy departed from him. And he
charged him to tell no man : but go, and
shew thyself to the priest, and offer for
thy cleansing, according as Moses commanded, for a testimony unto them.
15 But so much the more went there a fame
abroad of him : and great multitudes
came together to hear, and to be healed
16 by him of their infirmities. And he
withdrew himself into the wilderness,
and prayed.
17 And it came to pass on a certain day,
as he was teaching, that there were
Pharisees and doctors of the law sitting
by, which were come out of every town
of Galilee and Judea, and Jerusalem:
and the power of the Lord was present
18 to heal them. And, behold, men brought
in a bed a man which was taken with a
palsy : and they sought means to bring
19 him in, and to lay him before him. And
when they could not find by what way
they might bring him in because of the
multitude, they went upon the housetop, and let him down through the tiling
with his couch into the midst before
20 Jesus. And when he saw their faith, he
said unto him, Man, thy sins are forgiven
21 thee. And the scribes and the Pharisees
began to reason, saying, Who is this
which speaketh blasphemies? Who can
22 forgive sins, but God alone? But when
Jesus perceived their thoughts, he answering, said unto them, What reason
23 ye in your hearts? Whether is easier to
say, Thy sins be forgiven thee; or to say,
24 Rise up and walk? But that ye may
know that the Son of man hath power
upon earth to forgive sins, (he said unto
the sick of the palsy,) I say unto thee,
Arise, and take up thy couch, and go
25 unto thine house. And immediately he
rose up before them, and took up that
whereon he lay, and departed to his own
26 house, glorifying God. And they were

all amazed, and they glorified God, and
were filled with fear, saying, We have
seen strange things to-day.
27 And after these things he went forth,
and saw a publican, named Levi, sitting
at the receipt of custom : and he said
28 unto him, Follow me. And he left all,
29 rose up, and followed him. And Levi
made him a great feast in his own house :
and there was a great company of publicans and of others that sat down with
30 them. But their scribes and Pharisees
murmured against his disciples, saying,
Why do ye eat and drink with publicans
31 and sinners? And Jesus answering, said
unto them, They that are whole need not
32 a physician ; but they that are sick. I
came not to call the righteous, but sin-
33 ners to repentance. And they said unto
him, Why do the disciples of John fast
often, and make prayers, and likewise
the disciples of the Pharisees ; but thine
34 eat and drink? And he said unto them,
Can ye make the children of the bridechamber fast, while the bridegroom is
35 with them? But the days will come,
when the bridegroom shall be taken away
from them, and then shall they fast in
36 those days. And he spake also a parable
unto them ; No man putteth a piece of
a new garment upon an old ; if otherwise, then both the new maketh a rent,
and the piece that was taken out of the
37 new agreeth not with the old. And no
man putteth new wine into old bottles ;
else the new wine will burst the bottles,
and be spilled, and the bottles shall
38 perish. But new wine must be put into
new bottles ; and both are preserved.
39 No man also having drunk old wine
straightway desireth new ; for he saith,
The old is better.
6 And it came to pass on the second
sabbath after the first, that he went
through the corn-fields ; and his disciples
plucked the ears of corn, and did eat,
2 rubbing them in their hands. And certain of the Pharisees said unto them,
Why do ye that which is not lawful to
3 do on the sabbath-days ? And Jesus answering them said, Have ye not read so
much as this, what David did, when
himself was an hungered, and they which
4 were with him ; how he went into the
house of God, and did take and eat the
shewbread, and gave also to them that
were with him ; which it is not lawful
5 to eat but for the priests alone? And he
said unto them, That the Son of man is
Lord also of the sabbath.
6 And it came to pass also on another
sabbath, that he entered into the synagogue and taught : and there was a man
7 whose right hand was withered. And
the scribes and Pharisees watched him,
whether he would heal on the sabbath-

S. LUKE.

day; that they might find an accusa- 8 tion against him. But he knew their thoughts, and said to the man which had the withered hand, Rise up, and stand forth in the midst. And he arose and 9 stood forth. Then said Jesus unto them, I will ask you one thing; Is it lawful on the sabbath-days to do good, or to do 10 evil? to save life, or to destroy it? And looking round about upon them all, he said unto the man, Stretch forth thy hand. And he did so: and his hand was 11 restored whole as the other. And they were filled with madness; and communed one with another what they might do to Jesus.

12 And it came to pass in those days, that he went out into a mountain to pray, and continued all night in prayer to God. 13 And when it was day, he called unto him his disciples: and of them he chose twelve, whom also he named Apostles; 14 Simon, (whom he also named Peter,) and Andrew his brother, James and John, 15 Philip and Bartholomew, Matthew and Thomas, James the son of Alpheus, and 16 Simon called Zelotes, and Judas the brother of James, and Judas Iscariot, 17 which also was the traitor. And he came down with them, and stood in the plain, and the company of his disciples, and a great multitude of people out of all Judea and Jerusalem, and from the sea-coast of Tyre and Sidon, which came to hear him, and to be healed of their 18 diseases; and they that were vexed with unclean spirits: and they were healed. 19 And the whole multitude sought to touch him: for there went virtue out of him, and healed them all.

20 And he lifted up his eyes on his disciples, and said, Blessed be ye poor: for 21 yours is the kingdom of God. Blessed are ye that hunger now: for ye shall be filled. Blessed are ye that weep now: 22 for ye shall laugh. Blessed are ye, when men shall hate you, and when they shall separate you from their company, and shall reproach you, and cast out your name as evil, for the Son of man's sake. 23 Rejoice ye in that day, and leap for joy: for, behold, your reward is great in heaven: for in the like manner did their 24 fathers unto the prophets. But woe unto you that are rich! for ye have 25 received your consolation. Woe unto you that are full! for ye shall hunger. Woe unto you that laugh now! for ye 26 shall mourn and weep. Woe unto you, when all men shall speak well of you! for so did their fathers to the false prophets.

27 But I say unto you which hear, Love your enemies, do good to them which 28 hate you, bless them that curse you, and pray for them which despitefully use you. 29 And unto him that smiteth thee on the one cheek, offer also the other; and him that taketh away thy cloak, forbid not 30 to take thy coat also. Give to every man that asketh of thee; and of him that taketh away thy goods ask them 31 not again. And as ye would that men should do to you, do ye also to them 32 likewise. For if ye love them which love you, what thank have ye? for sinners also love those that love them. 33 And if ye do good to them which do good to you, what thank have ye? for 34 sinners also do even the same. And if ye lend to them of whom ye hope to receive, what thank have ye? for sinners also lend to sinners, to receive as much 35 again. But love ye your enemies, and do good, and lend, hoping for nothing again; and your reward shall be great, and ye shall be the children of the Highest: for he is kind unto the un- 36 thankful and to the evil. Be ye therefore merciful, as your Father also is 37 merciful. Judge not, and ye shall not be judged: condemn not, and ye shall not be condemned: forgive, and ye shall 38 be forgiven: give, and it shall be given unto you: good measure, pressed down, and shaken together, and running over, shall men give into your bosom. For with the same measure that ye mete withal it shall be measured to you again.

39 And he spake a parable unto them, Can the blind lead the blind? shall they 40 not both fall into the ditch? The disciple is not above his master: but every one that is perfect shall be as his master. 41 And why beholdest thou the mote that is in thy brother's eye, but perceivest not the beam that is in thine own eye? 42 Either how canst thou say to thy brother, Brother, let me pull out the mote that is in thine eye, when thou thyself beholdest not the beam that is in thine own eye? Thou hypocrite, cast out first the beam out of thine own eye, and then shalt thou see clearly to pull out the mote 43 that is in thy brother's eye. For a good tree bringeth not forth corrupt fruit; neither doth a corrupt tree bring forth 44 good fruit. For every tree is known by his own fruit. For of thorns men do not gather figs, nor of a bramble-bush gather 45 they grapes. A good man out of the good treasure of his heart bringeth forth that which is good; and an evil man out of the evil treasure of his heart bringeth forth that which is evil: for of the abundance of the heart his mouth speaketh.

46 And why call ye me, Lord, Lord, and 47 do not the things which I say? Whosoever cometh to me, and heareth my sayings, and doeth them, I will shew you to 48 whom he is like: he is like a man which

built an house, and digged deep, and laid the foundation on a rock: and when the flood arose, the stream beat vehemently upon that house, and could not shake it: for it was founded upon a
49 rock. But he that heareth, and doeth not, is like a man that without a foundation built an house upon the earth; against which the stream did beat vehemently, and immediately it fell; and the ruin of that house was great.

7 Now when he had ended all his sayings in the audience of the people, he entered into Capernaum.
2 And a certain centurion's servant, who was dear unto him, was sick, and ready
3 to die. And when he heard of Jesus, he sent unto him the elders of the Jews, beseeching him that he would come and
4 heal his servant. And when they came to Jesus, they besought him instantly, saying, That he was worthy for whom
5 he should do this: for he loveth our nation, and he hath built us a synagogue.
6 Then Jesus went with them. And when he was now not far from the house, the centurion sent friends to him, saying unto him, Lord, trouble not thyself: for I am not worthy that thou shouldest
7 enter under my roof: wherefore neither thought I myself worthy to come unto thee: but say in a word, and my servant
8 shall be healed. For I also am a man set under authority, having under me soldiers, and I say unto one, Go, and he goeth; and to another, Come, and he cometh; and to my servant, Do this,
9 and he doeth it. When Jesus heard these things, he marvelled at him, and turned him about, and said unto the people that followed him, I say unto you, I have not found so great faith, no, not
10 in Israel. And they that were sent, returning to the house, found the servant whole that had been sick.
11 And it came to pass the day after, that he went into a city called Nain; and many of his disciples went with him, and
12 much people. Now when he came nigh to the gate of the city, behold, there was a dead man carried out, the only son of his mother, and she was a widow: and much people of the city was with her.
13 And when the Lord saw her, he had compassion on her, and said unto her,
14 Weep not. And he came and touched the bier: and they that bare him stood still. And he said, Young man, I say
15 unto thee, Arise. And he that was dead sat up, and began to speak. And he
16 delivered him to his mother. And there came a fear on all; and they glorified God, saying, That a great prophet is risen up among us; and, That God hath
17 visited his people. And this rumour of him went forth throughout all Judea,

and throughout all the region round about.
18 And the disciples of John shewed him
19 of all these things. And John calling unto him two of his disciples sent them to Jesus, saying, Art thou he that should
20 come? or look we for another? When the men were come unto him, they said, John Baptist hath sent us unto thee, saying, Art thou he that should come?
21 or look we for another? And in the same hour he cured many of their infirmities and plagues, and of evil spirits; and unto many that were blind he gave
22 sight. Then Jesus answering, said unto them, Go your way, and tell John what things ye have seen and heard; how that the blind see, the lame walk, the lepers are cleansed, the deaf hear, the dead are raised, to the poor the gospel is preached.
23 And blessed is he, whosoever shall not be offended in me.
24 And when the messengers of John were departed, he began to speak unto the people concerning John, What went ye out into the wilderness for to see?
25 A reed shaken with the wind? But what went ye out for to see? A man clothed in soft raiment? Behold, they which are gorgeously apparelled, and
26 live delicately, are in kings' courts. But what went ye out for to see? A prophet? Yea, I say unto you, and much
27 more than a prophet. This is he, of whom it is written,
Behold, I send my messenger before thy face,
Which shall prepare thy way before thee.
28 For I say unto you, Among those that are born of women there is not a greater prophet than John the Baptist: but he that is least in the kingdom of God is
29 greater than he. And all the people that heard him, and the publicans, justified God, being baptized with the
30 baptism of John. But the Pharisees and lawyers rejected the counsel of God against themselves, being not baptized
31 of him. And the Lord said, Whereunto then shall I liken the men of this genera-
32 tion? and to what are they like? They are like unto children sitting in the market-place, and calling one to another, and saying, We have piped unto you, and ye have not danced; we have mourned to you, and ye have not wept.
33 For John the Baptist came neither eating bread nor drinking wine; and ye say,
34 He hath a devil. The Son of man is come eating and drinking; and ye say, Behold a gluttonous man, and a winebibber, a friend of publicans and sinners!
35 But Wisdom is justified of all her children.
36 And one of the Pharisees desired him

that he would eat with him. And he went into the Pharisee's house, and sat 37 down to meat. And, behold, a woman in the city, which was a sinner, when she knew that Jesus sat at meat in the Pharisee's house, brought an alabaster 38 box of ointment, and stood at his feet behind him weeping, and began to wash his feet with tears, and did wipe them with the hairs of her head, and kissed his feet, and anointed them with the 39 ointment. Now when the Pharisee which had bidden him saw it, he spake within himself, saying, This man, if he were a prophet, would have known who and what manner of woman this is that 40 toucheth him: for she is a sinner. And Jesus answering, said unto him, Simon, I have somewhat to say unto thee. And 41 he saith, Master, say on. There was a certain creditor which had two debtors: the one owed five hundred pence, and 42 the other fifty. And when they had nothing to pay, he frankly forgave them both. Tell me therefore, which of them 43 will love him most? Simon answered and said, I suppose that he, to whom he forgave most. And he said unto him, 44 Thou hast rightly judged. And he turned to the woman, and said unto Simon, Seest thou this woman? I entered into thine house, thou gavest me no water for my feet: but she hath washed my feet with tears, and wiped them with 45 the hairs of her head. Thou gavest me no kiss: but this woman since the time I came in hath not ceased to kiss my 46 feet. My head with oil thou didst not anoint: but this woman hath anointed 47 my feet with ointment. Wherefore, I say unto thee, Her sins, which are many, are forgiven; for she loved much: but to whom little is forgiven, the same 48 loveth little. And he said unto her, 49 Thy sins are forgiven. And they that sat at meat with him began to say within themselves, Who is this that forgiveth 50 sins also? And he said to the woman, Thy faith hath saved thee: go in peace.

8 And it came to pass afterward, that he went throughout every city and village, preaching and shewing the glad tidings of the kingdom of God: and the twelve 2 were with him, and certain women, which had been healed of evil spirits and infirmities, Mary called Magdalene, out 3 of whom went seven devils, and Joanna the wife of Chuza, Herod's steward, and Susanna, [and many others, which ministered unto him of their substance.] 4 And when much people were gathered together, and were come to him out of 5 every city, he spake by a parable: A sower went out to sow his seed: and as he sowed, some fell by the way-side; and it was trodden down, and the fowls 6 of the air devoured it. And some fell upon a rock; and as soon as it was sprung up, it withered away, because it lacked 7 moisture. And some fell among thorns; and the thorns sprang up with it, and 8 choked it. And other fell on good ground, and sprang up, and bare fruit an hundred-fold. And when he had said these things, he cried, He that hath ears to hear, let him hear. 9 And his disciples asked him, saying, 10 What might this parable be? And he said, Unto you it is given to know the mysteries of the kingdom of God: but to others in parables; that seeing they might not see, and hearing they might 11 not understand. Now the parable is 12 this: The seed is the word of God. Those by the way-side are they that hear; then cometh the devil, and taketh away the word out of their hearts, lest they should 13 believe and be saved. They on the rock are they, which, when they hear, receive the word with joy; and these have no root, which for a while believe, and in 14 time of temptation fall away. And that which fell among thorns are they, which, when they have heard, go forth, and are choked with cares, and riches, and pleasures of this life, and bring no fruit to 15 perfection. But that on the good ground are they, which in an honest and good heart, having heard the word, keep it, and bring forth fruit with patience. 16 No man, when he hath lighted a candle, covereth it with a vessel, or putteth it under a bed; but setteth it on a candlestick, that they which enter 17 in may see the light. For nothing is secret, that shall not be made manifest; neither any thing hid, that shall not be 18 known and come abroad. Take heed therefore how ye hear: for whosoever hath, to him shall be given; and whosoever hath not, from him shall be taken even that which he seemeth to have. 19 Then came to him his mother and his brethren, and could not come at him for 20 the press. And it was told him by certain 21 which said, Thy mother and thy brethren stand without, desiring to see thee. And he answered and said unto them, My mother and my brethren are these which hear the word of God, and do it. 22 Now it came to pass on a certain day, that he went into a ship with his disciples: and he said unto them, Let us go over unto the other side of the lake. 23 And they launched forth. But as they sailed, he fell asleep: and there came down a storm of wind on the lake; and they were filled with water, and were in 24 jeopardy. And they came to him, and awoke him, saying, Master, master, we perish. Then he arose, and rebuked the wind and the raging of the water: and

P

they ceased, and there was a calm.
25 And he said unto them, Where is your faith? And they being afraid wondered, saying one to another, What manner of man is this! for he commandeth even the winds and water, and they obey him.
26 And they arrived at the country of the Gadarenes, which is over against Galilee.
27 And when he went forth to land, there met him out of the city a certain man, which had devils long time, and ware no clothes, neither abode in any house, but in the tombs.
28 When he saw Jesus, he cried out, and fell down before him, and with a loud voice said, What have I to do with thee, Jesus, thou Son of God most high? I beseech thee, torment me not.
29 (For he had commanded the unclean spirit to come out of the man. For oftentimes it had caught him: and he was kept bound with chains and in fetters; and he brake the bands, and was driven of the devil into the wilderness.)
30 And Jesus asked him, saying, What is thy name? And he said, Legion: because many devils were entered unto him.
31 And they besought him that he would not command them to go out into the deep.
32 And there was there an herd of many swine feeding on the mountain: and they besought him that he would suffer them to enter into them.
33 And he suffered them. Then went the devils out of the man, and entered into the swine: and the herd ran violently down a steep place into the lake, and were choked.
34 When they that fed them saw what was done, they fled, and went and told it in the city and in the country.
35 Then they went out to see what was done; and came to Jesus, and found the man, out of whom the devils were departed, sitting at the feet of Jesus, clothed, and in his right mind: and they were afraid.
36 They also which saw it told them by what means he that was possessed of the devils was healed.
37 Then the whole multitude of the country of the Gadarenes round about besought him to depart from them; for they were taken with great fear: and he went up into the ship, and returned back again.
38 Now the man out of whom the devils were departed besought him that he might be with him: but Jesus sent him away, saying,
39 Return to thine own house, and shew how great things God hath done unto thee. And he went his way, and published throughout the whole city how great things Jesus had done unto him.
40 And it came to pass, that, when Jesus was returned, the people gladly received him: for they were all waiting for him.
41 And, behold, there came a man named Jairus, and he was a ruler of the synagogue: and he fell down at Jesus' feet, and besought him that he would come
42 into his house: for he had one only daughter, about twelve years of age, and she lay a dying. But as he went the people thronged him.
43 And a woman having an issue of blood twelve years, which had spent all her living upon physicians, neither could be
44 healed of any, came behind him, and touched the border of his garment: and immediately her issue of blood stanched.
45 And Jesus said, Who touched me? When all denied, Peter and they that were with him said, Master, the multitude throng thee and press thee, and
46 sayest thou, Who touched me? And Jesus said, Somebody hath touched me: for I perceive that virtue is gone out of
47 me. And when the woman saw that she was not hid, she came trembling, and falling down before him, she declared unto him before all the people for what cause she had touched him, and how she
48 was healed immediately. And he said unto her, Daughter, be of good comfort: thy faith hath made thee whole; go in peace.
49 While he yet spake, there cometh one from the ruler of the synagogue's house, saying to him, Thy daughter is dead;
50 trouble not the Master. But when Jesus heard it, he answered him, saying, Fear not: believe only, and she shall be made
51 whole. And when he came into the house, he suffered no man to go in, save Peter, and James, and John, and the father and the mother of the maiden.
52 And all wept, and bewailed her: but he said, Weep not; she is not dead, but
53 sleepeth. And they laughed him to
54 scorn, knowing that she was dead. And he put them all out, and took her by the hand, and called, saying, Maid, arise.
55 And her spirit came again, and she arose straightway: and he commanded to give
56 her meat. And her parents were astonished: but he charged them that they should tell no man what was done.

9 Then he called his twelve disciples together, and gave them power and authority over all devils, and to cure
2 diseases. And he sent them to preach the kingdom of God, and to heal the
3 sick. And he said unto them, Take nothing for your journey, neither staves, nor scrip, neither bread, neither money;
4 neither have two coats apiece. And
5 whatsoever house ye enter into, there abide, and thence depart. And whosoever will not receive you, when ye go out of that city, shake off the very dust from your feet for a testimony against
6 them. And they departed, and went through the towns, preaching the gospel, and healing every where.

S. LUKE.   179

7 Now Herod the tetrarch heard of all that was done by him: and he was perplexed, because that it was said of some, 8 that John was risen from the dead; and of some, that Elias had appeared; and of others, that one of the old prophets 9 was risen again. And Herod said, John have I beheaded: but who is this, of whom I hear such things? And he desired to see him.

10 And the apostles, when they were returned, told him all that they had done. And he took them, and went aside privately into a desert place belonging 11 [to the city called Bethsaida. And the people, when they knew it, followed him: and he received them, and spake unto them of the kingdom of God, and healed them that had need of healing.]

Belongs after xviii. 14. Vide Ciasca, "Diatessaron," p. 67.

12 And when the day began to wear away, then came the twelve, and said unto him, Send the multitude away, that they may go into the towns and country round about, and lodge, and get victuals: 13 for we are here in a desert place. But he said unto them, Give ye them to eat. And they said, We have no more but five loaves and two fishes; except we should go and buy meat for all this 14 people. For they were about five thousand men. And he said to his disciples, Make them sit down by fifties in a com-15 pany. And they did so, and made them 16 all sit down. Then he took the five loaves and the two fishes, and looking up to heaven, he blessed them, and brake, and gave to the disciples to set 17 before the multitude. And they did eat, and were all filled: and there was taken up of fragments that remained to them twelve baskets.

18 And it came to pass, as he was alone praying, his disciples were with him: and he asked them, saying, Whom say 19 the people that I am? They answering, said, John the Baptist; but some say, Elias; and others say, that one of the 20 old prophets is risen again. He said unto them, But whom say ye that I am? Peter answering, said, The Christ of God. 21 And he straitly charged them, and commanded them to tell no man that thing; 22 saying, The Son of man must suffer many things, and be rejected of the elders, and chief priests, and scribes, and be slain, and be raised the third day. 23 And he said to them all, If any man will come after me, let him deny himself, and take up his cross daily, and follow 24 me. For whosoever will save his life shall lose it: but whosoever will lose his life for my sake, the same shall save it. 25 For what is a man advantaged, if he gain the whole world, and lose himself, 26 or be cast away? For whosoever shall be ashamed of me and of my words, of him shall the Son of man be ashamed, when he shall come in his own glory, and in his Father's, and of the holy angels. 27 But I tell you of a truth, there be some standing here, which shall not taste of death, till they see the kingdom of God.

28 And it came to pass about an eight days after these sayings, he took Peter, and John, and James, and went up into 29 a mountain to pray. And as he prayed, the fashion of his countenance was altered, and his raiment was white and 30 glistering. And, behold, there talked with him two men, [which were Moses 31 and Elias: who appeared in glory, and spake of his decease which he should 32 accomplish at Jerusalem.] But Peter and they that were with him were heavy with sleep: and when they were awake, they saw his glory, and the two men 33 that stood with him. And it came to pass, as they departed from him, Peter said unto Jesus, Master, it is good for us to be here: and let us make three tabernacles; one for thee, and one for Moses, and one for Elias: not knowing what he 34 said. While he thus spake, there came a cloud, and overshadowed them: and they feared as they entered into the 35 cloud. And there came a voice out of the cloud, saying, This is my beloved 36 Son: hear him. And when the voice was past, Jesus was found alone. And they kept it close, and told no man in those days any of those things which they had seen.

37 And it came to pass, that on the next day, when they were come down from 38 the hill, much people met him. And, behold, a man of the company cried out, saying, Master, I beseech thee, look upon 39 my son: for he is mine only child. And, lo, a spirit taketh him, and he suddenly crieth out; and it teareth him that he foameth again, and bruising him, hardly 40 departeth from him. And I besought thy disciples to cast him out; and they 41 could not. And Jesus answering, said, O faithless and perverse generation, how long shall I be with you, and suffer you? 42 Bring thy son hither. And as he was yet a coming, the devil threw him down, and tare him. And Jesus rebuked the unclean spirit, and healed the child, and 43 delivered him again to his father. And they were all amazed at the mighty power of God.

But while they wondered every one at all things which Jesus did, he said unto 44 his disciples, Let these sayings sink down into your ears: for the Son of man shall 45 be delivered into the hands of men. But they understood not this saying, and it was hid from them, that they perceived it not: and they feared to ask him of that saying.

S. LUKE.

46 Then there arose a reasoning among them, which of them should be greatest.
47 And Jesus, perceiving the thought of their heart, took a child, and set him by
48 him, and said unto them, Whosoever shall receive this child in my name, receiveth me: and whosoever shall receive me, receiveth him that sent me: for he that is least among you all, the same shall be great.
49 And John answered and said, Master, we saw one casting out devils in thy name; and we forbade him, because he
50 followeth not with us. And Jesus said unto him, Forbid him not: for he that is not against us is for us.
51 And it came to pass, when the time was come that he should be received up, he stedfastly set his face to go to Jeru-
52 salem, and sent messengers before his face: and they went, and entered into a village of the Samaritans, to make
53 ready for him. And they did not receive him, because his face was as though he
54 would go to Jerusalem. And when his disciples James and John saw this, they said, Lord, wilt thou that we command fire to come down from heaven, and
55 consume them, even as Elias did? But he turned, and rebuked them, and said, Ye know not what manner of spirit ye
56 are of. For the Son of man is not come to destroy men's lives, but to save them. And they went to another village.
57 And it came to pass, that, as they went in the way, a certain man said unto him, Lord, I will follow thee whithersoever
58 thou goest. And Jesus said unto him, Foxes have holes, and birds of the air have nests; but the Son of man hath not
59 where to lay his head. And he said unto another, Follow me. But he said, Lord, suffer me first to go and bury my father.
60 Jesus said unto him, Let the dead bury their dead: but go thou and preach the
61 kingdom of God. And another also said, Lord, I will follow thee; but let me first go bid them farewell, which are at home
62 at my house. And Jesus said unto him, No man, having put his hand to the plough, and looking back, is fit for the kingdom of God.

10 After these things the Lord appointed other seventy also, and sent them two and two before his face into every city and place, whither he himself would
2 come. Therefore said he unto them, The harvest truly is great, but the labourers are few: pray ye therefore the Lord of the harvest, that he would send
3 forth labourers into his harvest. Go your ways: behold, I send you forth
4 as lambs among wolves. Carry neither purse, nor scrip, nor shoes: and salute
5 no man by the way. And into whatsoever house ye enter, first say, Peace be
6 to this house. And if the son of peace be there, your peace shall rest upon it:
7 if not, it shall turn to you again. And in the same house remain, eating and drinking such things as they give: for the labourer is worthy of his hire. Go
8 not from house to house. And into whatsoever city ye enter, and they receive you, eat such things as are set
9 before you: and heal the sick that are therein, and say unto them, The kingdom
10 of God is come nigh unto you. But into whatsoever city ye enter, and they receive you not, go your ways out into the streets
11 of the same, and say, Even the very dust of your city, which cleaveth on us, we do wipe off against you: notwithstanding be ye sure of this, that the kingdom of
12 God is come nigh unto you. But I say unto you, that it shall be more tolerable in that day for Sodom, than for that city.
13 Woe unto thee, Chorazin! woe unto thee, Bethsaida! for if the mighty works had been done in Tyre and Sidon, which have been done in you, they had a great while ago repented, sitting in sackcloth and
14 ashes. But it shall be more tolerable for Tyre and Sidon at the judgment,
15 than for you. And thou, Capernaum, which art exalted to heaven, shalt be
16 thrust down to hell. He that heareth you heareth me; and he that despiseth you despiseth me; and he that despiseth me despiseth him that sent me.
17 And the seventy returned again with joy, saying, Lord, even the devils are
18 subject unto us through thy name. And he said unto them, I beheld Satan as
19 lightning fall from heaven. Behold, I give unto you power to tread on serpents and scorpions, and over all the power of the enemy: and nothing shall by any
20 means hurt you. Notwithstanding in this rejoice not, that the spirits are subject unto you; but rather rejoice, because your names are written in heaven.
21 In that hour Jesus rejoiced in spirit, and said, I thank thee, O Father, Lord of heaven and earth, that thou hast hid these things from the wise and prudent, and hast revealed them unto babes: even so, Father; for so it seemed good in thy
22 sight. All things are delivered to me of my Father; and no man knoweth who the Son is, but the Father; and who the Father is, but the Son, and he to whom
23 the Son will reveal him. And he turned him unto his disciples, and said privately, Blessed are the eyes which see the things
24 that ye see: for I tell you, that many prophets and kings have desired to see those things which ye see, and have not seen them; and to hear those things which ye hear, and have not heard them.
25 And, behold, a certain lawyer stood up, and tempted him, saying, Master,

what shall I do to inherit eternal life?
26 He said unto him, What is written in
27 the law? how readest thou? And he
answering, said, Thou shalt love the
Lord thy God with all thy heart, and with
all thy soul, and with all thy strength,
and with all thy mind; and thy neigh-
28 bour as thyself. And he said unto him,
Thou hast answered right: this do, and
29 thou shalt live. But he, willing to justify himself, said unto Jesus, And who is
30 my neighbour? And Jesus answering,
said, A certain man went down from
Jerusalem to Jericho, and fell among
thieves, which stripped him of his raiment, and wounded him, and departed,
31 leaving him half dead. And by chance
there came down a certain priest that
way: and when he saw him, he passed
32 by on the other side. And likewise a
Levite, when he was at the place, came
and looked on him, and passed by on the
33 other side. But a certain Samaritan, as
he journeyed, came where he was: and
when he saw him, he had compassion on
34 him, and went to him, and bound up his
wounds, pouring in oil and wine, and set
him on his own beast, and brought him
35 to an inn, and took care of him. And
on the morrow when he departed, he
took out two pence, and gave them to
the host, and said unto him, Take care
of him; and whatsoever thou spendest
more, when I come again, I will repay
36 thee. Which now of these three, thinkest thou, was neighbour unto him that
37 fell among the thieves? And he said,
He that shewed mercy on him. Then
said Jesus unto him, Go, and do thou
likewise.
38 Now it came to pass, as they went,
that he entered into a certain village:
and a certain woman named Martha re-
39 ceived him into her house. And she had
a sister called Mary, which also sat at
40 Jesus' feet, and heard his word. But
Martha was cumbered about much serv-
ing, and came to him, and said, Lord,
dost thou not care that my sister hath
left me to serve alone? bid her therefore
41 that she help me. And Jesus answered
and said unto her, Martha, Martha, thou
art careful and troubled about many
42 things: but one thing is needful: and
Mary hath chosen that good part, which
shall not be taken away from her.

11 And it came to pass, that, as he was
praying in a certain place, when he
ceased, one of his disciples said unto
him, Lord, teach us to pray, as John
2 also taught his disciples. And he said
unto them, When ye pray, say, Our
Father which art in heaven, Hallowed
be thy name. Thy kingdom come. Thy
will be done, as in heaven, so in earth.
3 Give us day by day our daily bread.

4 And forgive us our sins; for we also
forgive every one that is indebted to us.
And lead us not into temptation; but
deliver us from evil.
5 And he said unto them, Which of you
shall have a friend, and shall go unto
him at midnight, and say unto him,
6 Friend, lend me three loaves; for a
friend of mine in his journey is come to
me, and I have nothing to set before
7 him? And he from within shall answer
and say, Trouble me not: the door is
now shut, and my children are with me
in bed; I cannot rise and give thee.
8 I say unto you, Though he will not rise
and give him, because he is his friend,
yet because of his importunity he will
rise and give him as many as he needeth.
9 And I say unto you, Ask, and it shall
be given you; seek, and ye shall find;
knock, and it shall be opened unto you.
10 For every one that asketh receiveth;
and he that seeketh findeth; and to him
11 that knocketh it shall be opened. If a
son shall ask bread of any of you that is
a father, will he give him a stone? or if
he ask a fish, will he for a fish give him
12 a serpent? Or if he shall ask an egg,
13 will he offer him a scorpion? If ye then,
being evil, know how to give good gifts
unto your children: how much more
shall your heavenly Father give the Holy
Spirit to them that ask him?
14 And he was casting out a devil, and it
was dumb. And it came to pass, when
the devil was gone out, the dumb spake;
15 and the people wondered. But some of
them said, He casteth out devils through
16 Beelzebub the chief of the devils. And
others, tempting him, sought of him a
17 sign from heaven. But he, knowing
their thoughts, said unto them, Every
kingdom divided against itself is brought
to desolation; and a house divided
18 against a house falleth. If Satan also
be divided against himself, how shall
his kingdom stand? because ye say that
I cast out devils through Beelzebub.
19 And if I by Beelzebub cast out devils,
by whom do your sons cast them out?
20 therefore shall they be your judges. But
if I with the finger of God cast out devils,
no doubt the kingdom of God is come
21 upon you. When a strong man armed
keepeth his palace, his goods are in
22 peace: but when a stronger than he
shall come upon him, and overcome
him, he taketh from him all his armour
wherein he trusted, and divideth his
23 spoils. He that is not with me is against
me: and he that gathereth not with me
24 scattereth. When the unclean spirit is
gone out of a man, he walketh through
dry places, seeking rest; and finding
none, he saith, I will return unto my
25 house whence I came out. And when

he cometh, he findeth it swept and garnished. 26 Then goeth he, and taketh to him seven other spirits more wicked than himself; and they enter in, and dwell there: and the last state of that man is worse than the first.

27 And it came to pass, as he spake these things, a certain woman of the company lifted up her voice, and said unto him, Blessed is the womb that bare thee, and 28 the paps which thou hast sucked. But he said, Yea rather, blessed are they that hear the word of God, and keep it.

29 And when the people were gathered thick together, he began to say, This is an evil generation: they seek a sign; and there shall no sign be given it, but the 30 sign of Jonas the prophet. For as Jonas was a sign unto the Ninevites, so shall also the Son of man be to this genera-31 tion. The queen of the south shall rise up in the judgment with the men of this generation, and condemn them: for she came from the utmost parts of the earth to hear the wisdom of Solomon; and, behold, a greater than Solomon is 32 here. The men of Nineveh shall rise up in the judgment with this generation, and shall condemn it: for they repented at the preaching of Jonas; and, behold, a greater than Jonas is here.

33 No man, when he hath lighted a candle, putteth it in a secret place, neither under a bushel, but on a candlestick, that they which come in may see 34 the light. The light of the body is the eye: therefore when thine eye is single, thy whole body also is full of light; but when thine eye is evil, thy body also is 35 full of darkness. Take heed therefore that the light which is in thee be not 36 darkness. If thy whole body therefore be full of light, having no part dark, the whole shall be full of light, as when the bright shining of a candle doth give thee light.

37 And as he spake, a certain Pharisee besought him to dine with him: and he 38 went in, and sat down to meat. And when the Pharisee saw it, he marvelled that he had not first washed before 39 dinner. And the Lord said unto him, Now do ye Pharisees make clean the outside of the cup and the platter; but your inward part is full of ravening and 40 wickedness. Ye fools, did not he that made that which is without make that 41 which is within also? But rather give alms of such things as ye have; and, behold, all things are clean unto you.

42 But woe unto you, Pharisees! for ye tithe mint and rue and all manner of herbs, and pass over judgment and the love of God: these ought ye to have done, and not to leave the other un-43 done. Woe unto you, Pharisees! for ye love the uppermost seats in the synagogues, and greetings in the markets. 44 Woe unto you; scribes and Pharisees, hypocrites! for ye are as graves which appear not, and the men that walk over them are not aware of them.

45 Then answered one of the lawyers, and said unto him, Master, thus saying 46 thou reproachest us also. And he said, Woe unto you also, ye lawyers! for ye lade men with burdens grievous to be borne, and ye yourselves touch not the 47 burdens with one of your fingers. Woe unto you! for ye build the sepulchres of the prophets, and your fathers killed 48 them. Truly ye bear witness that ye allow the deeds of your fathers: for they indeed killed them, and ye build 49 their sepulchres. Therefore also said the wisdom of God, I will send them prophets and apostles, and some of them 50 they shall slay and persecute: that the blood of all the prophets, which was shed from the foundation of the world, may be required of this generation; 51 from the blood of Abel unto the blood of Zacharias, which perished between the altar and the temple: verily I say unto you, It shall be required of this 52 generation. Woe unto you, lawyers! for ye have taken away the key of knowledge: ye enter not in yourselves, and them that were entering in ye hindered.

53 And as he said these things unto them, the scribes and the Pharisees began to urge him vehemently, and to provoke 54 him to speak of many things: laying wait for him, and seeking to catch something out of his mouth, that they might accuse him.

12 In the mean time, when there were gathered together an innumerable multitude of people, insomuch that they trode one upon another, he began to say unto his disciples first of all, Beware ye of the leaven of the Pharisees, which is 2 hypocrisy. For there is nothing covered, that shall not be revealed; neither hid 3 that shall not be known. Therefore whatsoever ye have spoken in darkness shall be heard in the light; and that which ye have spoken in the ear in closets shall be proclaimed upon the 4 housetops. And I say unto you my friends, Be not afraid of them that kill the body, and after that have no more 5 that they can do. But I will forewarn you whom ye shall fear: Fear him, which after he hath killed hath power to cast into hell; yea, I say unto you, Fear 6 him. Are not five sparrows sold for two farthings, and not one of them is for-7 gotten before God? But even the very hairs of your head are all numbered. Fear not therefore: ye are of more value

S. LUKE.

8 than many sparrows. Also I say unto you, Whosoever shall confess me before men, him shall the Son of man also con-
9 fess before the angels of God: but he that denieth me before men shall be
10 denied before the angels of God. And whosoever shall speak a word against the Son of man, it shall be forgiven him: but unto him that blasphemeth against the Holy Ghost it shall not be forgiven.
11 And when they bring you unto the synagogues, and unto magistrates, and powers, take ye no thought how or what thing ye shall answer, or what ye shall
12 say: for the Holy Ghost shall teach you in the same hour what ye ought to say.
13 And one of the company said unto him, Master, speak to my brother, that
14 he divide the inheritance with me. And he said unto him, Man, who made me a
15 judge or a divider over you? And he said unto them, Take heed, and beware of covetousness: for a man's life consisteth not in the abundance of the
16 things which he possesseth. And he spake a parable unto them, saying, The ground of a certain rich man brought
17 forth plentifully: and he thought within himself, saying, What shall I do, because I have no room where to bestow
18 my fruits? And he said, This will I do: I will pull down my barns, and build greater; and there will I bestow all my
19 fruits and my goods. And I will say to my soul, Soul, thou hast much goods laid up for many years; take thine ease,
20 eat, drink, and be merry. But God said unto him, Thou fool, this night thy soul shall be required of thee: then whose shall those things be, which thou hast
21 provided? So is he that layeth up treasure for himself, and is not rich toward God.
22 And he said unto his disciples, Therefore I say unto you, Take no thought for your life, what ye shall eat; neither for
23 the body, what ye shall put on. The life is more than meat, and the body
24 is more than raiment. Consider the ravens: for they neither sow nor reap; which neither have storehouse nor barn; and God feedeth them: how much more
25 are ye better than the fowls? And which of you with taking thought can add to
26 his stature one cubit? If ye then be not able to do that thing which is least, why
27 take ye thought for the rest? Consider the lilies how they grow: they toil not, they spin not; and yet I say unto you, that Solomon in all his glory was not
28 arrayed like one of these. If then God so clothe the grass, which is to day in the field, and to morrow is cast into the oven; how much more will he clothe
29 you, O ye of little faith? And seek not ye what ye shall eat, or what ye shall drink, neither be ye of doubtful mind.
30 For all these things do the nations of the world seek after: and your Father knoweth that ye have need of these
31 things. But rather seek ye the kingdom of God; and all these things shall be
32 added unto you. Fear not, little flock; for it is your Father's good pleasure to
33 give you the kingdom. Sell that ye have, and give alms; provide yourselves bags which wax not old, a treasure in the heavens that faileth not, where no thief approacheth, neither moth cor-
34 rupteth. For where your treasure is, there will your heart be also.
35 Let your loins be girded about, and
36 your lights burning; and ye yourselves like unto men that wait for their lord, when he will return from the wedding; that when he cometh and knocketh, they may open unto him immediately.
37 Blessed are those servants, whom the lord when he cometh shall find watching: verily I say unto you, that he shall gird himself, and make them to sit down to meat, and will come forth and serve
38 them. And if he shall come in the second watch, or come in the third watch, and find them so, blessed are
39 those servants. And this know, that if the goodman of the house had known what hour the thief would come, he would have watched, and not have suffered his house to be broken through.
40 Be ye therefore ready also: for the Son of man cometh at an hour when ye think not.
41 Then Peter said unto him, Lord, speakest thou this parable unto us, or even to
42 all? And the Lord said, Who then is that faithful and wise steward, whom his lord shall make ruler over his household, to give them their portion of meat
43 in due season? Blessed is that servant, whom his lord when he cometh shall find
44 so doing. Of a truth I say unto you, that he will make him ruler over all
45 that he hath. But and if that servant say in his heart, My lord delayeth his coming; and shall begin to beat the menservants and maidens, and to eat and
46 drink, and to be drunken; the lord of that servant will come in a day when he looketh not for him, and at an hour when he is not aware, and will cut him in sunder, and will appoint him his por-
47 tion with the unbelievers. And that servant, which knew his lord's will, and prepared not himself, neither did according to his will, shall be beaten with
48 many stripes. But he that knew not, and did commit things worthy of stripes, shall be beaten with few stripes. For unto whomsoever much is given, of him shall be much required; and to whom

men have committed much, of him they will ask the more.

49 I am come to send fire on the earth; and what will I, if it be already kindled?
50 But I have a baptism to be baptized with; and how am I straitened till it be
51 accomplished! Suppose ye that I am come to give peace on earth? I tell you,
52 Nay; but rather division: for from henceforth there shall be five in one house divided, three against two, and
53 two against three. The father shall be divided against the son, and the son against the father; the mother against the daughter, and the daughter against the mother; the mother in law against her daughter in law, and the daughter in law against her mother in law.
54 And he said also to the people, When ye see a cloud rise out of the west, straightway ye say, There cometh a
55 shower; and so it is. And when ye see the south wind blow, ye say, There will
56 be heat; and it cometh to pass. Ye hypocrites, ye can discern the face of the sky and of the earth; but how is it that
57 ye do not discern this time? Yea, and why even of yourselves judge ye not
58 what is right? When thou goest with thine adversary to the magistrate, as thou art in the way, give diligence that thou mayest be delivered from him; lest he hale thee to the judge, and the judge deliver thee to the officer, and the officer
59 cast thee into prison. I tell thee, thou shalt not depart thence, till thou hast paid the very last mite.

13 There were present at that season some that told him of the Galilæans,
2 whose blood Pilate had mingled with their sacrifices. And Jesus answering said unto them, Suppose ye that these Galilæans were sinners above all the Galilæans, because they suffered such
3 things? I tell you, Nay: but, except ye
4 repent, ye shall all likewise perish. Or those eighteen, upon whom the tower in Siloam fell, and slew them, think ye that they were sinners above all men that
5 dwelt in Jerusalem? I tell you, Nay: but, except ye repent, ye shall all like-
6 wise perish. He spake also this parable; A certain man had a fig tree planted in his vineyard; and he came and sought
7 fruit thereon, and found none. Then said he unto the dresser of his vineyard, Behold, these three years I come seeking fruit on this fig tree, and find none: cut it down; why cumbereth it the
8 ground? And he answering said unto him, Lord, let it alone this year also, till
9 I shall dig about it, and dung it: and if it bear fruit, well: and if not, then after that thou shalt cut it down.
10 And he was teaching in one of the
11 synagogues on the sabbath. And, behold, there was a woman which had a spirit of infirmity eighteen years, and was bowed together, and could in no
12 wise lift up herself. And when Jesus saw her, he called her to him, and said unto her, Woman, thou art loosed from
13 thine infirmity. And he laid his hands on her: and immediately she was made
14 straight, and glorified God. And the ruler of the synagogue answered with indignation, because that Jesus had healed on the sabbath day, and said unto the people, There are six days in which men ought to work: in them therefore come and be healed, and not
15 on the sabbath day. The Lord then answered him, and said, Thou hypocrite, doth not each one of you on the sabbath loose his ox or his ass from the stall, and
16 lead him away to watering? And ought not this woman, being a daughter of Abraham, whom Satan hath bound, lo, these eighteen years, be loosed from
17 this bond on the sabbath day? And when he had said these things, all his adversaries were ashamed: and all the people rejoiced for all the glorious things that were done by him.
18 Then said he, Unto what is the kingdom of God like? and whereunto shall I
19 resemble it? It is like a grain of mustard seed, which a man took, and cast into his garden; and it grew, and waxed a great tree; and the fowls of the air
20 lodged in the branches of it. And again he said, Whereunto shall I liken the
21 kingdom of God? It is like leaven, which a woman took and hid in three measures of meal, till the whole was leavened.
22 And he went through the cities and villages, teaching, and journeying to-
23 ward Jerusalem. Then said one unto him, Lord, are there few that be saved?
24 And he said unto them, Strive to enter in at the strait gate: for many, I say unto you, will seek to enter in, and shall
25 not be able. When once the master of the house is risen up, and hath shut to the door, and ye begin to stand without, and to knock at the door, saying, Lord, Lord, open unto us; and he shall answer and say unto you, I know you not whence
26 ye are: then shall ye begin to say, We have eaten and drunk in thy presence,
27 and thou hast taught in our streets. But he shall say, I tell you, I know you not whence ye are; depart from me, all ye
28 workers of iniquity. There shall be weeping and gnashing of teeth, when ye shall see Abraham, and Isaac, and Jacob, and all the prophets, in the kingdom of God, and you yourselves thrust out.
29 And they shall come from the east, and from the west, and from the north, and from the south, and shall sit down in the
30 kingdom of God. And, behold, there are

S. LUKE.

last which shall be first, and there are first which shall be last.

31 The same day there came certain of the Pharisees, saying unto him, Get thee out, and depart hence: for Herod will 32 kill thee. And he said unto them, Go ye, and tell that fox, Behold, I cast out devils, and I do cures to day and to morrow, and the third day I shall be 33 perfected. Nevertheless I must walk to day, and to morrow, and the day following: for it cannot be that a prophet 34 perish out of Jerusalem. O Jerusalem, Jerusalem, which killest the prophets, and stonest them that are sent unto thee; how often would I have gathered thy children together, as a hen doth gather her brood under her wings, and 35 ye would not! Behold, your house is left unto you desolate: and verily I say unto you, Ye shall not see me, until the time come when ye shall say, Blessed is he that cometh in the name of the Lord.

14 And it came to pass, as he went into the house of one of the chief Pharisees to eat bread on the sabbath day, that 2 they watched him. And, behold, there was a certain man before him which had 3 the dropsy. And Jesus answering spake unto the lawyers and Pharisees, saying, Is it lawful to heal on the sabbath day? 4 And they held their peace. And he took him, and healed him, and let him go; 5 and answered them, saying, Which of you shall have an ass or an ox fallen into a pit, and will not straightway pull him 6 out on the sabbath day? And they could not answer him again to these things.

7 And he put forth a parable to those which were bidden, when he marked how they chose out the chief rooms; saying 8 unto them, When thou art bidden of any man to a wedding, sit not down in the highest room; lest a more honourable 9 man than thou be bidden of him; and he that bade thee and him come and say to thee, Give this man place; and thou begin with shame to take the lowest 10 room. But when thou art bidden, go and sit down in the lowest room; that when he that bade thee cometh, he may say unto thee, Friend, go up higher: then shalt thou have worship in the presence of them that sit at meat with thee. 11 For whosoever exalteth himself shall be abased; and he that humbleth himself shall be exalted.

12 Then said he also to him that bade him, When thou makest a dinner or a supper, call not thy friends, nor thy brethren, neither thy kinsmen, nor thy rich neighbours; lest they also bid thee again, and a recompence be made thee. 13 But when thou makest a feast, call the poor, the maimed, the lame, the blind: 14 and thou shalt be blessed; for they cannot recompense thee: for thou shalt be recompensed at the resurrection of the just.

15 And when one of them that sat at meat with him heard these things, he said unto him, Blessed is he that shall 16 eat bread in the kingdom of God. Then said he unto him, A certain man made a 17 great supper, and bade many: and sent his servant at supper time to say to them that were bidden, Come; for all things 18 are now ready. And they all with one consent began to make excuse. The first said unto him, I have bought a piece of ground, and I must needs go and see it: 19 I pray thee have me excused. And another said, I have bought five yoke of oxen, and I go to prove them: I pray 20 thee have me excused. And another said, I have married a wife, and there-21 fore I cannot come. So that servant came, and shewed his lord these things. Then the master of the house being angry said to his servant, Go out quickly into the streets and lanes of the city, and bring in hither the poor, and the maimed, 22 and the halt, and the blind. And the servant said, Lord, it is done as thou hast commanded, and yet there is room. 23 And the lord said unto the servant, Go out into the highways and hedges, and compel them to come in, that my house 24 may be filled. For I say unto you, That none of those men which were bidden shall taste of my supper.

25 And there went great multitudes with him: and he turned, and said unto them, 26 If any man come to me, and hate not his father, and mother, and wife, and children, and brethren, and sisters, yea, and his own life also, he cannot be my 27 disciple. And whosoever doth not bear his cross, and come after me, cannot be 28 my disciple. For which of you, intending to build a tower, sitteth not down first, and counteth the cost, whether he 29 have sufficient to finish it? Lest haply, after he hath laid the foundation, and is not able to finish it, all that behold it 30 begin to mock him, saying, This man began to build, and was not able to 31 finish. Or what king, going to make war against another king, sitteth not down first, and consulteth whether he be able with ten thousand to meet him that cometh against him with twenty 32 thousand? Or else, while the other is yet a great way off, he sendeth an ambassage, and desireth conditions of peace. 33 So likewise, whosoever he be of you that forsaketh not all that he hath, he cannot 34 be my disciple. Salt is good: but if the salt have lost his savour, wherewith shall 35 it be seasoned? It is neither fit for the land, nor yet for the dunghill; but men

Q

S. LUKE.

cast it out. He that hath ears to hear, let him hear.

15 Then drew near unto him all the publicans and sinners for to hear him.
2 And the Pharisees and scribes murmured, saying, This man receiveth sinners, and eateth with them.
3 And he spake this parable unto them,
4 saying, What man of you, having an hundred sheep, if he lose one of them, doth not leave the ninety and nine in the wilderness, and go after that which
5 is lost, until he find it? And when he hath found it, he layeth it on his shoul-
6 ders, rejoicing. And when he cometh home, he calleth together his friends and neighbours, saying unto them, Rejoice with me; for I have found my sheep
7 which was lost. I say unto you, that likewise joy shall be in heaven over one sinner that repenteth, more than over ninety and nine just persons, which need no repentance.
8 Either what woman having ten pieces of silver, if she lose one piece, doth not light a candle, and sweep the house, and
9 seek diligently till she find it? And when she hath found it, she calleth her friends and her neighbours together, saying, Rejoice with me; for I have
10 found the piece which I had lost. Likewise, I say unto you, there is joy in the presence of the angels of God over one sinner that repenteth.
11 And he said, A certain man had two
12 sons: and the younger of them said to his father, Father, give me the portion of goods that falleth to me. And he
13 divided unto them his living. And not many days after the younger son gathered all together, and took his journey into a far country, and there wasted his substance with riotous living.
14 And when he had spent all, there arose a mighty famine in that land; and he
15 began to be in want. And he went and joined himself to a citizen of that country; and he sent him into his fields
16 to feed swine. And he would fain have filled his belly with the husks that the swine did eat: and no man gave unto
17 him. And when he came to himself, he said, How many hired servants of my father's have bread enough and to spare,
18 and I perish with hunger! I will arise and go to my father, and will say unto him, Father, I have sinned against
19 heaven, and before thee, and am no more worthy to be called thy son: make
20 me as one of thy hired servants. And he arose, and came to his father. But when he was yet a great way off, his father saw him, and had compassion, and ran, and fell on his neck, and kissed
21 him. And the son said unto him, Father, I have sinned against heaven, and in thy sight, and am no more worthy to
22 be called thy son. But the father said to his servants, Bring forth the best robe, and put it on him; and put a ring
23 on his hand, and shoes on his feet: and bring hither the fatted calf, and kill it;
24 and let us eat, and be merry: for this my son was dead, and is alive again; he was lost, and is found. And they began
25 to be merry. Now his elder son was in the field: and as he came and drew nigh to the house, he heard music and
26 dancing. And he called one of the servants, and asked what these things
27 meant. And he said unto him, Thy brother is come; and thy father hath killed the fatted calf, because he hath
28 received him safe and sound. And he was angry, and would not go in: therefore came his father out, and entreated
29 him. And he answering said to his father, Lo, these many years do I serve thee, neither transgressed I at any time thy commandment: and yet thou never gavest me a kid, that I might
30 make merry with my friends: but as soon as this thy son was come, which hath devoured thy living with harlots, thou hast killed for him the fatted calf.
31 And he said unto him, Son, thou art ever with me, and all that I have is
32 thine. It was meet that we should make merry, and be glad: for this thy brother was dead, and is alive again: and was lost, and is found.

16 And he said also unto his disciples, There was a certain rich man, which had a steward; and the same was accused unto him that he had wasted his goods.
2 And he called him, and said unto him, How is it that I hear this of thee? give an account of thy stewardship; for thou
3 mayest be no longer steward. Then the steward said within himself, What shall I do? for my lord taketh away from me the stewardship: I cannot dig; to beg I
4 am ashamed. I am resolved what to do, that, when I am put out of the stewardship, they may receive me into their
5 houses. So he called every one of his lord's debtors unto him, and said unto the first, How much owest thou unto my
6 lord? And he said, An hundred measures of oil. And he said unto him, Take thy bill, and sit down quickly, and write
7 fifty. Then said he to another, And how much owest thou? And he said, An hundred measures of wheat. And he said unto him, Take thy bill, and write
8 fourscore. And the lord commended the unjust steward, because he had done wisely: for the children of this world are in their generation wiser than the
9 children of light. And I say unto you, Make to yourselves friends of the mammon of unrighteousness; that, when ye

S. LUKE.

10 fail, they may receive you into everlasting habitations. He that is faithful in that which is least is faithful also in much: and he that is unjust in the least is un-
11 just also in much. If therefore ye have not been faithful in the unrighteous mammon, who will commit to your trust
12 the true riches? And if ye have not been faithful in that which is another man's, who shall give you that which is
13 your own? No servant can serve two masters: for either he will hate the one, and love the other; or else he will hold to the one, and despise the other. Ye cannot serve God and mammon.
14 And the Pharisees also, who were covetous, heard all these things: and
15 they derided him. And he said unto them, Ye are they which justify yourselves before men: but God knoweth your hearts: for that which is highly esteemed among men is abomination in
16 the sight of God. The law and the prophets were until John: since that time the kingdom of God is preached, and
17 every man presseth into it. And it is easier for heaven and earth to pass, than
18 one tittle of the law to fail. Whosoever putteth away his wife, and marrieth another, committeth adultery: and whosoever marrieth her that is put away from her husband committeth adultery.
19 There was a certain rich man, which was clothed in purple and fine linen,
20 and fared sumptuously every day: and there was a certain beggar named Lazarus, which was laid at his gate, full of
21 sores, and desiring to be fed with the crumbs which fell from the rich man's table: moreover the dogs came and
22 licked his sores. And it came to pass, that the beggar died, and was carried by the angels into Abraham's bosom: the
23 rich man also died, and was buried; and in hell he lift up his eyes, being in torments, and seeth Abraham afar off, and
24 Lazarus in his bosom. And he cried and said, Father Abraham, have mercy on me, and send Lazarus, that he may dip the tip of his finger in water, and cool my tongue; for I am tormented in this
25 flame. But Abraham said, Son, remember that thou in thy lifetime receivedst thy good things, and likewise Lazarus evil things: but now he is comforted,
26 and thou art tormented. And beside all this, between us and you there is a great gulf fixed: so that they which would pass from hence to you cannot; neither can they pass to us, that would
27 come from thence. Then he said, I pray thee therefore, father, that thou wouldest send him to my father's house:
28 for I have five brethren; that he may testify unto them, lest they also come
29 into this place of torment. Abraham saith unto him, They have Moses and
30 the prophets; let them hear them. And he said, Nay, father Abraham: but if one went unto them from the dead, they
31 will repent. And he said unto him, If they hear not Moses and the prophets, neither will they be persuaded, though one rose from the dead.

17 Then said he unto the disciples, It is impossible but that offences will come: but woe unto him, through whom they
2 come! It were better for him that a millstone were hanged about his neck, and he cast into the sea, than that he should offend one of these little ones.
3 Take heed to yourselves: If thy brother trespass against thee, rebuke him; and
4 if he repent, forgive him. And if he trespass against thee seven times in a day, and seven times in a day turn again to thee, saying, I repent; thou shalt forgive him.
5 And the apostles said unto the Lord,
6 Increase our faith. And the Lord said, If ye had faith as a grain of mustard seed, ye might say unto this sycamine tree, Be thou plucked up by the root, and be thou planted in the sea; and it
7 should obey you. But which of you, having a servant plowing or feeding cattle, will say unto him by and by, when he is come from the field, Go and
8 sit down to meat? And will not rather say unto him, Make ready wherewith I may sup, and gird thyself, and serve me, till I have eaten and drunken; and after-
9 ward thou shalt eat and drink? Doth he thank that servant because he did the things that were commanded him? I
10 trow not. So likewise ye, when ye shall have done all those things which are commanded you, say, We are unprofitable servants: we have done that which was our duty to do.
11 And it came to pass, as he went to Jerusalem, that he passed through the
12 midst of Samaria and Galilee. And as he entered into a certain village, there met him ten men that were lepers, which
13 stood afar off: and they lifted up their voices, and said, Jesus, Master, have
14 mercy on us. And when he saw them, he said unto them, Go shew yourselves unto the priests. And it came to pass, that, as they went, they were cleansed.
15 And one of them, when he saw that he was healed, turned back, and with a
16 loud voice glorified God, and fell down on his face at his feet, giving him thanks;
17 and he was a Samaritan. And Jesus answering said, Were there not ten cleansed? but where are the nine?
18 There are not found that returned to give glory to God, save this stranger.
19 And he said unto him, Arise, go thy way: thy faith hath made thee whole.

S. LUKE.

20 And when he was demanded of the Pharisees, when the kingdom of God should come, he answered them and said, The kingdom of God cometh not 21 with observation. Neither shall they say, Lo here! or, lo there! for, behold, the kingdom of God is within you.
22 And he said unto the disciples, The days will come, when ye shall desire to see one of the days of the Son of man, 23 and ye shall not see it. And they shall say to you, See here; or, see there: go 24 not after them, nor follow them. For as the lightning, that lighteneth out of the one part under heaven, shineth unto the other part under heaven; so shall also 25 the Son of man be in his day. But first must he suffer many things, and be re-26 jected of this generation. And as it was in the days of Noe, so shall it be also in 27 the days of the Son of man. They did eat, they drank, they married wives, they were given in marriage, until the day that Noe entered into the ark, and the flood came, and destroyed them all. 28 Likewise also as it was in the days of Lot; they did eat, they drank, they bought, they sold, they planted, they 29 builded; but the same day that Lot went out of Sodom it rained fire and brimstone from heaven, and destroyed them 30 all. Even thus shall it be in the day 31 when the Son of man is revealed. In that day, he which shall be upon the housetop, and his stuff in the house, let him not come down to take it away: and he that is in the field, let him likewise not return 32 back. Remember Lot's wife. Whoso-33 ever shall seek to save his life shall lose it; and whosoever shall lose his life shall 34 preserve it. I tell you, in that night there shall be two men in one bed; the one shall be taken, and the other shall 35 be left. Two women shall be grinding together; the one shall be taken, and 36 the other left. Two men shall be in the field; the one shall be taken, and the 37 other left. And they answered and said unto him, Where, Lord? And he said unto them, Wheresoever the body is, thither will the eagles be gathered together.

18 And he spake a parable unto them to this end, that men ought always to pray, 2 and not to faint; saying, There was in a city a judge, which feared not God, 3 neither regarded man: and there was a widow in that city; and she came unto him, saying, Avenge me of mine adver-4 sary. And he would not for a while: but afterward he said within himself, Though I fear not God, nor regard man; 5 yet because this widow troubleth me, I will avenge her, lest by her continual 6 coming she weary me. And the Lord said, Hear what the unjust judge saith.

7 And shall not God avenge his own elect, which cry day and night unto him, 8 though he bear long with them? I tell you that he will avenge them speedily. Nevertheless when the Son of man cometh, shall he find faith on the earth?
9 And he spake this parable unto certain which trusted in themselves that they were righteous, and despised others: 10 Two men went up into the temple to pray; the one a Pharisee, and the other 11 a publican. The Pharisee stood and prayed thus with himself, God, I thank thee, that I am not as other men are, extortioners, unjust, adulterers, or even 12 as this publican. I fast twice in the week, I give tithes of all that I possess. 13 And the publican, standing afar off, would not lift up so much as his eyes unto heaven, but smote upon his breast, saying, God be merciful to me a sinner. 14 I tell you, this man went down to his house justified rather than the other: for every one that exalteth himself shall be abased; and he that humbleth himself shall be exalted.
15 And they brought unto him also infants, that he would touch them: but when his disciples saw it, they rebuked 16 them. But Jesus called them unto him, and said, Suffer little children to come unto me, and forbid them not: for of 17 such is the kingdom of God. Verily I say unto you, Whosoever shall not receive the kingdom of God as a little child shall in no wise enter therein.
18 And a certain ruler asked him, saying, Good Master, what shall I do to inherit 19 eternal life? And Jesus said unto him, Why callest thou me good? none is good, 20 save one, that is, God. Thou knowest the commandments, Do not commit adultery, Do not kill, Do not steal, Do not bear false witness, Honour thy 21 father and thy mother. And he said, All these have I kept from my youth 22 up. Now when Jesus heard these things, he said unto him, Yet lackest thou one thing: sell all that thou hast, and distribute unto the poor, and thou shalt have treasure in heaven: and come, 23 follow me. And when he heard this, he was very sorrowful: for he was very 24 rich. And when Jesus saw that he was very sorrowful, he said, How hardly shall they that have riches enter into 25 the kingdom of God! For it is easier for a camel to go through a needle's eye, than for a rich man to enter into 26 the kingdom of God. And they that heard it said, Who then can be saved? 27 And he said, The things which are impossible with men are possible with God. 28 Then Peter said, Lo, we have left all, 29 and followed thee. And he said unto them, Verily, I say unto you, There is

S. LUKE. 189

no man that hath left house, or parents, or brethren, or wife, or children, for the
30 kingdom of God's sake, who shall not receive manifold more in this present time, and in the world to come life everlasting.
31 Then he took unto him the twelve, and said unto them, Behold, we go up to Jerusalem, and all things that are written by the prophets concerning the
32 Son of man shall be accomplished. For he shall be delivered unto the Gentiles, and shall be mocked, and spitefully
33 entreated, and spitted on: and they shall scourge him, and put him to death: and the third day he shall rise again.
34 And they understood none of these things: and this saying was hid from them, neither knew they the things which were spoken.
35 And it came to pass, that as he was come nigh unto Jericho, a certain blind
36 man sat by the way side begging: and hearing the multitude pass by, he asked
37 what it meant. And they told him, that
38 Jesus of Nazareth passeth by. And he cried, saying, Jesus, thou son of David,
39 have mercy on me. And they which went before rebuked him, that he should hold his peace: but he cried so much the more, Thou son of David, have mercy
40 on me. And Jesus stood, and commanded him to be brought unto him: and when he was come near, he asked
41 him, saying, What wilt thou that I shall do unto thee? And he said, Lord, that
42 I may receive my sight. And Jesus said unto him, Receive thy sight: thy faith
43 hath saved thee. And immediately he received his sight, and followed him, glorifying God: and all the people, when they saw it, gave praise unto God.

19 And Jesus entered and passed through Jericho. And, behold, there was a man
2 named Zacchæus, which was the chief among the publicans, and he was rich.
3 And he sought to see Jesus who he was; and could not for the press, because he
4 was little of stature. And he ran before, and climbed up into a sycomore tree to see him: for he was to pass that way.
5 And when Jesus came to the place, he looked up, and saw him, and said unto him, Zacchæus, make haste, and come
6 down; for to day I must abide at thy house. And he made haste, and came
7 down, and received him joyfully. And when they saw it, they all murmured, saying, That he was gone to be guest
8 with a man that is a sinner. And Zacchæus stood, and said unto the Lord; Behold, Lord, the half of my goods I give to the poor; and if I have taken any thing from any man by false accusation,
9 I restore him fourfold. And Jesus said unto him, This day is salvation come to this house, forsomuch as he also is a son
10 of Abraham. For the Son of man is come to seek and to save that which was lost.
11 And as they heard these things, he added and spake a parable, because he was nigh to Jerusalem, and because they thought that the kingdom of God should
12 immediately appear. He said therefore, A certain nobleman went into a far country to receive for himself a king-
13 dom, and to return. And he called his ten servants, and delivered them ten pounds, and said unto them, Occupy till
14 I come. But his citizens hated him, and sent a message after him, saying, We will not have this man to reign over us.
15 And it came to pass, that when he was returned, having received the kingdom, then he commanded these servants to be called unto him, to whom he had given the money, that he might know how much every man had gained by trading.
16 Then came the first, saying, Lord, thy
17 pound hath gained ten pounds. And he said unto him, Well, thou good servant: because thou hast been faithful in a very little, have thou authority over ten cities.
18 And the second came, saying, Lord, thy
19 pound hath gained five pounds. And he said likewise to him, Be thou also over
20 five cities. And another came, saying, Lord, behold, here is thy pound, which
21 I have kept laid up in a napkin: for I feared thee, because thou art an austere man: thou takest up that thou layedst not down, and reapest that thou didst
22 not sow. And he saith unto him, Out of thine own mouth will I judge thee, thou wicked servant. Thou knewest that I was an austere man, taking up that I laid not down, and reaping that I did
23 not sow: wherefore then gavest not thou my money into the bank, that at my coming I might have required mine own
24 with usury? And he said unto them that stood by, Take from him the pound, and give it to him that hath ten pounds.
25 (And they said unto him, Lord, he hath
26 ten pounds.) For I say unto you, That unto every one which hath shall be given; and from him that hath not, even that he hath shall be taken away from
27 him. But those mine enemies, which would not that I should reign over them, bring hither, and slay them before me.
28 And when he had thus spoken, he went before, ascending up to Jerusalem.
29 And it came to pass, when he was come nigh to Bethphage and Bethany, at the mount called the mount of Olives,
30 he sent two of his disciples, saying, Go ye into the village over against you; in the which at your entering ye shall find a colt tied, whereon yet never man sat:
31 loose him, and bring him hither. And

S. LUKE.

if any man ask you, Why do ye loose him? thus shall ye say unto him, Because
32 the Lord hath need of him. And they that were sent went their way, and found
33 even as he had said unto them. And as they were loosing the colt, the owners thereof said unto them, Why loose ye the
34 colt? And they said, The Lord hath
35 need of him. And they brought him to Jesus: and they cast their garments upon the colt, and they set Jesus there-
36 on. And as he went, they spread their
37 clothes in the way. And when he was come nigh, even now at the descent of the mount of Olives, the whole multitude of the disciples began to rejoice and praise God with a loud voice for all the mighty works that they had seen:
38 saying, Blessed be the King that cometh in the name of the Lord: peace in hea-
39 ven, and glory in the highest. And some of the Pharisees from among the multitude said unto him, Master, rebuke
40 thy disciples. And he answered and said unto them, I tell you that, if these should hold their peace, the stones would immediately cry out.
41 And when he was come near, he be-
42 held the city, and wept over it, saying, If thou hadst known, even thou, at least in this thy day, the things which belong unto thy peace! but now they are hid
43 from thine eyes. For the days shall come upon thee, that thine enemies shall cast a trench about thee, and compass thee round, and keep thee in on every
44 side. And shall lay thee even with the ground, and thy children within thee; and they shall not leave in thee one stone upon another; because thou knewest not the time of thy visitation.
45 And he went into the temple, and began to cast out them that sold there-
46 in, and them that bought; saying unto them, It is written, My house is the house of prayer: but ye have made it a den of thieves.
47 And he taught daily in the temple. But the chief priests and the scribes and the chief of the people sought to destroy
48 him, and could not find what they might do: for all the people were very attentive to hear him.
20 And it came to pass, that on one of those days, as he taught the people in the temple, and preached the gospel, the chief priests and the scribes came
2 upon him with the elders, and spake unto him, saying, Tell us, by what authority doest thou these things? or who is
3 he that gave thee this authority? And he answered and said unto them, I will also ask you one thing; and answer me:
4 The baptism of John, was it from heaven,
5 or of men? And they reasoned with themselves, saying, If we shall say, From heaven; he will say, Why then believed
6 ye him not? But and if we say, Of men; all the people will stone us: for they be persuaded that John was a prophet.
7 And they answered, that they could not
8 tell whence it was. And Jesus said unto them, Neither tell I you by what authority I do these things.
9 Then began he to speak to the people this parable; A certain man planted a vineyard, and let it forth to husbandmen, and went into a far country for a
10 long time. And at the season he sent a servant to the husbandmen, that they should give him of the fruit of the vineyard: but the husbandmen beat him,
11 and sent him away empty. And again he sent another servant: and they beat him also, and entreated him shamefully,
12 and sent him away empty. And again he sent a third: and they wounded him
13 also, and cast him out. Then said the lord of the vineyard, What shall I do? I will send my beloved son: it may be they will reverence him when they see
14 him. But when the husbandmen saw him, they reasoned among themselves, saying, This is the heir: come, let us kill him, that the inheritance may be
15 ours. So they cast him out of the vineyard, and killed him. What therefore shall the lord of the vineyard do unto
16 them? He shall come and destroy these husbandmen, and shall give the vineyard to others. And when they heard it, they
17 said, God forbid. And he beheld them, and said, What is this then that is written,

The stone which the builders rejected,
The same is become the head of the corner?

18 Whosoever shall fall upon that stone shall be broken; but on whomsoever it shall fall, it will grind him to powder.
19 And the chief priests and the scribes the same hour sought to lay hands on him; and they feared the people: for they perceived that he had spoken this
20 parable against them. And they watched him, and sent forth spies, which should feign themselves just men, that they might take hold of his words, that so they might deliver him unto the power
21 and authority of the governor. And they asked him, saying, Master, we know that thou sayest and teachest rightly, neither acceptest thou the person of any,
22 but teachest the way of God truly: Is it lawful for us to give tribute unto Cæsar,
23 or no? But he perceived their craftiness, and said unto them, Why tempt
24 ye me? Shew me a penny. Whose image and superscription hath it? They an-
25 swered and said, Cæsar's. And he said unto them, Render therefore unto Cæsar the things which be Cæsar's, and unto

S. LUKE.

26 God the things which be God's. And they could not take hold of his words before the people: and they marvelled at his answer, and held their peace.

27 Then came to him certain of the Sadducees, which deny that there is any resurrection; and they asked him, saying, Master, Moses wrote unto us, If any man's brother die, having a wife, and he die without children, that his brother should take his wife, and raise up seed 29 unto his brother. There were therefore seven brethren: and the first took a wife, 30 and died without children. And the second took her to wife, and he died 31 childless. And the third took her; and in like manner the seven also: and they 32 left no children, and died. Last of all 33 the woman died also. Therefore in the resurrection whose wife of them is she? 34 for seven had her to wife. And Jesus answering said unto them, The children of this world marry, and are given in 35 marriage: but they which shall be accounted worthy to obtain that world, and the resurrection from the dead, neither marry, nor are given in marriage: 36 neither can they die any more: for they are equal unto the angels; and are the children of God, being the children of 37 the resurrection. Now that the dead are raised, even Moses shewed at the bush, when he calleth the Lord the God of Abraham, and the God of Isaac, and 38 the God of Jacob. For he is not a God of the dead, but of the living: for all 39 live unto him. Then certain of the scribes answering said, Master, thou 40 hast well said. And after that they durst not ask him any question at all.

41 And he said unto them, How say they 42 that Christ is David's son? And David himself saith in the book of Psalms,
The Lord said unto my Lord,
Sit thou on my right hand,
43 Till I make thine enemies thy footstool.

44 David therefore calleth him Lord, how is he then his son?

45 Then in the audience of all the people 46 he said unto his disciples, Beware of the scribes, which desire to walk in long robes, and love greetings in the markets, and the highest seats in the synagogues, 47 and the chief rooms at feasts; which devour widows' houses, and for a shew make long prayers: the same shall receive greater damnation.

21 And he looked up, and saw the rich men casting their gifts into the trea- 2 sury. And he saw also a certain poor widow casting in thither two mites. 3 And he said, Of a truth I say unto you, that this poor widow hath cast in more 4 than they all: for all these have of their abundance cast in unto the offerings of God: but she of her penury hath cast in all the living that she had.

5 And as some spake of the temple, how it was adorned with goodly stones and 6 gifts, he said, As for these things which ye behold, the days will come, in the which there shall not be left one stone upon another, that shall not be thrown 7 down. And they asked him, saying, Master, but when shall these things be? and what sign will there be when these 8 things shall come to pass? And he said, Take heed that ye be not deceived: for many shall come in my name, saying, I am Christ; and the time draweth near: 9 go ye not therefore after them. But when ye shall hear of wars and commotions, be not terrified: for these things must first come to pass; but the end is not by and by.

10 Then said he unto them, Nation shall rise against nation, and kingdom against 11 kingdom: and great earthquakes shall be in divers places, and famines, and pestilences; and fearful sights and great 12 signs shall there be from heaven. But before all these, they shall lay their hands on you, and persecute you, delivering you up to the synagogues, and into prisons, being brought before kings 13 and rulers for my name's sake. And it 14 shall turn to you for a testimony. Settle it therefore in your hearts, not to medi- 15 tate before what ye shall answer: for I will give you a mouth and wisdom, which all your adversaries shall not be able to 16 gainsay nor resist. And ye shall be betrayed both by parents, and brethren, and kinsfolks, and friends; and some of you shall they cause to be put to death. 17 And ye shall be hated of all men for my 18 name's sake. But there shall not an 19 hair of your head perish. In your patience possess ye your souls.

20 And when ye shall see Jerusalem compassed with armies, then know that the 21 desolation thereof is nigh. Then let them which are in Judea flee to the mountains; and let them which are in the midst of it depart out; and let not them that are in the country enter 22 thereinto. For these be the days of vengeance, that all things which are 23 written may be fulfilled. But woe unto them that are with child, and to them that give suck, in those days! for there shall be great distress in the land, and 24 wrath upon this people. And they shall fall by the edge of the sword, and shall be led away captive into all nations: and Jerusalem shall be trodden down of the Gentiles, until the times of the Gen- 25 tiles be fulfilled. And there shall be signs in the sun, and in the moon, and in the stars; and upon the earth distress of nations, with perplexity; the sea and

S. LUKE.

26 the waves roaring; men's hearts failing them for fear, and for looking after those things which are coming on the earth: for the powers of heaven shall be 27 shaken. And then shall they see the Son of man coming in a cloud with 28 power and great glory. And when these things begin to come to pass, then look up, and lift up your heads; for your redemption draweth nigh.
29 And he spake to them a parable; Behold the fig tree, and all the trees; 30 When they now shoot forth, ye see and know of your own selves that summer is 31 now nigh at hand. So likewise ye, when ye see these things come to pass, know ye that the kingdom of God is nigh at 32 hand. Verily I say unto you, This generation shall not pass away, till all be 33 fulfilled. Heaven and earth shall pass away: but my words shall not pass away.
34 And take heed to yourselves, lest at any time your hearts be overcharged with surfeiting, and drunkenness, and cares of this life, and so that day come 35 upon you unawares. For as a snare shall it come on all them that dwell on the 36 face of the whole earth. Watch ye therefore, and pray always, that ye may be accounted worthy to escape all these things that shall come to pass, and to stand before the Son of man.
37 And in the day time he was teaching in the temple; and at night he went out, and abode in the mount that is 38 called the mount of Olives. And all the people came early in the morning to him in the temple, for to hear him.

22 Now the feast of unleavened bread drew nigh, which is called the Pass-2 over. And the chief priests and scribes sought how they might kill him; for 3 they feared the people.
Then entered Satan into Judas surnamed Iscariot, being of the number of 4 the twelve. And he went his way, and communed with the chief priests and captains, how he might betray him unto 5 them. And they were glad, and cove-6 nanted to give him money. And he promised, and sought opportunity to betray him unto them in the absence of the multitude.
7 Then came the day of unleavened bread, when the passover must be killed. 8 And he sent Peter and John, saying, Go and prepare us the passover, that we 9 may eat. And they said unto him, 10 Where wilt thou that we prepare? And he said unto them, Behold, when ye are entered into the city, there shall a man meet you, bearing a pitcher of water; follow him into the house where he 11 entereth in. And ye shall say unto the goodman of the house, The Master saith

unto thee, Where is the guestchamber, where I shall eat the passover with my 12 disciples? And he shall shew you a large upper room furnished: there make 13 ready. And they went, and found as he had said unto them: and they made ready the passover.
14 And when the hour was come, he sat down, and the twelve apostles with 15 him. And he said unto them, With desire I have desired to eat this pass-16 over with you before I suffer: for I say unto you, I will not any more eat thereof, until it be fulfilled in the kingdom of 17 God. And he took the cup, and gave thanks, and said, Take this, and divide 18 it among yourselves: for I say unto you, I will not drink of the fruit of the vine, until the kingdom of God shall come. 19 And he took bread, and gave thanks, and brake it, and gave unto them, saying, This is my body which is given for you: this do in remembrance of me. 20 Likewise also the cup after supper, saying, This cup is the new testament in 21 my blood, which is shed for you. But, behold, the hand of him that betrayeth 22 me is with me on the table. And truly the Son of man goeth, as it was determined: but woe unto that man by whom 23 he is betrayed! And they began to enquire among themselves, which of them it was that should do this thing.
24 And there was also a strife among them, which of them should be accounted 25 the greatest. And he said unto them, The kings of the Gentiles exercise lordship over them; and they that exercise authority upon them are called bene-26 factors. But ye shall not be so: but he that is greatest among you, let him be as the younger; and he that is chief, 27 as he that doth serve. For whether is greater, he that sitteth at meat, or he that serveth? is not he that sitteth at meat? but I am among you as he that 28 serveth. Ye are they which have continued with me in my temptations. 29 And I appoint unto you a kingdom, as my Father hath appointed unto me; 30 that ye may eat and drink at my table in my kingdom, and sit on thrones judg-31 ing the twelve tribes of Israel. And the Lord said, Simon, Simon, behold, Satan hath desired to have you, that he 32 may sift you as wheat: but I have prayed for thee, that thy faith fail not: and when thou art converted, strengthen 33 thy brethren. And he said unto him, Lord, I am ready to go with thee, both 34 into prison, and to death. And he said, I tell thee, Peter, the cock shall not crow this day, before that thou shalt thrice deny that thou knowest me.
35 And he said unto them, When I sent you without purse, and scrip, and shoes,

lacked ye anything? And they said, 36 Nothing. Then said he unto them, But now, he that hath a purse, let him take it, and likewise his scrip: and he that hath no sword, let him sell his garment, 37 and buy one. For I say unto you, that this that is written must yet be accomplished in me, And he was reckoned among the transgressors: for the things 38 concerning me have an end. And they said, Lord, behold here are two swords. And he said unto them, It is enough.

39 And he came out, and went, as he was wont, to the mount of Olives; and 40 his disciples also followed him. And when he was at the place, he said unto them, Pray that ye enter not into temp- 41 tation. And he was withdrawn from them about a stone's cast, and kneeled 42 down, and prayed, saying, Father, if thou be willing, remove this cup from me: nevertheless not my will, but thine, 43 be done. And there appeared an angel unto him from heaven, strengthening 44 him. And being in an agony he prayed more earnestly: and his sweat was as it were great drops of blood falling down 45 to the ground. And when he rose up from prayer, and was come to his disciples, he found them sleeping for sorrow, 46 and said unto them, Why sleep ye? rise and pray, lest ye enter into temptation.

47 And while he yet spake, behold a multitude, and he that was called Judas, one of the twelve, went before them, and drew near unto Jesus to kiss him. 48 But Jesus said unto him, Judas, betrayest thou the Son of man with a kiss? 49 When they which were about him saw what would follow, they said unto him, Lord, shall we smite with the sword? 50 And one of them smote the servant of the high priest, and cut off his right 51 ear. And Jesus answered and said, Suffer ye thus far. And he touched his 52 ear, and healed him. Then Jesus said unto the chief priests, and captains of the temple, and the elders, which were come to him, Be ye come out, as against 53 a thief, with swords and staves? When I was daily with you in the temple, ye stretched forth no hands against me: but this is your hour, and the power of darkness.

54 Then took they him, and led him, and brought him into the high priest's house. 55 And Peter followed afar off. And when they had kindled a fire in the midst of the hall, and were set down together, 56 Peter sat down among them. But a certain maid beheld him as he sat by the fire, and earnestly looked upon him, and said, This man was also with him. 57 And he denied him, saying, Woman, I 58 know him not. And after a little while another saw him, and said, Thou art also of them. And Peter said, Man, I 59 am not. And about the space of one hour after another confidently affirmed, saying, Of a truth this fellow also was 60 with him: for he is a Galilæan. And Peter said, Man, I know not what thou sayest. And immediately, while he yet 61 spake, the cock crew. And the Lord turned, and looked upon Peter. And Peter remembered the word of the Lord, how he had said unto him, Before the cock crow, thou shalt deny me thrice. 62 And Peter went out, and wept bitterly. 63 And the men that held Jesus mocked 64 him, and smote him. And when they had blindfolded him, they struck him on the face, and asked him, saying, Pro- 65 phesy, who is it that smote thee? And many [other] things blasphemously spake they against him.

66 And as soon as it was day, the elders of the people and the chief priests and the scribes came together, and led him 67 into their council, saying, Art thou the Christ? tell us. And he said unto them, 68 If I tell you, ye will not believe: and if I also ask you, ye will not answer me, 69 nor let me go. Hereafter shall the Son of man sit on the right hand of the 70 power of God. Then said they all, Art thou then the Son of God? And he said 71 unto them, Ye say that I am. And they said, What need we any further witness? for we ourselves have heard of his own mouth.

23 And the whole multitude of them arose, and led him unto Pilate, and 2 they began to accuse him, saying, We found this fellow perverting the nation, and forbidding to give tribute to Cæsar, saying that he himself is Christ a King. 3 And Pilate asked him, saying, Art thou the King of the Jews? And he answered 4 him and said, Thou sayest it. Then said Pilate to the chief priests and to the 5 people, I find no fault in this man. And they were the more fierce, saying, He stirreth up the people, teaching throughout all Jewry, beginning from Galilee to 6 this place. When Pilate heard of Galilee, he asked whether the man was a 7 Galilæan. And as soon as he knew that he belonged unto Herod's jurisdiction, he sent him to Herod, who himself also was at Jerusalem at that time.

8 And when Herod saw Jesus, he was exceeding glad: for he was desirous to see him of a long season, because he had heard many things of him; and he hoped to have seen some miracle done by him. 9 Then he questioned with him in many words; but he answered him nothing. 10 And the chief priests and scribes stood 11 and vehemently accused him. And Herod with his men of war set him at nought, and mocked him, and arrayed him in a

R

S. LUKE.

gorgeous robe, and sent him again to
12 Pilate. And the same day Pilate and Herod were made friends together: for before they were at enmity between themselves.
13 And Pilate, when he had called together the chief priests and the rulers
14 and the people, said unto them, Ye have brought this man unto me, as one that perverteth the people: and, behold, I, having examined him before you, have found no fault in this man touching those things whereof ye accuse him:
15 no, nor yet Herod: for I sent you to him; and, lo, nothing worthy of death
16 is done unto him. I will therefore
17 chastise him, and release him. (For of necessity he must release one unto them
18 at the feast.) And they cried out all at once, saying, Away with this man, and
19 release unto us Barabbas: (who for a certain sedition made in the city, and
20 for murder, was cast into prison.) Pilate, therefore, willing to release Jesus, spake
21 again to them. But they cried, saying,
22 Crucify him, crucify him. And he said unto them the third time, Why, what evil hath he done? I have found no cause of death in him: I will therefore
23 chastise him, and let him go. And they were instant with loud voices, requiring that he might be crucified. And the voices of them and of the chief priests
24 prevailed. And Pilate gave sentence
25 that it should be as they required. And he released unto them him that for sedition and murder was cast into prison, whom they had desired; but he delivered Jesus to their will.
26 And as they led him away, they laid hold upon one Simon, a Cyrenian, coming out of the country, and on him they laid the cross, that he might bear it after Jesus.
27 And there followed him a great company of people, and of women, which
28 also bewailed and lamented him. But Jesus turning unto them said, Daughters of Jerusalem, weep not for me, but weep for yourselves, and for your children.
29 For, behold, the days are coming, in the which they shall say, Blessed are the barren, and the wombs that never bare, and the paps that never gave suck.
30 Then shall they begin to say to the mountains, Fall on us; and to the hills,
31 Cover us. For if they do these things in a green tree, what shall be done in the dry?
32 And there were also two other, malefactors, led with him to be put to death.
33 And when they were come to the place, which is called Calvary, there they crucified him, and the malefactors, one on the right hand, and the other on the
34 left. Then said Jesus, Father, forgive

them: for they know not what they do. And they parted his raiment, and cast
35 lots. And the people stood beholding. And the rulers also with them derided him, saying, He saved others; let him save himself, if he be Christ, the chosen
36 of God. And the soldiers also mocked him, coming to him, and offering him
37 vinegar, and saying, If thou be the king
38 of the Jews, save thyself. And a superscription also was written over him in letters of Greek, and Latin, and Hebrew, THIS IS THE KING OF THE JEWS.
39 And one of the malefactors which were hanged railed on him, saying, If thou be
40 Christ, save thyself and us. But the other answering rebuked him, saying, Dost not thou fear God, seeing thou art
41 in the same condemnation? And we indeed justly; for we receive the due reward of our deeds: but this man hath
42 done nothing amiss. And he said unto Jesus, Lord, remember me when thou
43 comest into thy kingdom. And Jesus said unto him, Verily I say unto thee, To day shalt thou be with me in paradise.
44 And it was about the sixth hour, and there was a darkness over all the earth
45 until the ninth hour. And the sun was darkened, and the veil of the temple
46 was rent in the midst. And when Jesus had cried with a loud voice, he said, Father, into thy hands I commend my spirit: and having said thus, he gave up
47 the ghost. Now when the centurion saw what was done, he glorified God, saying, Certainly this was a righteous
48 man. And all the people that came together to that sight, beholding the things which were done, smote their breasts,
49 and returned. And all his acquaintance, and the women that followed him from Galilee, stood afar off, beholding these things.
50 And, behold, there was a man named Joseph, a counsellor; and he was a good
51 man, and a just: (the same had not consented to the counsel and deed of them;) he was of Arimathæa, a city of the Jews: who also himself waited for the kingdom
52 of God. This man went unto Pilate, and
53 begged the body of Jesus. And he took it down, and wrapped it in linen, and laid it in a sepulchre that was hewn in stone, wherein never man before was
54 laid. And that day was the preparation,
55 and the sabbath drew on. And the women also, which came with him from Galilee, followed after, and beheld the sepulchre, and how his body was laid.
56 And they returned, and prepared spices and ointments;
And rested the sabbath day according
24 to the commandment. Now upon the first day of the week, very early in the

S. LUKE.

morning, they came unto the sepulchre, bringing the spices which they had prepared, and certain others with them. 2 And they found the stone rolled away 3 from the sepulchre. And they entered in, and found not the body of the Lord 4 Jesus. And it came to pass, as they were much perplexed thereabout, behold, two men stood by them in shining 5 garments: and as they were afraid, and bowed down their faces to the earth, they said unto them, Why seek ye the 6 living among the dead? He is not here, but is risen: remember how he spake unto you when he was yet in Galilee, 7 saying, The Son of man must be delivered into the hands of sinful men, and be crucified, and the third day rise 8 again. And they remembered his words, 9 and returned from the sepulchre, and told all these things unto the eleven, 10 and to all the rest. It was Mary Magdalene, [and Joanna,] and Mary the mother of James, and other women that were with them, which told these things 11 unto the apostles. And their words seemed to them as idle tales, and they 12 believed them not. Then arose Peter, and ran into the sepulchre; and stooping down, he beheld the linen clothes laid by themselves, and departed, wondering in himself at that which was come to pass.

13 And, behold, two of them went that same day to a village called Emmaus, which was from Jerusalem about three-14 score furlongs. And they talked together of all these things which had happened. 15 And it came to pass, that, while they communed together and reasoned, Jesus himself drew near, and went with them 16 But their eyes were holden that they 17 should not know him. And he said unto them, What manner of communications are these that ye have one to another, 18 as ye walk, and are sad? And the one of them, whose name was Cleopas, answering said unto him, Art thou only a stranger in Jerusalem, and hast not known the things which are come to 19 pass there in these days? And he said unto them, What things? And they said unto him, Concerning Jesus of Nazareth, which was a prophet mighty in deed and word before God and all the 20 people: and how the chief priests and our rulers delivered him to be condemned 21 to death, and have crucified him But we trusted that it had been he which should have redeemed Israel: and beside all this, to day is the third day since 22 these things were done. Yea, and certain women also of our company made us astonished, which were early at the 23 sepulchre; and when they found not his body, they came, saying, that they had also seen a vision of angels, which said 24 that he was alive. And certain of them which were with us went to the sepulchre, and found it even so as the women 25 had said: but him they saw not. Then he said unto them, O fools, and slow of heart to believe all that the prophets 26 have spoken: ought not Christ to have suffered these things, and to enter into 27 his glory? And beginning at Moses and all the prophets, he expounded unto them in all the scriptures the things 28 concerning himself. And they drew nigh unto the village, whither they went: and he made as though he would have 29 gone further. But they constrained him, saying, Abide with us: for it is toward evening, and the day is far spent. And 30 he went in to tarry with them. And it came to pass, as he sat at meat with them, he took bread, and blessed it, and 31 brake, and gave to them. And their eyes were opened, and they knew him; 32 and he vanished out of their sight. And they said one to another, Did not our heart burn within us, while he talked with us by the way, and while he opened to 33 us the scriptures? And they rose up the same hour, and returned to Jerusalem, and found the eleven gathered together, 34 and them that were with them, saying, The Lord is risen indeed, and hath ap-35 peared to Simon. And they told what things were done in the way, and how he was known of them in breaking of bread.

36 And as they thus spake, Jesus himself stood in the midst of them, and saith 37 unto them, Peace be unto you. But they were terrified and affrighted, and supposed that they had seen a spirit. 38 And he said unto them, Why are ye troubled? and why do thoughts arise in 39 your hearts? Behold my hands and my feet, that it is I myself: handle me, and see; for a spirit hath not flesh and bones, 40 as ye see me have. And when he had thus spoken, he shewed them his hands 41 and his feet. And while they yet believed not for joy, and wondered, he said unto them, Have ye here any meat? 42 And they gave him a piece of a broiled 43 fish, and of an honeycomb. And he took it, and did eat before them.

44 And he said unto them, These are the words which I spake unto you, while I was yet with you, that all things must be fulfilled, which were written in the law of Moses, and in the prophets, and 45 in the psalms, concerning me. Then opened he their understanding, that they 46 might understand the scriptures, and said unto them, Thus it is written, and thus it behoved Christ to suffer, and to 47 rise from the dead the third day: and that repentance and remission of sins

should be preached in his name among all nations, beginning at Jerusalem. 48 And ye are witnesses of these things. 49 And, behold, I send the promise of my Father upon you: but tarry ye in the city of Jerusalem, until ye be endued with power from on high. 50 And he led them out *a* as far as to Bethany, and he lifted up his hands, 51 and blessed them. And it came to pass, while he blessed them, he was parted from them, and carried up into heaven. 52 And they worshipped him, and returned to Jerusalem with great joy: and were continually in the temple, praising and blessing God. Amen.

a "Many authorities omit 'out.'"

THE END.

Printed by BALLANTYNE, HANSON & CO
Edinburgh and London